LIVING
WITH THE
ANTHROPOCENE

Living with the Anthropocene is an illuminating deep-dive in this 'storm of our own making'. With such a diverse and expansive collection of voices, what makes this book stand out is its unity. Thinking about climate change can be lonely and devastating but here you can be assured of being held, not only in thrall, but in great company.

Anna Krien

An important book that speaks to our time.

Tim Flannery

With this marvellous book the term Anthropocene loses its academic tinge to become a pervasive and pressing reality. A pantheon of Australia's finest environmental writers reveals the haunting personal costs of living in a world that humans have already turned upside down.

Iain McCalman

Scientists originated the term and concept of the Anthropocene. But this work takes a much deeper dive into what the Anthropocene really means for us humans now and into the future, and – importantly – what the Anthropocene means for the rest of life with which we share this planet.

Will Steffen

LIVING
WITH THE
ANTHROPOCENE
LOVE, LOSS AND HOPE
IN THE FACE OF
ENVIRONMENTAL
CRISIS

EDITED BY
**CAMERON MUIR,
KIRSTEN WEHNER AND
JENNY NEWELL**

NEWSOUTH

A NewSouth book

Published by
NewSouth Publishing
University of New South Wales Press Ltd
University of New South Wales
Sydney NSW 2052
AUSTRALIA
newsouthpublishing.com

 A catalogue record for this
book is available from the
National Library of Australia

ISBN   9781742236889 (paperback)
        9781742244815 (ebook)
        9781742249315 (ePDF)

Internal design Josephine Pajor-Markus
Cover design Sandy Cull, gogoGingko
Cover image Palmistry – Mediaeval Palmistry. A woodcut illustration from the
    influential Ciromantia of Barthelemy Cocles, published circa 1534. *Topham
    Partners LLP / Alamy Stock Photo*

All reasonable efforts were taken to obtain permission to use copyright material
reproduced in this book, but in some cases copyright could not be traced. The authors
welcome information in this regard.

CONTENTS

SHARING THE STORY

WALKING TOGETHER

CONTRIBUTORS

Michael Adams writes about nature and the human search for meaning, and teaches in Human Geography at the University of Wollongong. He is published in literary journals as well as academic journals and books. His essay 'Salt Blood' won the Australian Book Review 2017 Calibre Essay Prize.

Nadia Bailey is a writer and critic. She is the author of three books, and her essays and short stories have been widely represented in journals and anthologies. Nadia was awarded the 2019 Kraków UNESCO City of Literature Residency and was the recipient of the 2018 Midsumma Futures Fellowship.

Saskia Beudel is the author of *Borrowed Eyes*, *A Country in Mind* and *Curating Sydney: Imagining the City's Future* (with Jill Bennett). Her essays and articles have been published in a wide range of Australian and international publications, most recently in *Sydney Review of Books*, *Artist Profile* and the *Routledge Handbook of Ecocriticism and Environmental Communication*.

Tony Birch is a senior research fellow in the Moondani Balluk Academic Centre at Victoria University in Melbourne. His research and writing are concerned with climate justice and Indigenous knowledge. He also writes short fiction, poetry and novels including

Shadowboxing, *Blood*, *Ghost River* and *White Girl*. Tony received the Patrick White Award in 2017.

James Bradley is the author of five novels – *Wrack*, *The Deep Field*, *The Resurrectionist*, *Clade* and *Ghost Species* – and a book of poetry, *Paper Nautilus*. His fiction and nonfiction have won or been short-listed for several major Australian and international literary awards and have been widely translated.

Jo Chandler is an Australian journalist, science writer and educator. Her journalism has covered a wide range of subject areas, including science, the environment, and women's and children's issues. She is currently a lecturer at the University of Melbourne's Centre for Advancing Journalism. She edited *Best Australian Science Writing 2016* and is author of *Feeling the Heat*. Jo's writing has won or been shortlisted for several major prizes, including a Walkley Award, the Eureka Prize for Science Journalism and the Bragg UNSW Press Prize for Science Writing.

Adrienne Corradini is a writer, horsewoman and academic librarian based in Wollongong. In 2016, her short story 'Waste' was shortlisted for the Wollongong Writers Festival Prize. Her work has been published in *Tertangala* and *Baby Teeth Journal*. In 2014, she was part of a team that received an AsiaBound grant to collaborate with students in China's first creative writing program. Adrienne's work explores the ways people, land and animals attempt to communicate, listen to and fathom each other.

Sophie Cunningham is a former publisher and editor, and the author of five books, including *Melbourne* (2011) and *City of Trees: Essays on Life, Death and the Need for a Forest* (2019). She is an adjunct professor at RMIT University's Non/fiction Lab, Melbourne.

John Dargavel is honorary associate professor in the Fenner School of Environment and Society at the Australian National University. After sixty years of researching and writing about forestry, its politics and history, he is now enjoying slowly writing about how we experience the environment in everyday life: extinctions and sanctuaries, gardens, balconies and theme parks.

Penny Dunstan is a Newcastle-based artist, agronomist and soil scientist working with land rehabilitation after open-cut coal mining in the upper Hunter Valley. Her art practice employs analogue and digital photography, topographic and stratigraphic drawing, writing and soil exploration to derive lived encounters with terraformed lands.

Delia Falconer is the author of two novels, *The Service of Clouds* and *The Lost Thoughts of Soldiers*. Her 2010 nonfiction work, *Sydney*, won the CAL Waverley Library Award for Literature and was shortlisted for other major national prizes including the NSW Premier's History and National Biography awards. Delia won the Walkley-Pascall Award for Arts Criticism in 2018. She is a senior lecturer in Creative Writing at University of Technology, Sydney.

Laura Fisher is an artist and sociologist known for her cross-disciplinary work on the relationship between art and social change. She has published widely on Aboriginal art, urban cycling culture, rural transformation and cross-cultural arts exchange. Laura is a student of the Kandos School of Cultural Adaptation <ksca.land>. Her current art projects work to bridge the city/country divide to support sustainable land use.

Suzy Freeman-Greene is a Melbourne writer and the arts and culture editor of *The Conversation*. Suzy's essays, feature writing and criticism have appeared in *Good Weekend*, *Griffith Review*, *Meanjin* and

Australian Book Review. For many years she was a regular columnist with *The Age*.

Andrea Gaynor has a passion for the environment and social justice. After finishing her PhD in 2001, she rode her bicycle through China, Laos and Cambodia before returning to lecture in Australian History at the University of Western Australia. Andrea is the author of the widely acclaimed *Harvest of the Suburbs: An Environmental History of Growing Food in Australian Cities* and editor of *George Seddon: Selected Writings*. She convenes the Australian and New Zealand Environmental History Network.

Joëlle Gergis is an award-winning climate scientist and writer based at the Australian National University. She is the author of *Sunburnt Country: The History and Future of Climate Change in Australia*.

Billy Griffiths is an award-winning writer and historian. He is the author of *Deep Time Dreaming* (which won the Felicia A Holton Book Award, the Ernest Scott Prize and Book of the Year at the NSW Premier's Literary Awards), and *The China Breakthrough*. He lectures in Cultural Heritage and Museum Studies at Deakin University in Melbourne.

Ashley Hay is a novelist and essayist whose awards include the Foundation for Australian Literary Studies' Colin Roderick Award, the NSW Premier's Literary Awards People's Choice, and the Bragg UNSW Press Prize for Science Writing. Her most recent novel is *A Hundred Small Lessons*. She is the editor of *Griffith Review*.

Justine Hyde is a writer, critic and librarian who lives in Melbourne. Her essays, short fiction and reviews are published in *The Age, The Saturday Paper, The Australian, Meanjin, Lithub, Electric Literature, Kill Your Darlings* and a range of anthologies.

Lucas Ihlein uses socially engaged art to explore human–environment relations. His recent project 'Sugar vs the Reef?' in collaboration with Kim Williams investigates grassroots cultural leadership in the Queensland sugarcane industry. Lucas is a student at the Kandos School of Cultural Adaptation, and a researcher at University of Wollongong. <lucasihlein.net>

Jennifer Lavers is a research scientist at the Institute for Marine and Antarctic Studies, University of Tasmania. She studies anthropogenic pressures on the marine environment, including fishing activity and offshore oil development, and recently has focused on the impact of plastic pollution, especially on seabirds. Jennifer has had featuring roles in the documentaries *A Plastic Ocean* (2017) and *BLUE* (2018). Collaborating with artists and others, she works to tell the marine plastics story in new ways, to new audiences.

Ian Lunt is an ecologist and writer. He lives in the regional city of Albury, New South Wales.

Cameron Allan McKean is a PhD candidate in Anthropology at Deakin University in Geelong, Victoria. He studies what life and loss look like for those who have intimately experienced coral death on degraded reefs in the Pacific Ocean.

George Main is a curator, writer and environmental historian. He is the author of *Heartland: The Regeneration of Rural Place* and is the head of the Centre for the Anthropocene at the National Museum of Australia.

Gretchen Miller is a documentary podcast producer and writer. In her 20 years at ABC Radio National she made landmark citizen engagement series such as The Trees Project and Hot Summer Land,

and made over seventy audio documentaries. Now independent and completing a PhD, The Rescue Project, her aim is to use immersive citizen stories to help people come to terms with the climate crisis and feel they can make a difference.

Ruth A Morgan is a senior lecturer in the History Program at Monash University, Melbourne. She has published widely on the climate and water histories of Australia and the British Empire, including her award-winning book, *Running Out? Water in Western Australia* (2015).

Stephen Muecke is professor of Creative Writing in the College of Humanities, Arts and Social Sciences at Flinders University, South Australia, and is a fellow of the Australian Academy of the Humanities. Forthcoming books include *Recomposing the Humanities with Bruno Latour*, edited with Rita Felski, and *The Children's Country: The Creation of a Goolarabooloo Future in North-west Australia*, co-authored with Paddy Roe.

Cameron Muir is a writer, editor and researcher. His writing has appeared in *Griffith Review*, *Meanjin*, *Overland*, the *Guardian*, *Australian Book Review* and *Best Australian Science Writing*, among other publications. Cameron's work has been shortlisted in the NSW Premier's History Awards, the Eureka Prize for Science Journalism and the Bragg UNSW Press Prize for Science Writing.

Jenny Newell is manager of Climate Change Projects, Australian Museum, Sydney. Working in the environmental humanities and formerly with Pacific communities and collections at the British Museum and the American Museum of Natural History, she now focuses on fostering engagement in the climate crisis. Her books include *Trading Nature* and the coedited volume *Curating the Future*. She convenes the Museums & Climate Change Network.

Emily O'Gorman is an environmental historian with interdisciplinary research interests within the environmental humanities. Her research focuses on how people live with rivers, wetlands and climates. She is the author of *Flood Country: An Environmental History of the Murray-Darling Basin* and the forthcoming book *Imagined Ecologies: More-than-human Histories of Wetlands*. Emily is a senior lecturer at Macquarie University, Sydney.

Kate Phillips has curated twenty exhibitions in Australia and the United Kingdom, including award-winning exhibitions at Museums Victoria, on a diverse range of science themes. Her ideas about audiences and communication continue to evolve as a result of her work in creative teams and listening to and observing people of all ages.

Alison Pouliot is a natural historian, environmental photographer and honorary fellow at the Australian National University. She spends most of her time in the dirt with her loupe. Her recent book, *The Allure of Fungi*, explores the kooky curiosities of the fungal realm. <www.alisonpouliot.com>

Jane Rawson is the author of *From the Wreck*, *A Wrong Turn at the Office of Unmade Lists* and *Formaldehyde*, and the nonfiction book, *The Handbook: Surviving and Living with Climate Change*. Her short fiction and essays, mostly about the environment, have been published widely. Jane is writing a new novel about witches and fascists, funded by grants from the Copyright Agency and the Australia Council for the Arts. She recently relocated to the Huon Valley, Tasmania, from Melbourne.

Annalise Rees is a visual artist working in the expanded field of drawing. Her work is informed by historical practices of exploration, navigation and cartography. She has been an artist in residence and exhibited across Australia and overseas, including travelling to the sub-Antarctic on board the research vessel *Investigator*.

Lauren Rickards is an associate professor in the School of Global, Urban and Social Studies at RMIT University, Melbourne. A human geographer, she is a Lead Author for the Sixth Assessment Report of the Intergovernmental Panel on Climate Change. Her research explores the sociocultural dimensions of climate change and the Anthropocene.

David Ritter is CEO of Greenpeace Australia Pacific. He holds honorary appointments with Sydney University and the University of Western Australia, and his most recent book was *The Coal Truth* (2018). David lives in Sydney with his spouse and two daughters.

Libby Robin is an award-winning author and environmental historian currently writing about the response of museums to the Anthropocene. Her most recent book is *The Environment: A History of the Idea* (with Paul Warde and Sverker Sörlin). She is Emeritus Professor at the Australian National University.

John Charles Ryan holds research fellowships at the University of New England and the University of Western Australia. He is the coeditor of *The Language of Plants: Science, Philosophy, Literature* and *Australian Wetland Cultures: Swamps and the Environmental Crisis*.

Katrina Schlunke is a researcher and adjunct Associate Professor at the University of Tasmania. Her current research project is an ARC-funded Discovery Grant, 'Beyond Extinction: Reconstructing the Thylacine (Tasmanian Tiger) Archive' (with Hannah Stark). Her recent publications are concerned with art and the Anthropocene, more-than-human queerness, and Indigenous knowledges and the university.

Ray Thompson worked with the Soil Conservation Service in New South Wales on surveying and reclaiming scalded land from 1984. He retired in 2018 and has been flat out ever since surveying and building waterponds all over Australia, and advising internationally.

Angela Tiatia is a multidisciplinary artist. Over the past nine years as an artist, director, producer, activist and community educator, she has brought attention to the growing impacts of social media on global culture, representation of otherness, gender inequalities and climate change in the Pacific region. Angela has award-winning works in major Australian and international galleries and has been a finalist in the Archibald and Sir John Sulman prizes. She is of Sāmoan and Australian heritage.

Ellen van Neerven is a Mununjali Yugambeh writer of award-winning fiction, poetry and nonfiction. Her books include *Heat and Light*, *Comfort Food* and *Throat*.

Adriana Vergés is an associate professor of marine ecology at the University of New South Wales, Sydney. Her research focuses on climate change impacts and the conservation of the world's threatened algal forests and seagrass meadows. She was awarded a Green Globe Award in 2017 for her 'Operation Crayweed' work restoring underwater forests, and the UNSW Emerging Thought Leader prize in 2019.

Kirsten Wehner is a curator/designer who creates experiences that foster people's connections with each other and the more-than-human world. Now director of PhotoAccess, she was formerly a head curator at the National Museum of Australia. Around the edges, Kirsten publishes in the environmental humanities and develops multi-species urban spaces. She coedited *Curating the Future:*

Museums, Communities and Climate Change and coauthored *Land-marks: A History of Australia in 33 Places.*

Gib Wettenhall OAM, an award-winning author, publisher and editor, specialises in exploring cultural landscapes including those of the First Australians. A farm forester, he manages 12 hectares of native forest straddling the southern Divide at Mollongghip, and is actively involved with his community and local environmental organisations.

Josh Wodak works at the intersection of the environmental human-ities and science and technology studies. A senior research fellow at the Institute for Culture and Society, Western Sydney University, he researches the efficacy and ethics of experimental conservation – such as synthetic corals and atmospheric engineering – for countering human impacts on the biosphere.

Kate Wright works at the interface of community-based social and environmental activism and environemntal humanities research. She is currently a Fellow at the Rachel Carson Centre for Environment and Society, Luwig-Maximilians Universität in Munich, where she is finishing her second book – a collaborative and creative history of the Armidale Community Garden.

ACKNOWLEDGMENTS

Bringing this book to fruition has depended on the energy and generosity of an extended community. *Living with the Anthropocene* grew out of an Australian Research Council Discovery research project, 'Understanding Australia in the Age of Humans: Localising the Anthropocene' (DP 160102648), which ran from 2016 to 2019. As part of this project, the National Museum of Australia partnered with the Sydney Environment Institute (University of Sydney) to create *Everyday Futures* <everydayfutures.com.au/>. This online collection of 'object-stories', curated by Cameron Muir, began the process of weaving together the ideas and the network that evolved into this book.

We'd like to sincerely acknowledge the support of the Australia Research Council and the contributions to this project by our colleagues on the original research team, Professor Libby Robin (now Emeritus), Dr Martha Sear, Dr Josh Wodak, Dr Caitlin de Berigny and Marie Mackenzie, as well as advisors Professors Gregg Mitman, Jan Zalasiewicz and Mark Williams. We're particularly and deeply grateful for the trust and support provided to us by the project leader, the indomitable and ever inspiring Professor Iain McCalman (now Emeritus).

We'd like to thank the Sydney Environment Institute (University of Sydney), National Museum of Australia, Australian Museum and PhotoAccess, each of whom contributed financially to the project, enabled us to take time away from other tasks to work on it or provided facilities and office support. Our thanks to Marie Mackenzie for wrangling financial matters at the University of Sydney.

The Copyright Agency's Cultural Fund significantly supported this project through a grant to the National Museum of Australia. We're extremely grateful to the Agency for their visionary support and to the National Museum's Centre for the Anthropocene, and particularly its then Head, Martha Sear, for their commitment to bringing this book to life.

We'd like to thank *The Monthly* for permission to include Joëlle Gergis' essay, 'The Terrible Truth of Climate Change', which first appeared in their August 2019 edition. An earlier version of Delia Falconer's essay, 'Signs and Wonders of a New Age' appeared in the *Sydney Review of Books* in March 2019.

No book makes it out into the world without a great publisher and we've been blessed to work with the team at NewSouth, including Phillipa McGuinness, Emma Hutchinson and Joumana Awad. We particularly appreciate the eagle eyes and gentle companionship that copyeditor Diana Hill brought to the project. Thank you!

It's been an incredible experience to work with so many fine writers on this collection. Their heartfelt contributions have touched us in deep and diverse ways and we each feel that, by virtue of collaborating with them, our sense of who we are and where we fit in the world has been made anew. We're extremely grateful for their generous spirits and look forward to our friendships continuing to blossom.

Finally, we'd like to thank our families for their understanding that there had to be many evenings, late nights and weekend afternoons when we needed to talk on Zoom, read submissions, exchange emails and get upset about the state of the world, rather than hang out with them. Such quiet acts of love flow beneath every word in this book.

A STORM OF OUR OWN MAKING

*Cameron Muir, Kirsten Wehner
and Jenny Newell*

You're not alone.

On one of Canberra's luminous spring days, we three drew up our chairs around a table in the back space of the community arts centre where Kirsten works, and shared a small, excited smile. In front of us was a sizeable stack of paper, forty-two pieces of writing from people around the continent, submitted, selected and edited, and the job ahead of figuring out how these diverse stories might be shaped into a conversation – this book – about what it is like to live in, with and as part of the Australian Anthropocene, the 'age of humans'.

As Tony Birch writes in his contribution to this volume, we live now in a 'storm of our own making', a time of unpredictable environmental change caused by human impact on the Earth's biophysical systems. In other words, 'nature' is no more. People now shape the world everywhere, and in ways that are threatening the wellbeing of many species on the planet, including our own, today and into the distant future. It's a situation that, we decided as we chatted, tends to induce vertigo, a terrifying sensation of falling into an abyss without handholds or soft landing – and all while your feet remain on the ground and your everyday life carries you along with getting to and from work, making dinner and kissing your family goodnight.

As we sat around the table that day in Canberra, we talked about how this book started with the many people around Australia who we'd encountered in our work as curators and writers. Cameron recalled passionate conversations with irrigators on the Liverpool Plains of New South Wales who were fighting new coal and gas developments. Kirsten spoke of sitting on the banks of the Murrumbidgee with Wiradjuri Elders who described vanished animal species as 'ghosts in our Country'. And Jen told of talking with schoolkids who were deeply confused about how they could learn about climate change as they sat in the classroom but were then criticised for calling for action to protect their future.

In each of these discussions, and many others in diverse communities across the continent, people described that they know absolutely in their hearts and heads that something profound is happening with the living world, that the activities of industrial societies are at the core of it, and that rapid rethinking and reconfiguring of how we live is needed. They also spoke often about feeling that they are 'invisible'. That they are trying to communicate the troubling environmental and social shifts gathering momentum around them, but that nobody seems to be listening. They frequently felt desperate and, most commonly, isolated in a way that compounds their fear and grief over uncontrollable change.

Responding to these conversations, we developed a project dedicated to eliciting and collecting people's stories about their experiences of living with environmental change. We issued an open call, invited fellow curators and scholars, and challenged some of Australia's best-known writers to reflect on their own personal journeys grappling with climate change, disappearing species, soil exhaustion, air pollution and other challenges of the Anthropocene.

Historians, ecologists, walkers, gardeners, artists, activists and students responded with heartfelt, revealing and powerful stories, often tunnelling down into feelings of loss, sometimes evoking laughter, and frequently turning resolutely towards the future with hope and determination. Every submission expressed its author's love and care for living places, people, and plant and animal companions.

This book brings together a selection of the submissions we received, stories and reflections that bear witness to how diverse Australians are experiencing the current 'storm of our own making'. In creating this book, we are trying to build a small shelter at the heart of this maelstrom. A place for pausing and sitting quietly, sharing our stories, and finding space and fellow travellers with whom we might make plans. We hope to foster a conceptual and imaginative space where we can draw strength and inspiration from the fact that none of us is or need be alone in the work of coming to terms with the huge challenges of the Anthropocene, or in finding the courage and ideas to remake the world to ensure a flourishing future.

UNTIL RECENTLY, MUCH PUBLIC CONVERSATION ABOUT THE Anthropocene proceeded in a relatively scientific or technological mode focused on questions of systemic environmental change. The concept itself developed as scientists sought to recognise that humankind's activities – deforestation, soil erosion, chemical pollution, species extinction and greenhouse gas emissions – have collectively altered the Earth systems to such an extent that we have entered a new geological epoch, the Anthropocene, or 'age of humans'. These scholars point to the ways in which traces of our lives today will be visible in the planet's strata, the layers of rock that make up Earth's surface, for millions of years into the future.

Humans, for example, now move more sediment than natural

forces. The tonnes and tonnes of plastic we send to landfill or let flow into the oceans each year will accrete to form a new geological material (what one oceanographer calls plastiglomerate). With approximately 96 per cent of Earth's animal biomass now made up by humans and livestock (with just 4 per cent wildlife), the fossil record of our time will show an extraordinary proliferation of chicken and bovine bones and the sudden vanishing – a catastrophic silence – of tens of thousands of mammal, bird, insect, reptile, fish, seaweed, coral, tree and plant species. Radioactive material generated through nuclear power production and weapons testing and use will shape life into the unimaginably deep future.

The world's scientific community is yet to decide whether to formally adopt the Anthropocene as a geological unit of time, and a lively debate continues as to whether the Anthropocene started with the acceleration of global extraction of resources from the 1950s, the advent of the Industrial Revolution, the spread of agriculture ten to fifteen thousand years ago or our hominid ancestors' first use of fire. Yet the term has, in a sense, already escaped these questions of definition, entering the popular lexicon as it appears on the front page of the *Economist*, in headlines in the *New York Times*, *National Geographic*, *Time Magazine*, *Le Monde* and *Der Spiegel*, is explored by major museum exhibitions in Germany, the United States and Canada, and inspires the work of a rapidly growing number of artists, authors and songwriters.

The Anthropocene has emerged as a metaphor for our times, and as the geographer Lauren Rickards writes in *Geographical Research*, 'The value of a metaphor is not simply a matter of how accurately it depicts the world, but of what insights, storylines, emotions and aesthetics it offers'. The Anthropocene is an idea that captures the extent and profundity of the multiple and interacting changes that human beings have wreaked and are wreaking on Earth, and that suggests something of the sheer hugeness of the task we now all face in adapting to and healing those impacts. Perhaps most importantly, the term lays responsibility for the world's troubles directly at 'our' – human beings' – feet.

One of the key criticisms of the idea of the Anthropocene is that, as it charges humans with the profound environmental changes taking place across the planet, it tends to treat us as a species as a whole, obscuring the ways in which Anthropocene challenges have been overwhelmingly created by, and in the service of, a few highly privileged groups of people. Think of the steam engine, for example, a technology that kick-started the Industrial Revolution and is consequently a prime candidate for an Anthropocene catalyst. As social scientists Andreas Malm and Alf Hornborg have pointed out, however, the steam engine was not an accessible technology. Only the very wealthy few could afford one – and they must bear responsibility for 'pointing steam power as a weapon' at European colonies in Africa and the New World, using it to disrupt and reorganise Indigenous ecological and social relationships to enable European powers to extract local wealth.

A second important criticism relates to the way in which the Anthropocene tends to normalise and foster human hubris, the idea that just as people are destroying the planet, we are capable of 'fixing' it. This approach tends to reinforce the cultural trope deeply embedded in western cultures that holds that human beings are somehow outside 'nature', able to decide to exploit – or manage – it for their own good. Yet this is precisely the approach that has ended up in the Anthropocene, as we've used Earth's resources and beings without thought for their own integrity and longevity, let alone for how our own wellbeing is completely tied up with that of wider ecological communities.

Scholars have developed a range of alternative labels for the age in which we live: Capitalocene, Econocene, Plantationocene, Plasticene, Pyrocene, Plutocene, Misanthropocene, Manthropocene, Anthronot-seen, Homogenocene, Obscene, Nerocene and Cthulhucene. Each variation focuses on a different aspect of the Anthropocene's complex character and genesis, and arguably also expresses in their sometimes tortuous meshing of terms our need for a new kind of language to talk about this time. One of the most haunting ideas in this cavalcade of tongue-twisters is surely biologist EO Wilson's Eremocene, the 'age of loneliness', which draws attention to the prospect of a future in which we have extinguished so many of the Earth's life forms that we find ourselves bereft of most non-human companions. As Delia Falconer writes in *Sydney Review of Books*, we face the prospect of a future 'in which we are thrown back only upon ourselves'.

In this book, we have chosen to remain with the Anthropocene as our key focus, seeing it as an idea that helps us conceptualise the widespread changes in which we are all now caught up, as well as affording them the gravity and reach in time and space that we feel they deserve. To our minds, the Anthropocene also directly asks us – the privileged parts of humanity – to take responsibility for the world we have wrought. As we edited and curated the stories gathered in this book, we came to see the Anthropocene as about facing and responding with compassion and determination to legacies – processes of colonialism, dispossession and exploitation that began hundreds of years ago and that have picked up pace to give rise to our current predicament. If we feel any responsibility to provide our descendants with even a semblance of the world we now enjoy, we must deal with the runaway consequences of these histories of violence against Earth's human and non-human inhabitants.

From this perspective, the Anthropocene is not primarily about scientific definitions of an era of technogeological time but rather about cultural problems, about how we can understand and transform the circumstances, trajectories and possibilities of our everyday lives – as individuals, communities and societies – in order to build more ecologically and culturally sustainable, even flourishing and joyous, places. This is to shift the lens of the Anthropocene from the global and systemic – though this remains an important context – to the realm of everyday experience. It is also to shorten our gaze, focusing less on how our time will be remembered in the distant fossil record (though the future remains our ultimate benchmark) and more on how the Anthropocene is, even as we write and you read this introduction, unfolding around us and transforming where and how we live.

Cultural problems, to our minds, are addressed through stories, those marvellous human (and in perhaps a slightly different sense non-human) technologies for shaping locations, characters and events into narratives that help us notice the world, draw its messiness into comprehensible threads and enable us to share, debate and agree on what is important and how we should act on that knowledge. This book grew through our conviction that, as a society, we need to spend a lot more time talking about what is happening to us: how we live in Australia in the Anthropocene, how we relate to each other and the rest of the living world, what is important to us in this present moment and what we are doing about it all. In other words, our interest in drawing together the stories in this book is to reveal and acknowledge as important those aspects of the Anthropocene that won't be visible in the strata a thousand years from now: grief, hope, trauma, generosity, courage, politics, failures, successes and the determination of those finding their way through.

IN THE 1940s, AMERICAN CONSERVATIONIST ALDO LEOPOLD lamented that the ecologist's eye saw destruction of the natural world where others couldn't perceive or notice it. He wrote, 'One of the penalties of an ecological education is that one lives alone in a world of wounds'. Yet, many of us have a decent ecological literacy, knowing our own backyards and bush, the mountain ridges, beachside rock pools and inland rivers on and near which we have grown up, the strip of trees alongside a suburban stormwater drain or the patch of sand that blooms when it rains. And you don't need to be trained as a scientist to notice that these places are changing – a less symphonic morning chorus, fewer anemones beneath a tidal shelf, a complete absence of Christmas beetles, the decimation of communities by ferocious bushfires, the drying of entire rivers – and to feel the burden of these wounds.

As a society, we don't always see value in people expressing how they feel about these terrible changes. When the three of us began working on *Living with the Anthropocene*, we decided to address this legacy by asking people to contribute stories focusing on how a material 'thing' – an object, image or place – captured their experience of environmental change in a place important to them. We were interested to home in on people's relationships with the physical world around them. The richness of these submissions can be seen on the *Everyday Futures* website (<everydayfutures.com.au>).

Most people wrote back with stories of loss and grief, whether of the disappearance of familiar birds whose songs resonated with memories of a mother's care, the possibility of cold brew coffee in a Melbourne laneway café or the promise of a liveable future for our children. At first, we resisted this deluge, reflecting perhaps our desperation to put away our own sadness – which had inspired the project – and commit to a more can-do, let's-fix-it course of action. Over time, however, we came to accept this tenor of the book, as we read these stories more closely, discovering how loss was interwoven with love and care and anger, and as they were joined by contributions telling more directly of activist strategies and programs of regeneration.

The authors gathered in this collection have courageously decided to share some of their most intimate responses, opening themselves up to that terrifying sense that others might find them weak or mawkish or simply ridiculous. In a very important way, this book is about bearing witness to these stories, about recording and acknowledging and declaring as important that we feel loss and anger and grief, as well as hope, at all that is happening to us and our places. We hope that, as this book proclaims these stories publicly, it may help us all individually come to terms with the complex and confusing experience of living in the Anthropocene. But also that it may help ensure that nobody who feels bereft or furious or lost at the terrors of our age need agree with Leopold's maxim. For to be alone is to be powerless.

EARLY ON IN THE PROJECT, AS WE THREE EDITORS TALKED with people across the country about their stories concerning environmental change, we began to notice common threads and shared interests. We began to consider how we could link, for example, Perth residents rallying to save the Beeliar wetlands with artists in the Blue Mountains working in the shadow of a coalmine. They were divided by distance, and on the face of it their projects were completely different, but both their stories were about trying to renew community connection and resilience. As the book developed, we began to see that although it comprises a collection of personal, often highly individual stories, it is also a picture of collective endeavour – a national movement (however decentralised) towards cultures of attention, respect and care for each other and the non-human co-inhabitants of our places.

This book is organised to reflect our sense of this collective endeavour, and to cherish and nourish it. Thematic sections loosely group stories that we feel resonate with each other, with short reflections on the meaning and significance of objects, structures and places sitting alongside longer essays delving more deeply into aspects of Anthropocene life. We have curated these sections to magnify and complicate, to correspond and complement, while leaving enough space for you to generate your own meanings in the reading. Some sections attend more closely to the challenges of documenting and understanding change in the natural world; others focus on losing places of significance. One speaks of the mysteries and predicament of the watery world, while another narrates how people are regenerating loved country. But responding to the Anthropocene is not only about rebuilding ecologies in a hands-on way, and through several sections run stories about the strength and importance of the act of storytelling.

So, while *Living with the Anthropocene* is about witnessing and validating individual experience, it is equally about declaring how so many of us yearn for our values of respect and care and action to be reflected throughout our society, and how many of us are finding ways to come together to work for a more positive future. So few eyes and ears in political spheres and corporate boardrooms, in institutions and organisations that have power to act on a scale matching the complexity and enormity of the Anthropocene, seem to be listening to our calls. But all is not lost. In the wake of the 'climate change election' in May 2019, David Ritter, CEO of Greenpeace Australia Pacific, shared a post on social media:

> The government is not the country. Huge amounts of
> climate action can occur outside of what the Commonwealth
> government does. Cities, towns, states, territories, businesses,
> institutions of all kinds … all of these can take action.

Understanding how our everyday lives are connected to the material world, at multiple temporal and geographical scales, helps bridge the gap between individual experience and large-scale government policies. The more that people feel connected to their communities and join together to make small acts of regeneration, the more the positions of those with power who resist taking on this same work look anachronistic and untenable.

We hope *Living with the Anthropocene* is not so much a guidebook as a companion to help see us through these dark times; a modest contribution to the work of fostering a national community empowered and enabled to help us adapt to the changes that are occurring and to come, to prevent worse from happening, and to imagine and strive towards positive futures. Stories about the reality of the state of the environment can leave some people despairing, others angry, many motivated, or feeling a mix of all three emotions. What frustrates us most, we believe, are structural impediments to action. There are ways we can powerfully reimagine redesigned economies, expand the influence and integration of Indigenous cultures, and renew and reconnect our relationships with the rest of the living world.

In some ways, this book contributes a relatively limited range of voices to this complex conversation; it is a start rather than the final say. The authors and editors come from many different communities and backgrounds, but as a group we mostly circulate around a relatively privileged literary, museum and scholarly world. Into the future, we aim to expand the conversation started in these pages, through community-led workshops, storytelling parties, festivals, touring exhibitions and other modes of bolstering engagement and participation in sharing stories of what it is like to live in Australia in this 'age of humans'. We hope you will join us.

For, what is important, surely, is that we all see the Anthropocene happening – the turmoil, grief and disruption, the worst of it – but also that we keep finding ways to keep coming together around our shared predicament, tell our stories, gather strength from company, draw resolve from grief and create acts of care. As Tony Birch observes, in the first essay of this collection, how we traverse this Anthropocene, this storm of our own making, 'will determine the life and death of human and non-human species'. 'Believe in the crowd', Tony says, and we heartily endorse, 'gain energy from the actions of others' and 'be in the world'.

You're not alone.

Postscript: January 2020

In the final weeks of preparing this book for publication, as we flipped emails back and forth about sentence flow and permissions, bushfire overtook our daily lives. Fuelled by prolonged drought, long periods of extremely high temperatures and unpredictable winds, great swathes of Australia – in Queensland, then New South Wales, then Victoria, then many places across the rest of the continent – caught alight. Within a few weeks the flames consumed at least 17 million hectares of bush and farmland and decimated several towns.

Hunkered down in the south-east of Australia, the three of us exchanged stories: of spending New Year's Day locked inside to avoid the choking smoke that blanketed Canberra, of fleeing the town of Cobargo in coastal New South Wales as fires arrived in the night, of receiving a text from friends saying that they had miraculously saved their house but their neighbour was on his way over to shoot their badly burned livestock. Pretty soon, many of this book's authors were also writing to us to share their experiences, but also to ask how we could, even glancingly, add to this collection a few words that acknowledged how we all – like surely so many people across Australia – were feeling about what was happening.

The scale and depth of the devastation wrought this summer has staggered all of us. We feel that we have suddenly found ourselves in our worst climate change nightmares, and that they have claimed us years before we expected. We are perhaps just at the beginning of unpacking how this summer's events have affected us, but uniting us is a profound and searching grief over the loss of so many living beings – loved people and incomprehensible numbers of animals, birds, insects, fungi and forests. All kin, all gone.

It feels like a threshold has been crossed, and in one way, we hope it has. We developed this book to try to help prepare our communities for the emotional costs of rapid and disruptive environmental changes. We didn't expect this summer to so tragically demonstrate that these changes have arrived. Everything seems raw, as if over a few months Australia has become a less stable, less secure country. But, perhaps, people across our nation have also taken a more hopeful step over the edge and into this new world. We sense a strength, a new standing together, arms linked, of people who are sad, angry, more awake and determined to prevent our country sliding further into crisis. We are now people who must learn how to survive in our dear country of extremes, who must live prepared for experiences we can't anticipate, and who must, and will, look after each other more keenly, carefully and devotedly than ever before.

FACING THE STORM

HAVING GONE,
I WILL COME BACK

Tony Birch

Over the last five years, people have often asked me if I am optimistic or pessimistic in relation to climate change and our collective ability to confront the ecological crisis we are already experiencing. My response has commonly been that I do not allow my personal feelings to get in the way of the work I do, which is essentially researching climate (in)justice and the protection of Aboriginal Country. I usually add that I have no choice but to do whatever I am capable of, in union with the likeminded who think, write, protest and persuade others to join us in this struggle and demand that recalcitrant governments, such as our own in Australia, act decisively on climate change *now*, and that we call out and demand drastic change and attitudes from corporations that continue to vandalise Country.

Between you and me, privately I am quite pessimistic about tackling climate change, when considering the lack of leadership provided by political 'leaders', particularly members of our federal governments over recent decades, both Liberal and Labor. For many years, politicians in Australia have utilised energy policy and climate *in*action as little more than an opportunistic and dangerous plaything.

While confessing to pessimism, in the past I have at least been a proactive pessimist, combating my occasional despair with action. I have been regularly inspired by the commitment of others: individuals and groups who work passionately on behalf of the planet. I also remain indebted to the courage of Aboriginal and Torres Strait peoples throughout Australia who fight every day of their lives to protect Country, often in the most adverse circumstances.

Maintaining such a position has not been difficult – until recently. Without being able to clearly articulate why change occurred in me, late last year I found that my energy for writing and speaking about climate change and climate justice wearied. I put my despondency down to fatigue, both emotional and physical, at the end of a busy working year. As many people do, I restricted my summer holiday reading to crime fiction; big, fat, escapist books. As many people also do, as the new year cranked into action I created a list of jobs and goals for the coming year. My list was composed of the books on climate justice I hoped to be reading, essays I expected to write and conference papers I planned to deliver. And then nothing happened. My concentration lapsed even further, my enthusiasm suffered and I sensed the black dog of depression shadowing me.

I have previously been mildly critical of the notion of climate grief, a debilitating experience of contemplating loss – of species, of habitat, of hope – combined with a growing despair that little is being done to address the critical challenges we face. My response to the diagnosis of climate grief was stated bluntly, and in terms that I now consider to be simplistic. I had written that for a way out of the malaise people felt we need only look to history; for instance, to the struggles of Indigenous people around the globe who have fought for the protection of Country and ecologies over many centuries. On reflection, I now believe that my words had reduced a complex psychological and emotional condition to a slogan, projected as little more than the stock cliché, *Just Do It*. Additionally, to my own shame, I suddenly felt that I couldn't do much at all.

I had been reading the endless ream of media 'extinction' stories that could be collectively summed up in the two-word analysis, *We're Fucked*. I had read similar stories in the past, of course, but rather than be disabled by them, I had strategically harnessed headlines of impending doom as an agent of energy in order to continue writing, speaking and occasionally marching. I am now not certain that, in the end, it was the projected death toll of species, the loss of vital ecologies (often conveyed with detailed maps), the murders of Indigenous climate activists and wilful ignorance of so-called 'leaders' that got me. To be honest, it may have been a combination of the extinction narratives I was reading mixed with a lifelong relationship with depression that finally wore me down. After all, a person living with depression gets little comfort from scales, charts and numbers recording and predicting the end of the world.

In March of 2019, death of a more visceral type impacted on my family and myself in a more intimate manner when one of my younger brothers unexpectedly passed away. Climate change and mass extinction were no longer of central concern to me. In fact, as illogical as it appears, the concept of mass extinction held no meaning for me, after being confronted with the death of one person I loved so dearly. As a child, I had been protective of my shy younger brother, often taking his hand in mine, or placing an arm over his shoulder. (I return to these moments of intimacy, documented in the faded black-and-white photographs taken of us together, whenever I need convincing of our shared love.) What I did not need reminding of was that my brother's heart had stopped beating, he was gone from me and that I was lost.

In the world

In the months following my brother's death, I developed the habit of avoiding people, except for those closest to me – my immediate family, particular friends, my remaining brothers and sisters and, of course, my mother, who continues to shift from moments of light, witnessing her remaining children bond and support each other, to days of emotional and physical inertia. I didn't fear seeing other people. They simply made no sense to me any longer. Such a thought now embarrasses me a little. It lacks generosity and is dismissive of people's genuine concern for me. Relative to my recent lethargy about climate activism, I had also forgotten what it was that motivated me to work on climate change in the first place. It wasn't a response to an intellectual idea, a call to direct action or a provocation to write. It was an appreciation of the resilience of people, younger people in particular.

In 2014, I'd been invited to join a global project, *Weather Stations*, which centred around working on a climate project with fifteen-year-old schoolkids in Europe and Australia. Engaged as a writer, I worked in schools in Dublin, London, Berlin, Hel (a Polish city on the Baltic Sea), and a local school in Melbourne, Footscray City College. My job was (supposedly) to inspire kids to think about climate change and respond with creative ideas through writing, photography and film-making. The program culminated in a climate youth forum at the International Literature Festival Berlin in 2015. It was a great success. At the commencement of the project, while I was concerned about climate change, I possibly sat in the defeatist camp. But being around a group of teenagers, on and off, for over a year, changed my attitude and approach to the issue dramatically. I met a very poor group of kids living on the outskirts of Dublin who were demanding that something be done for the love of a shared pony they kept in a paddock down the street. I was invigorated by Bangladeshi immigrant families in London fighting for the protection of areas of their homeland threatened by rising sea levels. And I sat and listened to children in Melbourne's west pay respect to the deep-time history provided by Aboriginal people and Country. What I have forgotten over the last year or so, exacerbated by the grief of losing my brother, is that I had initially been motivated to take a proactive stance on climate change by being *in the world* with people, and being inspired by their tenacity.

Finding a way back came unexpectedly, and, as I should have expected, by being with others. In early July 2019, I was invited to the Geelong Library to speak about my most recent novel, *The White Girl*. It happened to be NAIDOC Week. Consequently, I was to be welcomed by members of the traditional owners of local Country, the Wathaurong Nation. I left home in the early afternoon and caught a tram into the city, planning to catch a train from Southern Cross station for the hour-long trip. It wasn't until I was seated on the tram that I felt suddenly immobilised by a deep sense of sadness about my brother's death. I became anxious, realising that in a few hours I would be speaking to an audience of around one hundred people; people who I did not know, and more importantly, people who did not know my brother.

I no longer felt capable of attending the literary event. I got off the tram and stood in front of the station. The train was leaving in twenty minutes and I needed to decide if I was getting on it. I was aware that people would be expecting me to turn up and entertain them. My sense of responsibility and associated guilt was exacerbated by the thought that an Aboriginal Elder would also be waiting to greet me. A no-show on my part would be an act of disrespect, unless I was able to explain the emotional turmoil I was experiencing, which was not possible.

Inside the railway station, I stood in front of the electronic 'Departures' noticeboard and looked up as the minutes ticked down. Incapable of deciding what to do, I bought a ticket and hopped on the train, with the idea, absent of any common sense, that I might just ride to the end of the line, stay on the train and return home. Occupying a window seat, I took a copy of Alistair MacLeod's *Island: Collected Stories* from my bag (a regular comfort read), and opened the book.

It was school holidays and the train became crowded in the final minutes before departure. The carriage was packed with teenagers who had come up to the city for the day. They were mildly raucous and I soon became distracted from my book. Kids were harmlessly teasing each other, sharing a laugh and reliving a scene from an action movie they'd just seen at one of the city's cinemas. Over the next half-hour or so I switched from reading a beautiful MacLeod story, set in Cape Breton in eastern Canada, the home of most of his fiction, to looking out at the flat but evocative western plains of Victoria, and back to the performance of my travelling companions.

As well as the rowdy teenagers, there were small children crawling along the aisle, wriggling between the legs of strangers; a mother breastfeeding a stunningly redheaded infant; an elderly couple holding hands; and a loner talking quietly to himself. I eventually put my book away, sat back and observed the world of the carriage. I no longer felt anxious. I was alone on the train, but did not feel lonely. Without realising how it had happened, I understood that these 'strangers on a train' had comforted me. If I'd refused the train journey, I'd have gone home and hidden beneath a blanket. Both alone and lonely.

The train pulled into Geelong and I left the station, feeling fortunate to have experienced the generosity of others, people who had done nothing more than be with each other and do no harm. When I spoke at the library an hour later, I reciprocated by extending my own generosity to others; an audience that had come out on a cold winter's night and listened to a writer speak about the courage of Aboriginal women. I was fortunate to experience the generosity of the Wathaurong people who had gathered for the event. When acknowledging

Country and welcoming visitors, traditional owners often tell a story of place, imparting vital knowledge of who they are and how Country governs life. Had I not been at the library to listen to and accept the generosity of the gift of Wathaurong storytelling, I would have denied myself the opportunity to offer a story of my own in return. Had I not caught the train to Geelong, my night would have been empty.

Under my feet

In addition to recognising the sustenance provided by being with people, recently I became conscious that I was able to think about my brother more clearly, to have him beside me, by walking. The thought should not have come as a revelation, as I've always walked and run long distances in order to understand both myself and the places I feel connected to. I have previously written about such experiences. My climate change research and writing has often included long walks on the Country I am writing about. Walking has long been regarded as meditative, providing inspiration for thought, creativity and action. I do experience periods of contemplation while walking and, more particularly, running. I like being *in* place, experiencing the privilege of being on Country as life is performed. I also believe that a disconnection from place can exacerbate our collective sense of powerlessness, disabling us at the very time we must confront those proactively damaging the planet. While Indigenous nations experience separation from Country with a profound sense of grief, historically, capitalist, 'modern' societies have justified the destruction of place and the loss of attachment to place as the necessary collateral damage that comes with 'progress'.

I first wrote about the death of my brother after presenting my work at a climate change gathering in Kyoto. The essay was based upon an initial walk through Melbourne followed by a 'fieldwork' walk along the Birrarung (Yarra) River. The walking and writing directly related to my climate change research, with attention focused on the cultural and geographic forces that have shaped the mouth and lower basin of the river since the period following the last ice age. After finishing the essay, I felt an urge to take another walk, from Dights Falls, on the same river, and along the riverbanks through Yarra Bend National Park. Initially, I felt no particular compulsion to write about the walk or relate it to my research. And yet, the urge to walk was so strong that I became convinced that if I didn't undertake it *very soon*, something terrible would happen.

On the first day around Yarra Bend Park I walked from my home in Carlton and past my younger brother's front gate a kilometre away. I followed a plantation beside the Eastern Freeway, where one of our childhood homes had stood, down to Dights Falls, where we had swum in the river as teenagers. My walk then followed the meandering bends of the river, cut across sports ovals and through abandoned industrial sites. I crossed the Fairfield 'pipe bridge' that we had jumped into the river from as kids, and looped back to the falls along 2 kilometres of a narrow muddy track that few people use. At the end of the walk I became fixated by two thoughts. Firstly, I felt my brother nearer to me than at any time since his death. And secondly, that it was absolutely necessary that I return to the river the following day and begin the process of mapping it.

Over several weeks I became consumed by my river excursions. They turned into daily runs of around 8 kilometres. As soon as I'd finished each run and begun walking home I would start thinking about a new run for the following day, one that, while remaining within the confines of the park, would explore additional tracks and banks. I created maps in my head. I also went online and researched historical maps of the area, including an aerial military map from 1942 that I have long been fascinated by. Running by the Birrarung, I shared the scent of its tannin-stained waters with my brother and listened to the birds and frogs at home in the remnant billabongs linked to the river. At night in bed I would revisit that day's run, visualising the route, returning to place, with my brother at my side.

Yarra Bend Park and the greater surrounds, including much of Melbourne, belong to the Wurundjeri Nation, who maintained Country unimpeded until the arrival of the British in the early nineteenth century. The invasion of land not only disrupted the lives and customs of Indigenous people but destroyed vital ecological systems. This included Country bordering the Birrarung and the greater river system, with wetlands across the lower basin of the river, many creeks linked to the river, and billabongs and wetlands from the source to the confluence. While it is often stated that sections of the river and wetlands have been lost as a result of almost 200 years of colonial development, in a spiritual sense the river of deep time remains in place, willing to respond to our desire to recognise its continued presence.

There are many parts of the inner city of Melbourne that I know well. I have lived in the city for over sixty years and I do not need a map, or even a street sign, to find my way around. I could have walked many, many places these last months, in an effort to commemorate my younger brother: back lanes, football grounds, schoolyards and street corners. Each would have conjured an aspect of his life, a moment when I would have felt his presence with ease; his beautiful face and smile, his adoration of his older brother and the anxieties that sometimes suffocated him in later life. But it was standing on the bank of the Birrarung where I sought him, and found him and now repeatedly return to with him. During my early mapping excursions, I felt no need to ask myself why I had chosen the river as the site for what has become a regular pilgrimage. I don't expect that I would have known why at the time. But I think I do know now.

The Birrarung River is truly sacred, in both a historic and contemporary sense. Despite the vandalisation it has suffered, the river has defied the ravages of colonialism, as has the Wurundjeri Nation.

I believe I sought my brother there, firstly, and simply, because we enjoyed so much happiness and freedom on the river when we were kids. A more profound reasoning, one that I am only beginning to come to terms with, is that I feel deeply indebted to the river. Its strength humbles me and invites me to celebrate my brother as a life force. He had struggled with his health in recent years, to the point that some people will unfortunately remember him as becoming permanently debilitated. The river reminds me that he was far from this. As I have written elsewhere, what I only now realise about my younger brother is that he was a person of tremendous courage and strength. He was far stronger than I will ever be.

Always Was, Always Will Be

The most recent global climate strike, in September 2019, attracted millions of people across the world. The conservative estimate of the number of people who took to the streets in Australia is 300 000. I joined the Melbourne event, on a sunny Friday afternoon, where more than 100 000 people gathered around the Treasury Gardens before marching through the CBD. The crowd was so large that when the lead marchers completed their circular journey of the city they almost swallowed the tail of this mighty serpent of collective action. I intended to document that march by taking photographs, which has been my practice for many years now. It was not until I pointed my camera at a young teenager carrying a sign – *POLITICIANS ARE KILLERS* – that I realised I had forgotten to return the memory card to the camera after downloading images of the Birrarung River days before. I decided to stand on a street corner and wait for the march to begin before joining the procession.

I was soon met by another writer, Robert Power, a friend I had not seen for some time. We talked about our admiration for the passion and energy of the young people about to lead the march. We spoke about the failure of politicians and the absence of moral leadership in nominal democracies such as Australia, the United States and the United Kingdom. I eventually mentioned the recent death of my brother and the effect it had had on me. I explained to Robert that I had found it difficult to do any work, including writing, and had spent most of my time walking and running, but doing little else. Robert, like me, is a university professor. But also like me, he comes from the other side of the tracks and is proudly a little rough around the edges.

He observed me closely as I spoke and said, 'What do you think you're going through?'

'I think I'm fucked', I shrugged.

Sceptical of my self-diagnosis, he placed a hand on my shoulder and offered, 'I don't reckon that's it'.

'What do you mean?' I asked.

'I'm sure you have been saddened by your loss', he said, 'but you're not fucked. Death is a deeply spiritual event and I think that what you've done is given yourself the time and space to experience it, rather than rush on and lie to yourself that you can leave it behind.'

He then winked at me. 'You'll be okay.'

The marchers gathered behind a cordon of police before heading off. I heard the beginning of a familiar chant. The climate strike march was being led by a group of young Aboriginal people, proudly waving the black, yellow and red tricolour. As they passed by, I tapped my foot to the beat of 'Always Was, Always Will Be, Aboriginal Land ... Always Was, Always Will Be ...' They were followed by many, many thousands of people, young and old, energised, angry, frustrated and ready to fight.

We are at a pivotal moment in time. We are also in the middle of a storm of our own making. Few of us know what will come next, not with any certainty, at least. There is no doubt though that the future will be challenging. How we meet that challenge will determine the life and death of human and non-human species. I fear for the future of my grandchildren. I fear deeply for the ongoing protection of Aboriginal Country. I'm not sure what to do next in the struggle for climate justice, although I am certain that, tactically, direct action will play an important role. I also know that I believe in the crowd, that I gain energy from the actions of others. I also know that I must be *in the world* in order to respect it.

THE TERRIBLE TRUTH
OF CLIMATE CHANGE

Joëlle Gergis

The latest science is alarming, even for climate scientists. In June 2019 I delivered a keynote presentation on Australia's vulnerability to climate change and our policy challenges at the annual meeting of the Australian Meteorological and Oceanographic Society, the main conference for those working in the climate science community. I saw it as an opportunity to summarise the post-election political and scientific reality we now face.

As one of the dozen or so Australian lead authors on the United Nations Intergovernmental Panel on Climate Change's (IPCC) sixth assessment report, currently underway, I have a deep appreciation of the speed and severity of climate change unfolding across the planet. Last year I was also appointed as one of the scientific advisors to the Climate Council, Australia's leading independent body providing expert advice to the public on climate science and policy. In short, I am in the confronting position of being one of the few Australians who sees the terrifying reality of the climate crisis.

Preparing for this talk I experienced something gut-wrenching. It was the realisation that there is now nowhere to hide from the terrible truth. The last time this happened to me, I was visiting my father in hospital following emergency surgery for a massive brain haemorrhage. As he lay unconscious in intensive care, I examined his CT scan with one of the attending surgeons, who gently explained that the dark patch covering nearly a quarter of the image of his brain was a pool of blood. Although they had done their best to drain the area and stem the bleeding, the catastrophic nature of the damage was undeniable. The brutality of the evidence was clear – the full weight of it sent my stomach into freefall.

The results coming out of the climate science community at the moment are, even for experts, similarly alarming.

One common metric used to investigate the effects of global warming is known as 'equilibrium climate sensitivity'. This is the full amount of global surface warming that will eventually occur in response to a doubling of atmospheric CO_2 concentrations compared to pre-industrial times. It's sometimes referred to as the holy grail of climate science because it helps quantify the specific risks posed to human society as the planet continues to warm.

We know that CO_2 concentrations have risen from pre-industrial levels of 280 parts per million (ppm) to approximately 410 ppm today, the highest recorded in at least three million years. Without major mitigation efforts, we are likely to reach 560 ppm by around 2060.

When the IPCC's fifth assessment report was published in 2013, it estimated that such a doubling of CO_2 was likely to produce warming within the range of 1.5 to 4.5°C as the Earth reaches a new equilibrium. However, preliminary estimates calculated from the latest global climate models (being used in the current IPCC assessment, due out in 2021) are far higher than with the previous generation of models. Early reports are predicting that a doubling of CO_2 may in fact produce between 2.8 and 5.8°C of warming. Incredibly, at least eight of the latest models produced by leading research centres in the United States, the United Kingdom, Canada and France are showing climate sensitivity of 5°C or warmer.

When these results were first released at a climate modelling workshop in March 2019, a flurry of panicked emails from my IPCC colleagues flooded my inbox. What if the models are right? Has the Earth already crossed some kind of tipping point? Are we experiencing abrupt climate change right now? The model runs aren't all available yet, but when many of the most advanced models in the world are independently reproducing the same disturbing results, it's hard not to worry.

When the UN's Paris Agreement was adopted in December 2015, it defined a specific goal: to keep global warming to well below 2°C and as close as possible to 1.5°C above pre-industrial levels (defined as the climate conditions experienced during the 1850–1900 period). While admirable in intent, the agreement did not impose legally binding limits on signatory nations and contained no enforcement mechanisms. Instead, each country committed to publicly disclosed Nationally Determined Contributions (NDCs) to reduce emissions. In essence, it is up to each nation to act in the public interest.

Even achieving the most ambitious goal of 1.5°C will see the further destruction of between 70 and 90 per cent of reef-building corals compared to today, according to the IPCC's *Special Report on Global Warming of 1.5°C*, released last October. With 2°C of warming, a staggering 99 per cent of tropical coral reefs disappear. An entire component of the Earth's biosphere – our planetary life-support system – would be eliminated. The knock-on effects on the 25 per cent of all marine life that depends on coral reefs would be profound and immeasurable.

So how is the Paris Agreement actually panning out?

In 2017, we reached 1°C of warming above global pre-industrial conditions. According to the UN Environment Programme's (UNEP) *Emissions Gap Report*, released in November 2018, current unconditional NDCs will see global average temperature rise by 2.9 to 3.4°C above pre-industrial levels by the end of this century.

To restrict warming to 2°C above pre-industrial levels, the world needs to triple its current emissions reduction pledges. If that's not bad enough, to restrict global warming to 1.5°C, global ambition needs to increase fivefold.

Meanwhile, the Australian federal government has a target of reducing emissions by 26 to 28 per cent below 2005 levels by 2030, which experts believe is more aligned with global warming of 3 to 4°C. Despite Prime Minister Scott Morrison's claim that we will meet our Paris Agreement commitments 'in a canter', the UNEP report clearly identifies Australia as one of the G20 nations that will fall short of achieving its already inadequate NDCs by 2030.

Even with the 1°C of warming we've already experienced, 50 per cent of the Great Barrier Reef is dead. We are witnessing catastrophic ecosystem collapse of the largest living organism on the planet. As I share this horrifying information with audiences around the country, I often pause to allow people to try and really take that information in.

Increasingly after my speaking events, I catch myself unexpectedly weeping in my hotel room or on flights home. Every now and then, the reality of what the science is saying manages to thaw the emotionally frozen part of myself I need to maintain to do my job. In those moments, what surfaces is pure grief. It's the only feeling that comes close to the pain I felt processing the severity of my dad's brain injury. Being willing to acknowledge the arrival of the point of no return is an act of bravery.

But these days my grief is rapidly being superseded by rage. Volcanically explosive rage. Because in the very same IPCC report that outlines the details of the impending apocalypse, the climate science community clearly stated that limiting warming to 1.5°C is geophysically possible.

Past emissions alone are unlikely to raise global average temperatures to 1.5°C above pre-industrial levels. The IPCC report states that any further warming beyond the 1°C already recorded would likely be less than 0.5°C over the next twenty to thirty years, if all anthropogenic greenhouse gas emissions were reduced to zero immediately. That is, if we act urgently, it is technically feasible to turn things around. The only thing missing is strong global policy.

Although the very foundation of human civilisation is at stake, the world is on track to seriously overshoot our UN targets. Worse still, global carbon emissions are still rising. In response, scientists are prioritising research on how the planet has responded during other warm periods in the Earth's history.

The most comprehensive summary of conditions experienced during past warm periods in the Earth's recent history was published in June 2018 in one of our leading journals, *Nature Geoscience*, by fifty-nine leading experts from seventeen countries. The report concluded that warming of between 1.5 and 2°C in the past was enough to see significant shifts in climate zones, and land and aquatic ecosystems 'spatially reorganize'.

These changes triggered substantial long-term melting of ice in Greenland and Antarctica, unleashing 6 to 13 metres of global sea-level rise lasting thousands of years.

Examining the Earth's climatic past tells us that even between 1.5 and 2°C of warming sees the world reconfigure in ways that people don't yet appreciate. All bets are off between 3 and 4°C, where we are currently headed. Parts of Australia will become uninhabitable, as other areas of our country become increasingly ravaged by extreme weather events.

In 2019 the Australian Meteorological and Oceanographic Society's annual conference was held in Darwin, where the infamous Cyclone Tracy struck on Christmas Day in 1974, virtually demolishing the entire city. More than 70 per cent of the city's buildings, including 80 per cent of its houses, were destroyed. Seventy-one people were killed and most of the 48 000 residents made homeless. Conditions were so dire that around 36 000 people were evacuated, many by military aircraft. It was a disaster of monumental proportions.

As I collated this information for my presentation, it became clear to me that Cyclone Tracy is a warning. Without major action, we will see tropical cyclones drifting into areas on the southern edge of current cyclone zones, into places such as south-east Queensland and northern New South Wales, where infrastructure is not ready to cope with cyclonic conditions.

These areas currently house more than 3.6 million people; we simply aren't prepared for what is upon us.

There is a very rational reason why Australian schoolkids are now taking to the streets – the immensity of what is at stake is truly staggering. Staying silent about this planetary emergency no longer feels like an option for me either. Given how disconnected policy is from scientific reality in this country, an urgent and pragmatic national conversation is now essential. Otherwise, living on a destabilised planet is the terrible truth that we will all face.

As a climate scientist at this fraught point in our history, the most helpful thing I can offer is the same professionalism that the doctor displayed late that night in Dad's intensive-care ward. A clear-eyed and compassionate look at the facts.

We still have time to try to avert the scale of the disaster, but we must respond as we would in an emergency. The question is, can we muster the best of our humanity in time?

HEARTS ON THE WIRE

Andrea Gaynor

The fences went up even before the court challenge failed. Police stood guard, relaxed but close, as workers laid panels of wire mesh into orange plastic bases. This land in southern Perth was reserved for an extension of the Roe Highway, Stage 8; a long-dormant plan which in 2014 became part of Tony Abbott's Perth Freight Link to Fremantle. The fence was the first step in making the plan a reality and the bushland into a death row; now only those involved in the execution would have access to the condemned.

The fence was despised, but artist Susie Waller dreamed up a project that refigured it as a canvas on which people could express their frustration, love and hopes for a commutation of the sentence, or at least a stay of execution. Inspired by the Noongar story of the rainbow serpent or Wagyl that created the nearby Beeliar wetlands – through which the highway would also pass – Waller provided colourful cardboard hearts for people to write on and tie to the fence. I wrote my own message on a yellow heart and tearfully fastened it among others declaring love for the wetlands, a desire to protect the endangered Carnaby's black cockatoo or, simply, 'No Roe 8'.

This wasn't my local patch, but it had all the tough and intriguing old beauty of Swan coastal plain woodland. My second childhood home had been built on similar woodland and I had played in remnants on the block next door until they, too, were flattened for a three-bedroom, two-bathroom home with a built-in garage.

The day bulldozing began in earnest, I took my two children to the Coolbellup bushland. As the dusty violence of bush annihilation took place inside the fence, we walked through the then-unfenced section to the west. We saw a tawny frogmouth in a small tree, still as a broken bough. A path led us under the reaching banksia and tall marri, between the grasstrees like frozen fireworks – so remarkable yet familiar – and the 'dinosaur plant' macrozamias. We lingered a while then returned to the fence, where we met a man with a camera. He had come – as he had been coming for years – to record the frogmouth family that had lived and bred in the same tree for generations.

Three weeks and three days later, after a Christmas reprieve, more than a thousand people gathered at dawn in a desperate bid to save the remaining bush. We pushed down the fence – hearts heavy on the sand – and occupied the site, surrounding the machinery until driven back by mounted police, or arrested. That afternoon the tawny frogmouths' tree was literally bulldozed out from under them, the startled birds flying off giddily in the sharp sunlight. Five days later, the fledgling was photographed lifeless at the base of a tree. He, along with the many bandicoots found dead of shock, exposure and car impact, became potent symbols of a community's outrage.

This was a small-scale re-enactment of a scene played out countless times on a massive scale: for the ever-expanding suburbs of Perth, for farms, for forestry. But the old, tired cry – the bushland must go! – is becoming less convincing as we awake to the reality of our shared vulnerability. The changing climate of the south-west of Australia is putting pressure on the bushland, perhaps outstripping its capacity to adapt, just as human demands – on people and nature alike – are intensifying.

Our hearts have been torn from the fence by the wind and broken by the devastation we have witnessed. And we, too, are changing hearts, and minds.

Postscript: After the March 2017 election, the Labor state government cancelled Roe 8. In an ironic reversal of the protest scenes, volunteers re-erected the fences to protect the cleared land, allowing it to regenerate while restoration plans were made.

TEARING

AWAY

BUT HOW ARE WE SUPPOSED TO HAVE ANY FUN?

Jane Rawson

Let me tell you about the things I have lost.

Not my home. Not my habitat. Not my family. Not my nation. Not my right to vote. Not my right to speak. Not my freedom. Not my life.

But I have lost:

- drinking two martinis, good ones, then walking to the cinema to sit quiet, delighted, drunk on ten-dollar ticket night; afterwards, the short train-ride home
- walking in Emporium shopping centre, making the sensuous circuit from Muji (linen bedding) to T2 (Melbourne Breakfast tea, loose leaf) to Mecca Cosmetica (a spray of Byredo Eleventh Hour, 'the smell of things ending ... the last perfume on Earth')
- sitting down to a start-of-summer café breakfast of cold brew coffee (a slice of orange; ice) and a serve of cherry pie with cream, my trolley loaded with vegetables from the market
- laughing in a Footscray alley, the scent of piss almost scrubbed away, listening to a friend perform his experimental music.

I love the bourgeois products of humanity. Books, films, music, architecture, travel, wine, coffee, fashion: I love all of it. I hear that a lot of environmentalists loathe humanity and its accomplishments, but I'm not one of them. Humans invented train travel and fountain pens, a winding path through a meadow and a small wooden bridge over a chattering rivulet; humans invented the double bass and custard tarts; humans invented velvet, bias-cut dresses, the Chrysler Building, Perfect Manhattans, picnics, preserved lemon and sleeping in. Humans invented mix tapes. We have a lot to be proud of.

For most of my life I have lived among the glorious fruits of human invention: Canberra's joyous 1990s DIY music scene; San Francisco's headlong online creativity at the turn of the century; Melbourne's adorably starry-eyed, self-infatuated food and literature obsession.

And now, suddenly, I don't.

I left Footscray and moved to regional Tasmania. Sold up, priced myself out of the market, packed my things and can't go back. I live in the bush now, where everything is a drive away, unless by everything you mean trees, birds, small jumping marsupials and the mountains wreathed in mist until 11 in the morning.

I am not the outdoor type. I like to walk home a little drunk along city streets, smiling at the antics of passers-by and flagging a taxi if I get too tired. I do not like to walk through scrub hour after hour with the sun flaking my skin and tiny flies climbing into my nostrils to drink my snot, dying in the bush if I get too tired.

So maybe I should say, let me tell you about the things I have lost:

- my dreams
- being me.

You know those apartments on the Upper East Side of Manhattan? The ones with picture rails and floor-to-ceiling bookshelves, faded Persian rugs and deep wooden windowsills? The kind of place you might sink into your armchair in front of a roaring fire to sip a glass of Syrah while you read the latest Ali Smith, the smell of home-made bread wafting from the kitchen (the sourdough starter a gift from friend and neighbour, Colson Whitehead). That kind of apart-ment: that's what I should have left Melbourne for. That was the next logical step. Not a falling-down cottage at the end of a long dirt road surrounded by trees in the south of Tasmania.

IN 2014 I WROTE (WITH MY FRIEND AND COLLEAGUE JAMES Whitmore) a book about climate change. In the couple of years previ-ous, every scientist we spoke to told us there was no getting out of it: climate change was here and it was ruining lives. But regular people and the media were still talking about climate change like it was a thing we were going to stop: no one seemed to be figuring out what they would do when it arrived. That worried us.

Our guide – *The Handbook* – laid out what people could do to prepare themselves, their families and their communities to survive the effects of climate change. The book was inspired by an interview on ABC Radio with Professor Jean Palutikof, director of the National Climate Change Adaptation Research Facility. She was talking about the effects a worsening climate would likely have on Australia. 'So where should I move?' host Waleed Aly jokingly asked her. She'd clearly been considering the matter for months, probably years. As an expert in climate adaptation, she must have thought about how to get through climate change a lot more often than the average person had.

He seemed surprised that she actually had an answer – that she really did think Melbourne wasn't a great choice. You should choose a developed country, she told him, definitely not in the tropics. Prob-ably Scandinavia or Canada: places where agriculture is limited now by temperature because it's too cold. A bit of warming will help in those places. If it had to be Australia, Tasmania, she supposed.

James and I wanted to know if she was right. In our chapter 'Where should I live?' we looked at all the different options and concluded there are no guaranteed safe havens.

'Living with climate change isn't just about worsening or unpredictable weather', we wrote:

> It's about society, and about how society will react to that worsening and unpredictable weather. It's about all kinds of complex inputs into agriculture, and how our food gets around. It's about whether you're the kind of person who does best by yourself or among others. It's about whether you're prepared to jettison a whole life – friends, family, job, your favourite bar – that you're probably very attached to and launch into something altogether different.

So, no clear answers. Nowhere safe to go. But I have always preferred easy answers and I couldn't let go of that one from Professor Palutikof: 'if it has to be Australia, Tasmania'.

I looked at a few real estate sites. I subscribed to Hobart's 'Farm Gate Market' newsletter. I lurked on the Cygnet community Facebook page. And meanwhile, I kept writing and kept publishing.

The writing paid off. I got kind of famous. My novel was longlisted for the Miles Franklin literary award. I was asked to launch books, to write blurbs. People started paying me to show up to things. The ABC seemed to be inviting me on the radio every five minutes. A major UK publisher picked up my book. I had long essays published in *Overland* and *Meanjin*. My career was about to go places. If someone hadn't done nail art based on my novel cover, they were going to any day. The Manhattan apartment was just over the horizon. But so was my move to Tasmania.

The problem was that I had become more and more afraid of the world humans were building. I was more and more disgusted by my part in it. We were heading for a time when almost everything would be human: the perverted climate, and the animal-denuded landscape. Human endeavour looks so much more beautiful when it appears in shining islands among a world mostly natural – an adornment to all the other wonders the Earth provides. By itself, it starts to look a bit gaudy: a bit much.

That essay in *Meanjin* was about a topic that had started bothering me not long after *The Handbook* was published: the death of wild animals. Not extinctions, so much, but precipitous drops in the numbers of nearly every animal on Earth, while the numbers of humans and of cows, sheep and chickens – definitely chickens – rose and rose and rose and rose. In the course of my research I was finding over and over again that there were almost no animals left on Earth who weren't us or the animals we'd bred to serve us.

It affected me. I tried to change my life to minimise the harm I caused to wild animals (having long since given up on making any dent in the massive quantities of emissions caused by heedless governments, overfunded defence forces and profit-maddened corporations). I stopped buying new clothes or food I wasn't really hungry for – agriculture is a massive destructor of wildlife habitat – but when it came to giving up books (they're unnecessary, right?) I baulked. I love books. I read about a hundred of them a year. I get a chunk of those from the library and others second-hand, but I probably buy fifty new books every year. And wine. I definitely buy wine. Perfume. I go to see bands; I listen to their music online and on vinyl. I drink coffee; also tea. I take trips, and some of them are to places where the roads are strewn with dead creatures.

I realised that everything I love to do destroys the world. All those wonderful things that make me so happy to be alive are making everything else dead. I sat in an overpriced café in a Melbourne laneway and drank a batch brew coffee and actually cried because I realised that I couldn't be a part of any of this anymore: not laneways, not batch brew coffee, not buying a gorgeous new dress off the internet, not anything. I cried because I was out of choices. And then I went somewhere where the things I love to do, weren't.

At least, I thought, I'll be safe.

IN *THE HANDBOOK*, DISCUSSING WHERE OR IF YOU SHOULD move to escape climate change, we wrote,

> [e]migration, even if it's within your own country, is expensive, exhausting and time-consuming. You don't want your resources depleted before you even head off, and you want plenty left to help you get settled. A new place is confusing at the best of times, and going while things are calm should give you time to gather plenty of information before you have to deal with crises. If you're going to be beset by bushfire or flood, you want to be somewhere you know the terrain, the way the weather behaves, the safe places to shift to.

Two days after I moved to bushland Tasmania, my new neighbourhood was on fire. I did not know the terrain, the way the weather behaved, or the safe places to shift to. I had no bushfire plan. I had no hoses, and no ladder to climb to clear out the gutters. I didn't even have a pair of sturdy gloves. I was screwed.

Honestly, I blame that stupid book I wrote. It said:

> On the off chance that we get around to significantly reducing our emissions, predictions are that there will be 5–25% more extreme fire danger days in south east Australia by 2020 and

10–50% by 2050. If we carry on as we are now, they'll go up 15–65% by 2020; by 2050 there will be double or triple the number of extreme fire days. Tasmania is a lucky exception as it's likely to have little increase in extreme fire days.

Lucky exception. Except that in the three years since I wrote that chapter, everything changed for Tasmania. As Richard Flanagan wrote in the *Guardian* during the fires, 'I had understood that climate change's effects on Tasmania would be significant but not disastrous … compared to much of the world it didn't seem catastrophic. But it wasn't so'. Tasmania has warmed and dried much faster than anticipated: a wet island full of foliage resistant to fire has become the opposite. Dry thunderstorms – a phenomenon largely new to the state, with multiple lightning strikes but no rain – have lit fires all over a landscape that is now just waiting to burn.

So there I was, in the Huon Valley where – having done my homework – I had fled to escape climate change and my contribution to ecocide, only to find myself fleeing again. A fire had taken hold to the south-west of us, and all week the radio had been telling us Friday would be an awful day, hot and very windy. 'As bad as 1967', experts and old people were saying: in February of that year, 110 fires burned 2640 square kilometres of southern Tasmania over the course of just five hours. Sixty-two people died, 900 were injured and more than 7000 lost their homes. I have never been in a bushfire, but my parents and husband lived in Canberra during the fires there, and I lived in Melbourne at the time of Black Saturday. Everything I knew about bushfire had convinced me it was fast, unpredictable and delivered death in the most horrible ways.

So when the howling wind woke us at 4 am that Friday, I decided we weren't going to stick around to see what happened. I suddenly had a bushfire plan: get out, right now. In the grey, smoky pre-dawn, we packed the car, kissed our new home goodbye and drove to

Hobart. We holed up in a motel in Bellerive, me, my husband and the cats, waiting for the danger to pass. I scrolled through Twitter, watching flurries of white ash swirl by the glass sliding doors, the smoke thick over Hobart and just about every other place in the state. We watched the cricket with the sound down and I wondered why Cheryl Strayed, a famous person, had followed my account. It turned out my latest novel had been mentioned in the *New York Times*, given a big thumbs-up by author Elizabeth McCracken in the 'By the Book' column. I could not have felt further from New York. I could not have felt further from the excited feelers that US agents and film production companies were stretching towards my publisher. Some other person wrote that book and some other person was going to reap a massive advance and a film tie-in book cover. Some other person will live in that New York apartment drinking martinis, because we have broken the world so thoroughly that only a person in an alternate timeline could possibly be living that life. On Saturday morning, when the weather had calmed a little, we went back to our home. Fire was still very much – as they like to say on the radio – 'in the landscape'.

By the second day of autumn 2019 here in the Huon Valley, the fires are still burning. It's 38 degrees outside, a hot wind blowing from the north. These fires started around Christmas, and for a full eight weeks they've been threatening property and lives. No one can relax. People are losing their minds. This is what it is now, the world. And some part of me wonders if I moved here on purpose, for this: to punish myself for my part in making things this way, to face the thing that's been frightening the crap out of me for so many years. As a man in Castle Forbes Bay tells ABC Radio, 'I've done all the preparing I can do. I just want it to come over the hill now. I need to know what happens next'.

What does happen next? Now we know that it's an endless cycle of this. Anyone who's listened to a few days' worth of ABC local radio's bushfire warnings – and that's now nearly everyone in Australia – has experienced a metaphor of our future under climate change: the same message of threat and destruction over and over and over again until you can't help but be numb to it but are unable to succumb to the boredom, because at any point it could be you getting the emergency warning, you who has to flee, but only if the path is clear.

'The fire will impact Bermuda Road, Frypan Road, Dickenson Creek Road, Tunbridges Road, Watsons Road, Lightwood Creek Road, through to Sunny Hills Road within the next sixty minutes. The fire is uncontrollable. Burning embers falling in this area will threaten your home before the main fire. Smoke and ash will make it difficult to see and breathe. What to do: If your home is well prepared for very high-risk fires and you can actively defend it, it should provide shelter. If your home is unprepared, evacuate now to a safer location only if the path is clear.'

None of our homes are prepared, there is no safer location and the path is never clear.

RETREAT IS NO ANSWER. 'AT WHAT POINT DO YOU PULL OUT of working/fighting for the common good and focus on saving yourself?' one scientist asked James Whitmore and me when we wondered where she would move to escape climate change, and we instantly felt shame for asking.

I can't let myself despair, though I desperately want to: I helped make this problem and it's my problem to solve. Conservative commentators accuse environmentalists of wanting to send everyone back to the Stone Age, of being advocates of hair-shirt-wearing guilt, of being anti-human. I never wanted to be that person, but here I am, turning my back on everything I love because of my guilt over my complicity.

I do believe that in this current rapacious capitalist system, it is impossible to be human and not do terrible damage. But it's not the being human that does it: it's the rapacious capitalist system. So now I am trying to understand how you live with all this, hold it, don't flinch away from it; how you try to change it; and how you still find room in your heart for creativity and joy. As Frances Flanagan bemoans in her *Inside Story* essay, 'Climate Change and the New Work Order', the struggle with climate change has narrowed to be about 'things I was supposed to say no to rather than the grand, existential puzzle of what to say yes to'.

Around me I see artists grappling with this question; or maybe they're grappling with something else entirely and I'm just so obsessed with my own problems that I think everyone else must be too. Natasha Lyonne's Netflix series, *Russian Doll*, follows a woman who can't stop dying, and whose every death destroys a little bit more of what she loves. Everything just keeps getting worse until she starts finding reasons to love the world, to find joy in life. In Sandra Newman's latest novel, *The Heavens*, a woman lives in one almost-perfect world and dreams another parallel life, but with every dream she alters something in the almost-perfect world until it becomes a terrible place, much the same as the one we're living in now. By being alive, even when she's trying to be good, she's breaking the world. Should she despair, hate herself, die? Or can she find a way to love life regardless?

In the newspapers, the novels, the essays of Australia, America, England there are hundreds of writers feeling the same way I do. Our future and our children's future have become uncertain. The world around us is exploited and ruined. Our politics are corrupted. There is so much more death than there should be and so much less hope. We are all feeling immensely sad. For so long our lives have been perfect; now that we have to live like other people, it is breaking our hearts.

A lot of the time I feel immensely sad for the terrible roll-call of loss. But here I am, surrounded by birds and trees, a sky full of stars, a sweet smell in the night air. What have I lost? Sure, my dreams. I can always make new ones.

What haven't I lost? Not my home. Not my habitat. Not my family. Not my nation. Not my right to vote. Not my right to speak. Not my freedom. Not my life.

Readings

Frances Flanagan, 'Climate Change and the New Work Order', *Inside Story*, online journal, 2019, <insidestory.org.au/climate-change-and-the-new-work-order/>.

Richard Flanagan, 'Tasmania Is Burning: The Climate Disaster Future Has Arrived While Those in Power Laugh at Us', *Guardian*, 5 February 2019.

Sandra Newman, *The Heavens*, Grove Atlantic, New York, 2019.

Jane Rawson and James Whitmore, *The Handbook: Surviving and Living with Climate Change*, Transit Lounge, Melbourne, 2019.

WHAT DOES A TEACUP HAVE TO DO WITH BUSHFIRES?

Kirsten Wehner

On 8 January 2003, lightning strikes ignited fires in the dense bush to the west of Canberra. Ten days later, fire fronts reached the edge of the city and around 3 pm they raced up the slopes of Mount Stromlo and engulfed the observatory on the summit. Most of the facility's telescopes were destroyed, along with the technical and workshop buildings, the historic director's house, residents' homes and the pine, tea tree and eucalypt forest that encircled the hill. In a few short hours, the mountain's landscape was transformed beyond recognition.

After the fire, someone – I'm not sure who – found a chipped and scorched white cafeteria-style teacup among the ruins of the 74-inch telescope. Fused to its handle was a splatter of aluminium, a remnant of the telescope dome which had melted in the intense heat, dripping and dropping onto objects on the ground floor then cooling into fantastical shapes. I discovered this curious artefact in the National Museum of Australia's collection several years after the fire and I've returned to see it many times since. For it captures for me the loss of the beloved landscape of my childhood, revealing as a personal and painful experience one of the key trajectories of the

Australian Anthropocene – the acceleration of our continent's bush-fire regime.

I grew up on Mount Stromlo, in one of the houses – No 8 – grouped just down the hill from the observatory offices. There was a relatively permeable barrier between work and home life on the mountain, and during school holidays I would often wander up to visit my dad in his corner room. I usually managed to turn up to knock on his window mid-morning, assured of a trip to the communal lounge where Milka, the tea lady, would ply me with a warm, milky drink and Arnotts packet biscuits. For a six-year-old – bliss!

The teacup was probably one of the many Milka set out and washed up each day. Perhaps I once drank from it. The twisted shard of aluminium came from one of the telescopes that were my father's pride and joy. These objects were part of the observatory's texture. They were participants in the myriad everyday experiences that made my self during my first decades, and now, charred and deformed, they express for me the observatory's violent transformation.

Mount Stromlo was evacuated before the bushfire swept through. There was no loss of human life on the mountain and in many ways the observatory recovered well. Much of the research infrastructure was rebuilt, with updated scientific and technical facilities, and the heritage offices were even restored to their original appearance. I often tell myself that I shouldn't be too sad about the burning of a bunch of buildings. My experience of bushfire, to date, has been gentle compared to that of many Australians who have lost their homes, livelihoods and families.

And yet, this teacup, with its weird aluminium wing, reminds me that losses do not need to be visible and truly tragic to be meaningful. I feel a persistent grief about the absence of the observatory of my childhood, an awareness that my memories of rambling around the mountain – building cubbies in the forest, talking to the cows that grazed the back of the hill, drinking tea with my dad –

are now forever disjointed from the living landscape. As our annual bushfire season lengthens and burns increase in severity and frequency, it seems all too likely that making sense of such experiences of dislocation will become as much a part of our lives as making and sharing tea and biscuits.

WEEKEND IN GONDWANA

Jo Chandler

Refugium: A geographical region that has remained unaltered by a climatic change affecting surrounding regions and that therefore forms a haven for relict fauna and flora.

It's a gloriously frigid, olde-worlde, 350 ppm-or-less kind of day when I haul out my backpack, lace up my adventure boots and head south to Gondwana.

With summers cycling closer, hotter, longer – sweating dread – I've lately been rummaging through my closet of high Holocene winters: soup on slow combustion stoves, spencers and stockings, coal briquettes, puddles that crack underfoot, frost over paddocks and breath hanging in air, chilblains – remember those? Cold will of course still come, in extremis, supercharged by wild shifts in the firmament. But the winters of my memory belong to a vanished epoch, and I'm bereft. This isn't nostalgia, rather a condition environmental philosopher Glenn Albrecht has identified as 'solastalgia', derived from solace (the lack of it) and desolation: 'the pain experienced when there is recognition that the place where one resides and that one loves is under immediate assault'. A fortifying wander back through the geological continuum promises some perspective. Comfort, cold or otherwise, is surely too much to ask.

The plane from Melbourne is scarcely up and it's down again in Launceston. A two-hour drive west and we're pulling up on Tasmania's Central Plateau. The southerly from the Antarctic is brutal but the plateau – the island's highest landscape – is washed in eye-watering, pale sunlight, the kind that doesn't warm so much as cook unprotected flesh. On a wide, wild plain not far from Lake Mackenzie, three figures are at work in the middle distance. They're ecologists mapping environmental *refugia*, locations where topography, geography and climate have contrived a sweet spot within which besieged species find nurturing conditions for survival.

Even a day or two will do me, in my own search for refuge.

Walking out to them, I'm lagging in the sure-footed wake of Ben French, a young ecologist who has enthused about the bush, the threats posed to it by climate change and his PhD subject – a rescue strategy for *Athrotaxis cupressoides*, Tasmania's endemic pencil pine – for the length of the ride from the airport. The venerable tree's majesty is rather lost in translation from the Latin. It dates back 150 million years, one of the oldest surviving plant lineages on Earth. 'There's just something about them', says French. 'Something charismatic ...' He's struggling for the words, as I will, and do. Google the images of the late, legendary nature photographer Peter Dombrovskis – 'Pencil pine at pool of Siloam, Walls of Jerusalem National Park, Tasmania, 1982'. You'll see our transcendent, gnarly, haunting, humbling, portentous, gobsmacking problem.

The ground beneath my boots feels rubbery, otherworldly – and it is. Sphagnum peat can take millennia to form. It belongs to the same Gondwanan landscape as the pencil pine – the understorey and overstorey of the same primeval narrative. It deserves worship, not clumsy intrusion. It sighs and shifts as I pick a route across spiky hummocks and between clumps of vivid green, velvety cushion plants – up to

1000 years old, sorry, so sorry! – weaving around littered lumps of dolerite and basalt; occasionally stumbling into the sucking quagmire that threads the entire plain.

The bog – but really, who could call it such? – extends over an area the size of several footy grounds, enclosed by stands of snow gums (*Eucalyptus coccifera*) and a tumble of Jurassic cliffs. It's a rare, precious ecosystem – a steeping sponge cake of decomposing plants and mosses that purifies and regulates water flows, nurtures biodiversity, and works heroically to cool the planet and mitigate humanity's spiralling atmospheric crimes. Barely 3 per cent of the Earth's surface hosts peatlands, yet they soak up and store more carbon than all the world's other vegetation combined. Damage to these carbon sinks is a major source of greenhouse gas emissions, and they are being whacked by ever more severe droughts and rampaging firestorms. Which is why efforts to try to restore them, like the one underway here, are imperative.

Everywhere, this plain sprouts ghostly clumps of knee-high, ash-grey antlers – the remains of *Richea scoparia*, an alpine heath which ordinarily paints a sublime springtime palette of pink and red and creamy yellow across the highlands. But these specimens won't bloom again. They were roasted in January 2016 when, after a record-breaking spell of heat and drought across the island, dry lightning strikes ignited even these historically non-combustible wetlands. Wildfires consumed almost 20 000 hectares of World Heritage-listed wilderness that summer. And that was merely the curtain-raiser. Three years later, in the summer of 2018–19, blazes sparked by massive dry lightning storms burned another 95 000-plus hectares of wilderness. Months later, these areas are still a no-go zone.

The bog is pockmarked with fire damage of various degrees. The only colours flowering in the rubble of rock, blackened trees and singed earth are fixed to tall rods planted in the ground by the field team – plastic squares of luminous orange, yellow, green, blue that will be used to plot aerial surveys. The crew, huddled in protective layers, is hard at work. Researcher Scott Nichols is doubled over, closely inspecting sphagnum mounds within the patchwork of survey squares. He calls out coordinates to Aimee Bliss, one of two research assistants, who scrawls them on a data sheet along with his diagnosis: 'Healthy', 'Damaged', 'Killed'.

Sphagnum is a bryophyte – the oldest of all land plants, and likely the surviving link between aquatic and land plants. The building block for the peatlands ecology, it has no defences against wildfire. The healthy specimens clinging on here, Nichols explains, are mostly edging the puddles in the bog. Understanding in granular detail the response of peatlands to fire is critical to informing evolving efforts to try to preserve and rehabilitate them. His data sheets document vegetation and animal scats, peat depth and acidity. Drone shots will add the microtopography of slope and aspect.

In the next phase Nichols, Bliss and the last of the trio, Cameron Geeves, will peg small canopies of shade cloth over some areas – sphagnum doesn't like ultraviolet radiation – scatter fertiliser to stimulate growth, transplant cuttings of healthy growth to burnt areas. Then they wait and watch and, over years to come, send in the drones to see what, if anything, works.

It's painstaking, physically battering and psychologically bruising work – these are, after all, lovers of the natural world; scientists with an unblinkered understanding of what is unfolding. I've met many like them over fifteen years, on and off, reporting on climate science, and observed the tenor of their distress rising with the temperatures and the parts per million. This is, surely, a doomed endeavour?

No, declares Professor David Bowman, the storied scientist whose work has brought me here, and who is overseeing these projects, when he strides into the picture, a six-foot-something, 61-year-old dervish of energy and flapping Gore-Tex, hollering questions and opinions over the wind. His forty-year scientific career has earned him recognition as one of the world's foremost fire ecologists. This trial may not save the bog, he concedes. But that won't constitute failure. What we may learn, he says, is that 'if we lose one of these bogs, it's basically gone forever …' Then the work would need to shift: identify unburnt bogs and 'make sure they never get burnt'.

But how would this be possible? Bowman starts reeling off strategies that smack of environmental heresy. 'It might be getting people with whipper-snippers and cutting a fire break around it. It might be getting solar-powered pumps and irrigating it during the summer. I have no bloody idea.' He expects many people will label such ideas as ridiculous. 'But everything's ridiculous now.'

Bowman was the lead author of a paper published by a cohort of distinguished Australian ecologists and biologists in 2018 urging a radical overhaul of conservation strategies in the Anthropocene, a shift to what they call 'renewal ecology'. The noble Edenic ambitions of existing conservation efforts, of recovering ecosystems, were now futile, they argued. Environmental change was 'inevitable and irrevocable'. The rate, scale and magnitude of the global crisis demanded hitherto unimaginable efforts to manage ecosystems to maximise the prospects for both biodiversity and humans. Whipper-snippering the wilderness, if that's what it takes, to salvage what is salvageable.

Renewal ecology is about pushing back, 'saying we've got nothing to lose', says Bowman. 'The precautionary principle made perfect sense in a non-Anthropocene environment, but once you are in the Anthropocene … it's pointless. "Oh, something bad *might* happen."

'No. Something bad *is* happening.'

AS THE CHUNK OF THE FRAGMENTED, FECUND SUPERCONtinent of Gondwanaland we recognise today as Australia meandered northward, eucalypts and acacias capitalised on warmer, drier conditions, evolving to tolerate and even regenerate through wild-fire. Gondwanan survivors like *A. cupressoides* clung on in damp, cool niches. Tasmania became the lifeboat for paleoendemic species, treasures that today underwrite the World Heritage status of the island's wilderness.

When Aboriginal people wandered into the scene via a land bridge around 35 000 years ago, they brought fire to manage the landscape – a practice that has long intrigued David Bowman. In all their thousands of years of occupancy, he says, Aboriginal fire regimes caused little disturbance to the Gondwanan forests. But since European colonisation, one-third of the island's pencil pines have gone. Around half the specimens on the Central Plateau were lost in a single summer, 1960–61, when graziers set the bush alight to renew grasslands for their livestock. Until the 1990s, most wildfires were the result of deliberate or inadvertent human ignition. They still are, though these days humanity doesn't need to strike the match.

Fire scars left on ancient trees and other paleo clues show that lightning has ignited Tasmania in deep history, but this occurred only rarely until 2000. Since then, dry lightning fires have become an almost annual event. In January 2016, after some of the driest and warmest months on record, eighty dry lightning fires ignited across western Tasmania. On 15 January 2019 – a single day – over 2000 strikes sparked more than sixty bushfires. Bowman likens what played out to 'an alien spaceship coming in and just attacking the island with lightning bolts'.

While there's been wide speculation that lightning activity is increasing, continuing work by scientists indicates that this is likely not the case. The lightning has always been there, they argue. What's changed is that these bolts find the kindling for an incendiary new regime. As the planet heats, the rains produced by the low-pressure systems that nurtured the ecosystems of southern Australia over the aeons have been drifting south, falling into the sea, while evaporation is increasing. 'Ongoing climate change is making dry spells longer and more frequent, increasing the fire prone area of Tasmania', scientists explained in *The Conversation* in the wake of the 2019 fires. 'Almost the whole state is becoming vulnerable to dry lightning.'

Leaving the sphagnum crew to their work, we set out across the singed landscape of Eagle Valley towards a site that the scientists unromantically identify as 'Unburnt South'. First we must traverse a swathe of desolate, burnt country, dropping in on locations where French has been doing some research gardening, planting pencil pine seeds under a range of conditions he will monitor for years to come.

Bowman, a hiker since his teens, is as weather-beaten as the country, but moves across it at a cracking pace. He launches into a running, unfiltered commentary on the scene. 'It was horrible', of course, what happened here, he says, surveying scorched rocks and trees. 'But it was amazing, there was so much learning and science, and then you are reframing thinking and breaking it down and building it up ... Do I really believe that we can restore these systems? Well, as the world's warming, it's probably a 1000-year program to be planting seeds. It's an amazing gesture.'

Lightning ignited what became the Mersey Forest Fire Complex on 13 January 2016, and over the next week blazes raged and merged, outrunning the capacity of local and interstate crews to respond. The firestorm gained such power it was spotting up to 9 kilometres ahead as it exploded up Devils Gullet – a deep, narrow glacial gorge – and onto the plateau here at Lake Mackenzie. The peatlands smouldered until May.

Images shot in late January by photographer Rob Blakers, who built his reputation capturing the beauty of the Tasmanian wilderness, revealed the shattering scale of the loss – one of the world's most treasured ecosystems reduced to a patchwork of char and toasted cushion plants. 'The Central Plateau is littered by the gaunt skeletons of burnt pencil pines', Blakers wrote in the Hobart *Mercury*, a tragedy that 'brings grief to anyone who has a sense of what the living tree is like'. Bowman told the *Age/Sydney Morning Herald* that the vanishing of these trees was akin to 'losing the thylacine'. He pulled no punches: 'I think I would be being unethical and unprofessional if I didn't form the diagnosis and say what it is – climate change. Under the current rate of warming I think this ecosystem will be gone in 50 years.'

That quote captured something of a seismic professional and personal moment, Bowman recalls. For years, he'd been tissue-wrapping his commentary with the customary caveats of science, 'always sort of dancing on the spot ... "Oh well, you know fires and the historical context, we can't really say what's climate change". And I just said, "This is what climate change looks like it. This is it". I just was over it'.

He argues for interventions like planned burnings, recognising that this looms as a 'philosophical rupture' with the concept of self-sustaining wilderness, one that offends many conservationists and greens. But the vulnerability of the bush in the Anthropocene 'has raised profound philosophical questions, and ongoing political discussion, about acceptable responses to the impacts of climate change on this world heritage area'.

Ben French summons us to look at one of his sites, where he's sown pencil pine seeds that happened – in a bit of cosmic good luck – to have been collected by the Royal Tasmanian Botanical Gardens for their seed bank not long before the fires. 'I'm trying to capture all the variability within a site', he explains, dispersing seeds between sphagnum hummocks, some up on the top, some down on the wet edges of the bog. Half of them are protected by small teepees of galvanised mesh, the remainder are at the mercy of herbivore grazers foreign and domestic – wallabies, wombats, rabbits and possums the lead culprits.

'Jo – you've walked between the markers!'

'Oh shit – did I just kill it?'

French assures me not. His anxious expression says otherwise.

Athrotaxis cupressoides can take fifty years to reach just 1 metre in height. Individual stems have been aged at over 1000 years, though it's suspected they may be much older. The pencil pine and the King Billy pine, *A. selaginoides*, are a rare pair, the only extant species of their ancient genus.

'Let's imagine this works', says Bowman. 'Let's be really optimistic – say some of these seeds take, and they germinate into little seedlings, then Ben will come here when he's my age and say, "I did that", that would be awesome.' The other possibility, he expands, is that 'we learn that it is just not going to work'. We learn that to salvage the species we're going to have to find locations where it survives 'and we're going to irrigate it, and we're going to have bloody fire breaks, and we're going to save these things because we love them … It would be quite possible, theoretically, to excavate a pencil pine, dig it up with a crane, put it on the back of a truck and take it somewhere and plant it'.

Translocation of vulnerable species – plants and animals – out of harm's way, once the solution of last resort, has gained pace and reluctant acceptance in triaging the Anthropocene emergency. Bowman raises the prospect of moving pencil pine specimens to botanic gardens, or cultivating them somewhere like Macquarie Island, where conditions may suit them for a while yet. This is the same guy who controversially argued in a *Nature* article a few years ago that one option for managing remote Australia's multiple ecological problems was to bring in elephants and rhinos to control invasive, highly combustible gamba grass. 'Of course, introducing large mammals cannot solve all of Australia's ecological-management conundrums', he wrote. 'But the usual approaches … aren't working. The full spectrum of options needs to be canvassed in an open and honest way.'

After an hour or so marching in the footprint of the inferno, surrounded by the agonies of ashen limbs reaching into blue sky, we finally find our way into Unburnt South. Indigo pools of water are surrounded by mounds of heath and greenery and stands of pencil pines. Surveying the growth under one of them, French leans in and gently teases out a young wild-sown pencil pine shoot – barely up to his first knuckle, it requires the keenest eye to find.

There's a dense glade of *A. cupressoides* gathered in the lee of a cliff, a cathedral of surviving Gondwana. Stepping inside, it's a tangle of moss and lichen, carpets of russet and yellow under labyrinthine branches. They've meandered over centuries of unhurried life, bulging joints wrapped in the wrinkled flesh of grey, flaking bark. The foliage, tendrils of delicate green, utterly unlike the familiar dressings of nearby eucalypts, turns to shades of pink and burgundy where it falls into the litter of magnificent decay.

The tree trunks are crowded close, sometimes leaning in unison, then suddenly individuals turning towards ... what? It's been discovered only lately that these are clonal organisms. 'They're all connected by underground stems and root suckers', explains Bowman. 'When you get your eye in, you can see they grow in clumps, or they grow in lines, and they're very, very, very old.' How old surviving clones like these might be is difficult to say, but as explained in a *Nature* paper he coauthored, at least some individuals may be survivors from the first seedlings that established on freshly exposed ground following the retreat of the ice sheet after the Last Glacial Maximum. 'It's not outside the realm of possibility they've been in situ for 10 000 years just spreading out', he expands.

Perhaps this glade is a single organism – communicating, socialising and supporting itself via an intricate web of hidden roots and fungal filaments, conspiracies of insects and the chemistry of scent. Science has only lately begun to crack the coded language of trees, the social network of what's being dubbed the 'wood wide web', which enables the forest community to share resources like water, to protect and care for its members and to warn them of dangers.

Shafts of sunlight insinuate themselves through the canopy, illuminating spiderwebs and bouquets of burnished moss that look more like they belong to the seabed than the forest floor. The light is dreamy. Breathing Gondwana, this inheritance of tens of millions of years of growth and renewal and survival provides some powerful solace. Wanting nothing so much as to lie down in this faerie dell and quietly metamorphose, I recall the theory that trees pump out perfumes to protect themselves from intruders. *A. cupressoides* is wafting something seductive, sedative. It's all I can do to return to my time.

Following our trio of lengthening shadows back out across the fire zone, the Anthropocene – or the Pyrocene, as Bowman's US colleague, Stephen J Pyne declares it – feels all the more achingly impoverished. But Bowman weighs in with an unexpected take. Ecology is complicated, he observes. Climate change adds to that complexity. 'It's shape-shifting, like those games people have with the strings between their fingers … the same stuff can be rearranged and you get different outcomes.' Many of these may seem to represent an undoing. But there are other shapes to conjure.

American environmental activist and deep ecology scholar Joanna Macy talks about the epic collision now playing out, of 'The Great Unravelling, under the pressure of the destruction caused by the industrial growth society' versus 'The Great Turning … the transition to a life-sustaining society' built on new and sometimes very old ways of holding the land, generating energy, producing food. 'The awesome thing about the moment that you and I share is that we don't know which is going to win out. How is the story going to end?' So she said in an interview she gave a decade ago. I wonder if she still believes the outcome is in the balance.

'The problem with the Anthropocene is that it can be presented as an end-of-times end, whereas really what it is is a threshold', says Bowman. 'It's going into a new state, things are reassembling.' We need to try to find a different, more optimistic lens, he argues, or to at least be striving to learn from what is unfolding, to not see everything through the prism of what we're losing or have lost. It will take another conversation or two for it to dawn that while I am flailing about in stages 3, 4 and 5 of my grieving (anger, bargaining, depression), Bowman has long since graduated through testing and acceptance and is craning his neck towards the sunlit uplands.

'Okay, I've got a confession to make', he says, pulling up and gesturing to a stand of casualties of the wildfires. 'Even those dead pencil pines to me have a fantastic beauty about them. It's killed, and it's sad, but I can't get angry about the fire … this was nature, nature started it.'

But it's not, I object. It's deeply unnatural – 'nature kicked in the arse by human-driven climate change'.

'Yes, there is the stupidity', he concedes, and pushes on. 'If you say, "Okay, we want to make war with the climate", then the climate is going to win. It's just going to crush us … [But] I can look at this and I go, "Well, you know it's changing. It got burnt. It's sad, but it's regenerating, and there is going to be life here, and it's still a beautiful landscape" … Even if all the pines get killed, it's still beautiful.'

French agrees to the extent that yes, 'the fact that it's copped a beating and has changed doesn't mean it is a write-off'. But the young man is less phlegmatic about what is playing out. 'I find it really tragic, personally. It's an area where I've spent a lot of time. Which I'm really attached to. I love pencil pines.'

'So do I', Bowman interjects.

'I find it hard to be optimistic about it, going forward', says French. 'I find it quite upsetting.'

WE REJOIN THE SPHAGNUM CREW FOR THE NIGHT IN A HUT on the parched shores of Lake Mackenzie, sharing a vat of spicy vegetables stewed on a wood stove by lamplight. We're stripped to our sweaty thermals, boots and socks drying by the hearth. Outside it's bitterly cold, and there are intergalactic views horizon to horizon. Inside it's cosy and convivial, albeit a little ripe.

As a non-scientist and serial intruder on fieldwork, I love the raw exhaustion and intimacy of this downtime, where scientific problems and camp menus are deliberated with equal weight; where clever, curious and often unconventional beings are cloistered with their histories, preoccupations and foibles away from the distractions of the workaday world. It's in these moments I've often found the most revelatory morsels for my notebooks. But this evening is just the warm-up.

Next morning, we take a short drive to the lookout over Devils Gullet, a platform levitating above sheer grey cliffs 'carved out by ice and water moving off the plateau', a sign advises. It allows 180-degree views over 200 million years of history: the 'intrusion of hard dolerite rocks from deep within the Earth', the uplift of the plateau, the advance and retreat of the ice sheet half-a-dozen times over the past two million years, the most recent glaciation peaking around 20 000 years ago. And, in all directions, the scars of the inferno that tore through here three summers gone. Spectral forests stripped of their canopy.

'Doesn't it break your heart, to see all that burnt?'

'No, not really', Bowman shrugs. 'They're eucalypts – it will regenerate. In fact, I'm surprised how much it has regenerated.' The lesson of so many years exploring biology is that 'life is spectacularly resilient ... I have no concern about life'. Which isn't to say that it will be life as we know it.

Bowman describes the intensity and pace of the fire as it powered along this gorge in 2016. The fallout could have been much worse. One small shift in the wind and we would have lost the last, large remaining *refugium* of *A. cupressoides*, a forest called Dixons Kingdom in the Walls of Jerusalem National Park, hiding out somewhere south of us. Climate models have underestimated aspects of fire behaviour in the Anthropocene, he says, and are having to be recalibrated in light of the real-world fallout of just one degree of warming. 'I've always found the whole thing vaguely hilarious', he says. 'People think that climate change is going to be staged. It's actually punctuated by these incredible … thresholds, stresses. And then *boom*, it just changes.'

Our comprehension of the Anthropocene falls short on so many fronts. We broadly blame humanity, but not all humans are equal in their contributions to the mess. 'Aboriginal cultures lived here pretty sustainably', he observes, and adapted as the ice ebbed and flowed across the landscape beneath us. 'There's a cultural dimension going on here, and I think that's the struggle that we're involved with. What sort of society are we going to have? How are we going to adapt to the planetary constraints?'

By now we're on the road, swerving around dead animals. Tasmania is unhappily recognised as the roadkill capital of the world, littered with bloodied carnage – possums, wallabies, pademelons, rabbits. Once these were kept in check by thylacines, and by Indigenous hunters, and then colonial trappers trading their pelts and meat. Today, the apex predators wince, ride the sickening bump and keep driving. Even in country cherished as World Heritage wilderness, so many cascading layers of disturbance. 'If I was a good person, I would stop and drag that off the road', Bowman says of the next casualty, a wallaby. He's not being sentimental. Endangered Tasmanian devils and quolls come to feast on the dead, only to get taken out by the next vehicle. But we push on, we're on the clock – he has a phone conference, and I have a flight to catch.

'What do the Gaians do?'

I'm stumped. Who?

'The Gaians are the society that comes after the Anthropocene.'

I admit I've not heard of them.

'I made them up. It's just an idea, for fun.' He's conjured up a population for the next Earth, named for Gaia, the Greek goddess of the Earth, who was famously also appropriated back in the 1960s by James Lovelock to capture his theory of the planet as a living, self-regulating organism.

Bowman's Gaians 'are the people who come out the other side. And you have to ask the question … what do they do? What animates them? What is their belief? I know they are going to exist, but I don't know what they do'. He's workshopping some ideas. Even in humanity's darkest moments, 'art somehow survives, people still value things'. Ultimately their life's work, their cultural work, will be about ecological restoration. 'Because their survival will depend on it. Everything will be about restoration. It's not about living with nature – it's tending and restoring nature because the system will have been crashed so badly.'

Bowman's not alone thinking about these next Earthlings. In her 2016 book *Hope and Grief in the Anthropocene*, University of Melbourne geographer Lesley Head has a chapter pondering 'The Anthropoceans', and how they (we?) remake ourselves and our world. They will 'have emotional work to do' in the fallout, 'they will practise hope rather than feel it', they will toil physically much harder for the basics of life, they will have to be good at sharing, they will understand the many ways we are 'embedded in the processes of the earth' but not 'green' as we now know it. Like Bowman, she argues the traditions of preservationist, conservationist environmentalism 'are insufficiently powerful to deal with current and projected reality'.

By now we're off the plateau, following the instructions of our iPhone navigator to our last stop before he drops me in Launceston. In between directions, Bowman's workshopping his thesis, wondering out loud about how the Gaians will manage questions of justice, how they will organise their resources, what the family unit might look like. 'I'm pretty certain that it's going to be more a matriarchy, more female dominated.'

He's hazy (evasive?) on what will play out between our reality and theirs. He's firmly directing his gaze somewhere past that conceivably apocalyptic horizon. Having witnessed the growing distress and anger of scientists who understand what we have done and where we are heading, I'm inclined to diagnose this as an insulating, self-care mechanism. Psychological *refugium*? I'm content to join him there, for now.

'Let's be a bit more optimistic and assume that we get through the Anthropocene. Obviously, you know, capitalism will end and everything is going to change, like it already has. What will they [humans] do? ... The narrative of the utopian stream or strand in the crisis we are in is not being tended.'

What if, he says, the Gaians look back at the work of people like the ones we've just left behind on the plateau nurturing sphagnum and pencil pines, 'and understand that humans had this capacity not only to destroy nature but to tend nature, and then the nature that we have is not about a binary – it's wilderness or not wilderness. It's us. It's our expression'.

Which is not to say it isn't going to be hellish. 'These people are going to be shit scared. The storms that are coming are just mad ... The capacity of an energised climate to create mayhem well ... the insurance industry's noticing what that's like, and it hasn't even started yet.'

And yet, he's feeling 'weirdly optimistic', partly because we owe that to the generations who will live with it – among them his students, working up there on the plateau. And because, as terrifying as this next Earth looms, 'as the shit hits the fan, now we can get on with it. We can snap out of our torpor and break out of our denial because it's the denial that is causing an amazing amount of the anxiety. People are so anxious'.

We pull up at a bushland property in the Liffey Valley at the foot of Drys Bluff, a steep precipice at the northern edge of the Central Plateau. We're visiting a native plant nursery where Sally and Herbert Staubmann have conjured hundreds of pencil pine seedlings, some from seeds collected by the botanic gardens team, some from seed they have collected themselves under permit, some from cuttings they've cultivated. These are the stock that will be used by Ben French and Scott Nichols to expand their restoration trials up on the plateau.

Herbert Staubmann, Austrian by birth, came to Australia as an electromechanic with Siemens. 'I worked in Darwin for a while on big motors and generators in a tin shed before the wet season. I met a Swiss guy who worked in a nursery and I said, "I've had this – I want to work outdoors".' Having given up machinery to get his hands dirty in horticulture, he found his way to this piece of magic country when he fell in love with Australian eucalypts and with Tasmanian-raised Sally.

While their nursery is a substantial operation, producing bulk quantities of some 400 varieties of natives, mostly Tasmanian endemics that they sell to councils, farmers, the hydro and parks and wildlife authorities, it sits seamlessly within the wildscape. Plants are raised on unfenced terraces; native creatures are encouraged to roam and graze beneath, birds to come in and control the pests; and stormwater drains are lush with rushes and sedges to keep the frogs happy. The couple are proud of what they have built here over twenty years. There's a rare aura about them, a contentment and gentleness, humility. Perhaps that is the gift of tending to seasons, to nature.

The couple show us their crop of *A. cupressoides* – rows and rows of what look like fragile green corals set in small black pots. They fuss protectively, plucking out invisible weeds, explaining how they've been experimenting with different techniques to try to raise sturdy specimens sufficient to meet the needs of the scientists. Cuttings are so far proving the easier option, but Herbert suspects that, long term, plants grown from seed will do better out in an increasingly hostile world.

'I sow them in autumn, let them germinate outside, leave them out over winter', Herbert explains. 'I've never had them dampen off – meaning succumb to a fungal infection.' But this year, trying to hurry things along to provide seedlings to Ben French, he put them for a spell in the propagation house 'and they just started keeling over – I got them out and salvaged what I could'.

Sally Staubmann chimes in: 'I think the strongest ones are the ones that come up outside over winter. That's my theory'.

Herbert spent all the previous day roaming up on the plateau looking for seeds, returning with a tiny bagful to show for his efforts. 'I'm not very confident that there's a lot of viable seed', he explains. 'They seem to be aborting early – see the small ones here? I need to put a couple of those under the dissecting lens to see if there is a viable embryo in there.'

They're excited to be part of the research effort, the restoration trials, to play a part in efforts to preserve *A. cupressoides* into the future, but they're mindful that they are in a trial-and-error race against time and more than a bit anxious about how it will all turn out. 'The important thing for Ben's project – for your project – is to get these to a good size', Herbert says.

Bowman reassures them. One way or another the trials will yield a result – he's not worried about that. As he's tried to impress on his students and field crews, failure is also success in what it teaches about how to go forward. But Herbert and Sally Staubmann are plainly more sentimentally inclined, hoping to see the survival of at least some proportion of their precious progeny. Herbert pulls up a punnet to show me what a plant sown from seed a year ago now looks like, forefinger prodding the soil to find the barely-there growth. 'You're looking at a couple of seed leaves in their initial stage, that are narrow and long ... so they're slow.'

I tell him I saw some wild-sown seedlings up on the plateau with Ben French yesterday.

'You actually found some? Some germinating seeds? Wow.'

It's time for us to go – beyond time, so it's a hurried round of farewells. The Staubmanns wave us off, smiling broadly. They are both small in stature, wearing skin and clothes weathered by the elements. They remind me of garden gnomes.

'What did you think of that?' Bowman asks as we pull away. The couple have already vanished into the landscape that they have contrived and preserved: architects and inheritors, consumers and custodians.

'It's them.' The realisation falls out of my mouth. 'They're them. They're Gaians.'

Readings

Glenn Albrecht and Gina Sartor, 'Solastalgia: The Distress Caused by Environmental Change', in *Australasian Psychiatry*, 15 Supp 1(1), February 2007, <www.researchgate.net/publication/5820433//>.

Rob Blakers, 'All at Risk of Being Lost Forever', *Mercury*, 29 January 2016, <bit.ly/mercury-blakers>.

David Bowman, 'Bring Elephants to Australia?', *Nature*, 482, 30, 2012, <doi:10.1038/482030a>.

David MJS Bowman, Stephen T Garnett, Snow Barlow, et al., 'Renewal Ecology: Conservation for the Anthropocene', in *Restoration Ecology*, vol. 25, issue 5, September 2017, pp. 674–80, <onlinelibrary.wiley.com/doi/abs/10.1111/rec.12560>.

Collins English Dictionary online, <www.collinsdictionary.com/dictionary/english/refugium>.

Nick Earl, Peter Love, Rebecca Harris and Tomas Remenyi, 'Dry Lightning Has Set Tasmania Ablaze, and Climate Change Makes It More Likely to Happen Again', *The Conversation*, 7 February 2019, <bit.ly/conversation-earl>.

Lesley Head, *Hope and Grief in the Anthropocene: Re-conceptualising Human-nature Relations*, Routledge, London and New York, 2016.

Alexandra Humphries and Rhiana Whitson, 'Response to Bushfires in Tasmania's World Heritage Wilderness Found Wanting, New Report Says', ABC News website, <bit.ly/abc-humphries>.

Joanna Macy, 'A Wild Love for the World', *On Being with Krista Tippett*, radio broadcast and podcast, 16 September 2010, <bit.ly/onbeing-macy>.

Adam Morton, '"Like Losing the Thylacine": Fire Burns Tasmanian Wilderness World Heritage Area', *Age/Sydney Morning Herald*, 31 January 2016, <bit.ly/smh-morton>.

Jennifer Styger, Jon B Marsden-Smedley and Jamie B Kirkpatrick, 'Changes in Lightning Fire Incidence in the Tasmanian Wilderness World Heritage Area, 1980–2016', *Fire*, vol. 1, no. 3, 2018, pp. 1–10 <doi:10.3390/fire1030038>.

James Worth, Shota Sakaguchi, Karl Rann, et al., 'Gondwanan Conifer Clones Imperilled by Bushfire', *Scientific Reports*, 6, 33930, 2016 <www.nature.com/articles/srep33930>.

LOST PADDOCKS

Michael Adams and Adrienne Corradini

To get here, drive west – away from the shining ocean and white beaches, across the hot flatlands below the escarpment. The dirt turn-off is abrupt, rusty fences and a locked gate leading into the weedy lane.

Landscapes like this are the fastest growing regions in Australia. Peri-urban space is what is left over as the urban disperses – slip-shod in its anthropocentric mission – further and further into what was once distinctly rural landscape, and sometimes bushland. Back-dropping this land, the escarpment is continuous forest, too steep for development or agriculture, instead preserved for conservation. Green fingers reach down to connect to the scrubby flood-zone banks of creeks and on to the lake foreshore.

A long time ago these alluvial flatlands and their streams were fished, hunted and harvested. They flooded seasonally, burned seasonally, dried out. Wetland birds gathered in great flocks, kangaroos and many other animals lived and wandered here. It continues to be known and loved by the descendants of those fishers and hunters.

Now it is pre-development. The materialisation of suburban, industrial or carceral built space is embedded in council web pages, draft plans for developments and neighbourhoods that do not (yet) exist. The abstract cadastre denies the reality of the underlying active land; seasonal floods will be engineered away, other changes are considered too distant to matter.

For now, it is a horse agistment paddock: land banked by developers, rented and managed by a middle-aged working mother, used by a rag-tag assemblage of horse addicts.

WHEN YOU ARRIVE AFTER WORK, YOU HAVE MISSED THE afternoon rush. Daylight saving: the sun is still well above the escarpment. You have the windows down, greeting each horse by name as you drive up the laneway. The median dividing the two narrow gravel ruts is unmown, paspalum and kikuyu scraping the underside of your car.

At this hour, your own horse is waiting at the gate. His bright bay coat is iridescent in the afternoon light, and he turns his head one way and then the other, vision criss-crossing in front of his face. As a prey animal, he sees much better what is beside and behind him: two other horses grazing, a willy-wagtail dancing at their noses, waiting for the insects the horses disturb. The birds and animals of open spaces live here with the horses: magpies, plovers, swallows, raptors, skinks, snakes. Behind you the laneway lines up precisely with the sharpest, lowest dip in the escarpment so that it is a grassy line meeting the obtuse angle of the mountain.

At certain times of the year, families of young hawks leave their nest to perch on the telephone wires and call to each other, high-pitched and infantile. Swallows swarm in the late afternoon, carving murmurations across the streaked sky lined with the glow of the just-sunk sun on the escarpment. You can see turtle eggs centimetres from fox scat in the laneway. You can scoop up a scruffy catatonic peewee and take him to the vet.

THIS IS NOT THE PLACE WHERE THIN IMMACULATE WOMEN IN English riding clothes park Volvos and Range Rovers. Here women arrive in beat-up sedans and utes as if working in shifts morning and afternoon to cart food to horses, heave off rugs and cast on new ones.

They are managers at leagues clubs or fast food establishments, the women who escort your kids to the sick bay in school offices, mattress saleswomen on maternity leave, hairdressers, nurses and vet nurses, firewomen who play Oztag. They talk about their endometriosis surgeries while rolling up dirty hoses, their wet horses grazing quietly. Incessant car horns from the vehicle storage lot and the squawking of seagulls hovering over the tip form the backdrop to their daily routine. Northerly winds blow the sickly-sweet smell of landfill across the paddocks.

These women have known many places like this. When the land is sold, the development approved, each woman has to find another place for her horse to live. She has to move her own small and humble depot: solar charger, car battery, big plastic boxes, buckets clipped to the fence. Halters and other tack loosely tied at each gate are thrown into the backs of cars and carted to wherever else she has managed to borrow land.

AS YOU RIDE YOUR HORSE PAST ALL THE OTHERS, OUT ONTO the track that snakes along the back of the paddocks, you see you are trailing a young red fox. You prepare for your horse's reaction; he has a stubborn hatred for one ibis who frequents this part of the track and you expect he will extend his aversion to this fox. But your horse does not notice him and the little flame-red flash slips into the long grass.

You are enjoying the sunset and the roll of his body when suddenly he stops dead square. Your attention and his ears are snapped forward. You look around and see nothing, facing the bush.

As you ask him to walk forward, he resists and then prances on the spot. He tries to turn and you snatch the other rein to keep him facing the trees. Get a horse to look at something for thirteen seconds and his fear turns into intrigue, you have read. You also know that your friend's horse spooked out here last year and threw her into a tree, shattering the bones in her leg.

Your eyes finally find it: a rusa deer stag. His body is entirely obscured by scrub. He is just a floating head, big gentle eyes, enormous antlers stretching up to meet the branches above him. He sinks back into the trees and you ask your horse to move forward but the stag steps out again. Your horse pigroots in protest at being made to endure this. You rebalance in the saddle, hands see-sawing each rein to keep your horse facing the deer.

The deer repeats this over and over, sinking back and stepping out of the trees, watching you watch him, seen by and seeing both horse and rider. Today he retains this territory. You are alone at the paddocks with no phone. There is no way you are going to get your horse past those scratched-up antlers, big black wet nose and peculiar way of expressing whatever fear or curiosity he experiences while all this hot horse blood pumps beneath you.

SOON, AFTER THE HORSES ARE GONE FROM THE PADDOCKS, to get here you will drive west, away from the shining ocean and white beaches, turning through the short streets with roundabouts and Aboriginal-sounding names. Your view of the escarpment will be obscured by the roofs of improbably large charcoal-grey houses selected from a catalogue, with names like 'Sanctuary' and 'Daintree'.

The bitumen will be smooth, the gutters curved, the lawns uniform and trimmed. There will be designer dogs behind Colorbond fences. In the driveways there will be shiny new hatchbacks and company dual cabs. There will be three yuccas in front of one house, a single agave in front of another. The morning birdsong will be faint and distant.

DUBBO DUST

Cameron Muir

I don't remember much about my first big dust storm in Dubbo except that our neighbours' two young girls went missing. Mum said we'd just come out of Victor's Fish and Chips in south Dubbo when she saw the storm coming from the west. We raced towards home in our Hillman car, across the bridge, with the orange cloud looming ahead of us. It was one of those rolling dust storms that appear to rise and tumble from the earth.

Other cars drove a little faster, windmill grass collected in the fences, trees started bending and whipping back, eucalyptus leaves fluttered through the air, and the sky turned a flat, grubby copper pink.

Once we were inside, Mum began shutting the windows. We'd made it before it hit. Mum said it was exciting once we were safe. The rest isn't clear, I just recall the feeling, everything charged, amplified: the neighbours back out on the street, loud voices, urgency, where were the girls? Red and dark now. They could have been gone five minutes or an hour, I don't know, but it felt like long enough to understand that we take order and security for granted, that a storm can expose vulnerabilities, that we are a part of the natural world and that it's larger than us. The girls had been hiding from the storm in a cupboard.

There were enough dust storms in Dubbo during the 1980s that the Lions Club began putting dirt in jars and selling it. We still have a few jars of 'Dubbo Dust'. The label guarantees it as 'famous, genuine'. It was a playful way of reclaiming the town's identity, countering the negative perception of it as a dusty, backward town by confidently embracing it. Towards the bottom of the label there's an asterisk, with the line 'Also known as Cobar Rain'. Dubbo is thought to mean 'red earth', derived from Wiradjuri (or for the ceremonial clay head-covering local Wiradjuri wore). Yet the red soil in dust storms comes from further west, from cropping land, but mostly from grazing land, from past Cobar, and sometimes from as far away as Lake Eyre. Airborne dust is a natural occurrence, but scientists have shown that over the last 150 years human activities such as agriculture and land-clearing have degraded Australia's soils and accelerated wind erosion.

Exposure to dust can trigger asthma and allergic reactions, lead to chronic breathing and lung problems, and contribute to heart disease. Dust can carry fungal spores that can cause disease in coral reefs. Degraded land is a threat to habitat and food security, reducing soil fertility, and leaving ecosystems susceptible to soil erosion and excessive nutrient runoff into waterways. Nearly half the world's population lives near regions affected by land degradation.

Over the past year, the dust storms in Dubbo and its surrounds have been so frequent I can no longer see the same confidence that was on the label for the mid-1980s jar of Dubbo Dust. Unless there's significant rain soon, the river is expected to stop running by May 2020. Small towns further west have water trucked in. Mum sent me a Happy New Year SMS with a photo showing a murky streetlight lit during the day. Video footage of that dust storm made international news. Friends and family have sent me brief messages throughout the year. Dad sent me a video of the Castlereagh, the sky bronze, and the riverbed pockmarked with silent hoof prints. The day after the school climate strike my in-laws sent a photo of the lurid orange sky, roof solar panels in the foreground. A few weeks ago, Mum said she needs to wipe down the clothesline and wash the pegs before hanging out the washing. Friends say they keep their washing inside, using a dryer even though it's spring. Mum said she sneezes red dust. The highway closed last week because of low visibility. Climate change will continue to exacerbate the dry conditions that give rise to erosion and dust.

Each dust storm is a kind a signal from somewhere distant: a reminder that an ecosystem is under stress, someone's livelihood is threatened. All this turmoil is happening out of sight. Every time I receive a message, a gritty photo, I know I'm safe from it in middle-class Canberra – even though, materially, I'm connected to these shadow-places, to the places where food, fibre and minerals come from. Sometimes it's easier to not look. I'm missing like the girls, in hiding.

The label on the Dubbo Dust jar urges, tongue-in-cheek, 'Buy now before stock runs out. Supply will not last indefinitely'. A haunting prescience.

SEEKING
VANTAGE
POINTS

SIGNS AND WONDERS OF A NEW AGE

Delia Falconer

I have lived near the harbour in eastern Sydney for twenty years and, because I walk, I have become an observer of local conditions. In autumn I watch for fish fry in the water and the swifts that circle like tiny warplanes above the navy dockyard. In winter, great gangs of corellas flock around the plane trees in Rushcutters Bay Park, while in summer the koels call with a grinding yearning. There have been surprises over the years: a fairy penguin off the end of Darling Point, or the metre-wide stingray gliding, on the high tide, up the middle of the Rushcutters Creek canal. But mostly I am looking for famil-iar creatures: the microbats that flit at dusk above the water near the stairs to the small beach; or the flying foxes in the Moreton Bay fig outside our apartment, though there are no longer enough of them to keep us awake with their squabbling at night.

One of my walks takes me around Mrs Macquarie's Chair in the Domain, through Woolloomooloo Bay. From the old boardwalk next to the marina, I always keep an eye out for the large mullet that nose around the floating moorings.

One day, in 2018, when I stopped to look there was nothing in the deep green water: not a mullet, nor even one of the usually ubiquitous smooth toadfish with fins like propellers. Once I would have put this down to the relative absence of fish in Sydney Harbour in winter, but this time it felt different: I found myself wondering if there were no longer any fish left to see. What if they had disappeared, like the sparrows that were such a common sight when I was a child, or the greengrocer cicadas that we used to catch in the school playground? I had been ticking off checklists of animals on my walks, I realised, to counter a growing sense of loss.

The knowledge that human activity was driving the Earth's creatures and systems to – or beyond – breaking point first struck me with full force in 2016, when I was in Buenos Aires. I went online to news that a bleaching event had killed 30 per cent of the Great Barrier Reef: a 2000-kilometre-long organism large enough to be seen from outer space. That I was on the other side of the world in a city that was itself experiencing unseasonal autumn humidity, which the locals were ascribing to the loss of rainforest in the country's north, made the sense of end times more urgent. The figures were already grim. In 2014, the World Wildlife Fund released its *Living Planet Report*, which concluded that human activity had killed off 52 per cent of the world's wildlife over the previous forty years.

That afternoon in Woolloomooloo, I realised the missing fish had become signs of catastrophic absence. Everything is carrying an awful symbolic freight. 'Every bird I see these days, every bee', my children's godmother says, 'I wonder if it's the last.' 'Are wombats endangered? Are echidnas?' asks my son, who has recently learned about the plight of koalas, as we drive through rainforest to our Airbnb tucked into the base of the Barren Grounds escarpment south of Sydney.

The global catastrophes underway are dizzying. Each day brings news of the ongoing crises we are starting to recognise under the umbrella of the Anthropocene, our new age of human-made change that has pushed us out of the stable 12 000-year Holocene.

Out-of-control fires in the Amazon; warming sea currents; record high summer temperatures in both hemispheres, leading to ice caps melting at a rate far faster than environmental modelling had anticipated: it's hard to grasp how quickly things are turning. This means that it is almost impossible now to look at the smallest details without a sense of deep unease.

AT SCHOOL I LEARNED HOW ROMAN PRIESTS AND OFFICIALS would look for omens of the future. Haruspices would examine the entrails of animals, augurs the flight patterns and songs of birds. In the 1980s, it was easy to feel a sense of smug distance from these ancient practitioners of prophecy; but now I notice that we are scrutinising the same things, through science, but also in our conversations. The great difference is that now we are trying to read not only the future but also the past as it intrudes more and more into our present. Instead of trying to divine the will of the gods from these same signs, we are trying to determine our own responsibility as a species.

Surely some of the most iconic images of the last decade have been Chris Jordan's photographs of dead albatross chicks on a beach in Midway Atoll National Wildlife Refuge. The atoll lies in the Hawaiian Archipelago, in the North Pacific Ocean, more than 2000 kilometres from the nearest continent, but in these pictures, which went viral, the birds' rib cages have collapsed to reveal, within the soft shapes of decomposing feather and bone, stomach cavities filled with dozens of bright pen lids, buttons and bottle tops. Scientists worldwide are studying seabirds' stomachs to assess the impact of decades of plastic pollution on their populations. In a 2018 issue of *Griffith Review*, Cameron Muir described watching scientists pump the stomachs of shearwater chicks emerging from their burrows for the first time on remote Lord Howe Island. The plastic objects the team discovered – as many as 276 pieces per bird – confirmed the catastrophic spread of the material through the oceans, with some studies suggesting 90 per cent of seabirds have now ingested some sort of plastic. Muir records the audible crunching of the belly of a young chick that was euthanised.

More recently, it is whale stomachs that have been going viral. Forensic videos show scientists pulling plastic, piece by piece, from these creatures' vast internal organs. One necroscopy, filmed at night, shows a 4.7-metre-long Cuvier's beaked whale, found dead of starvation in the Philippines. A man reaches into the young animal's insides to unfurl large pieces of soft plastic, which look like obscene intestinal tissue in the artificial light. The final tally will be 40 kilos of plastic, including sixteen rice sacks, plastic bags, snack bags and tangles of nylon rope: one of the worst poisoning cases scientists in the area had seen. These autopsies are themselves grim animations of the figures issued by UNESCO, which estimates that plastic pollution is killing 100 000 marine mammals every year.

Then there are the waves of multiple animal deaths – sudden die-offs of large numbers of living creatures. In spite of their abbreviation to the businesslike 'MEE', these mass extinction events retain the quality of epic portent. Here in Australia, an extreme heatwave in December 2018 killed an estimated 23 000 spectacled flying foxes in far north Queensland – almost one-third of this species on this continent – as they are unable to regulate their body temperature once the external temperature exceeds 40°C. Colony die-offs around the country are ongoing. That same summer up to one million native fish, including bream, silver perch and decades-old Murray cod, perished in the lower Darling River. Footage of NSW MP Jeremy Buckingham gagging and vomiting on camera as he held the rotting corpse of a cod from the mass floating in the Menindee weir pool seemed like a moment of visceral augury. An abnormal rise in water temperature is now also mooted as the cause of the 2013 die-off of hundreds of millions of sea stars along the west coast of North America from Alaska to Mexico, making the starfish vulnerable to a bacterial infection that destroys their limbs and wastes their bodies until they liquefy. This is the largest epidemic ever observed in wild marine animals.

For the ancients, changes of animal behaviour were also signs of the gods' will. Changes in the flight patterns of birds, or in their songs or feeding habits, or any other unusual activity such as a wolf, horse or dog in an unusual location, all required interpretation. Today, we are seeing such changes on a global scale. In 2017, a tally of 4000 species from around the world showed that roughly half were on the move in response to changing climate conditions. Others appear to be simply – and confoundingly – disappearing. In 2018, newspapers began reporting an apparent 'insect apocalypse', after German entomologists described a drop in biomass in their nets of 75 per cent over twenty-seven years of collecting. This confirmed an anecdotal sense of decline that had already been broached by writers like Michael McCarthy. In his 2016 book, *The Moth Snowstorm*, he described how many of the insects whose presence we had taken for granted, even if this was as brutally simple as registering the accumulation of moths on the car windscreen on childhood drives, were no longer a familiar part of our daily lives.

While it makes intuitive sense that these disappearances and deaths must be signs of drastic damage caused by human activity, direct links can prove elusive. For example, in 2018, in the northern hemisphere spring – calving season – an estimated 200 000 critically endangered saiga antelope were found dead in Kazakhstan. Many had stood grazing normally until a moment before they fell; as if, one scientist reported, 'a switch had been turned on'. This single event killed 60 per cent of the total global saiga population. It was only after performing post-mortems on thirty-two animals that scientists were able to conclude that the cause was the bacterium *Pasteurella multocida*: a recent 37°C heatwave and 80 per cent humidity had caused it to pass from the antelopes' tonsils, where it resided harmlessly, into their bloodstream, leading to haemorrhagic septicaemia. Here in Australia, a panel from the Australian Academy of Science would subsequently attribute the Darling River fish kills to a combination of drought and over-extraction by those managing the Murray-Darling river system. No action has yet been taken to put water back into the system. Meanwhile, science proceeds with necessary caution. Some scientists have expressed scepticism about catastrophic insect demise in the future, citing a lack of long-term data.

When scientists do confirm your suspicions, and even express uncharacteristic shock, it feels as if the earth has suddenly dropped away beneath your feet. In Australia, researchers have observed a fall in the bogong moth population that they describe as 'astonishing'. Each spring, an estimated two billion bogong moths used to make their 1000-kilometre migration from grasslands in Queensland and northern New South Wales to the alpine region in the country's south-east, where they would aestivate in the mountains' cracks and boulders. It was only as recently as 2018 that scientists worked out that they were using the Earth's magnetic field to navigate, the only insects in the world to do so. In 2019, when they searched the moths' usual summer hiding places, researchers could only count several individuals, or none. 'They haven't just declined. They've gone', ecologist Dr Ken Green told the *Guardian*. 'We have done mountains from down to the Victorian border all the way to Canberra. We have checked every cave we know.'

The cognitive dissonance this disappearance produces is profound, even for those of us who have lived for decades in cities, only registering the edge of the migration in the influx of lost moths through open windows or swarming around oval floodlights on hot nights. The last great influx of bogongs into Sydney I can remember was in 2007, when I walked back from lunch with my cousin in the city on an October afternoon. Dark clusters of moths crowded around the overhanging granite entryways of the buildings near Circular Quay, while those ousted from their cool resting places fluttered helplessly on the hot footpaths. When I moved back to Sydney from Melbourne in 2001, the bogongs were so ubiquitous that as I prepared to bite into my toasted focaccia at a hole-in-the-wall café in Potts Point, I noticed just in time the antennae of an insect that had self-immolated in the melted cheese. These moments feel like a mere eyeblink ago and at the same time irretrievable. These days, instead of living with a sense of futurity, I find that I am looking at my surroundings more and more through a forensic lens. When I do dare to look forward, these phenomena point to a future void that I realise is already here. It is the same story with Christmas beetles, a feature of past hot summers. I can't remember the last time I caught one pinging around my study, or felt its tickling strength in my cupped hands.

THESE ARE TRULY STRANGE TIMES BECAUSE, AT THE SAME moment that the Earth is throwing up signs of distress, it is also giving birth to phenomena of spectacular and haunting strangeness. On the one hand, my Facebook and Twitter feeds are studded with my friends' fear and grief about the environment. On the other, they are filled with a stream of postings in which beautiful and uncanny phenomena follow one after the other, imbued with a glamour that is weirdly incandescent. These 'wonders' are less obviously urgent but just as pernicious. Atomised, and quasi-magical, they turn a dying world into a modern cabinet of curiosities, or a suite of special effects.

The most miraculous of these modern wonders, surely, are the images of long-extinct animals that are emerging after tens of thousands of years from melting permafrost in the arctic north. In 2018, goldminers in Canada's Yukon unearthed a mummified prehistoric wolf cub, its fur, skin and muscles perfectly preserved. Eight weeks old at the time of its death 50 000 years ago, when the forest was empty tundra, the cub is the only one of its kind so far to appear. That same year, from the Batagaika Crater in Yakutia, Siberia, a Pleistocene-era Lenskaya, or Lena horse, two weeks old, emerged after 30 000 to 40 000 years in the permafrost; this was not long after a month-old cave lion, eyes not yet open, head resting on its paw, also turned up in Yakutia, on the banks of the Tirekhtykh River. Posted and re-posted, these images too are forensic – and yet, at the same time, shot in perfectly lit close-up they are also eerily compelling. 'Little hooves', 'Amazing detail', enthuses one site showcasing these oddly intimate photographs.

Throughout the northern hemisphere summer of 2018, the world's fourth-hottest year on record, other ancient things made themselves known. Severe drought in Europe, in which rainfall in some places was 3 per cent of the usual quota, caused rivers in Germany to disgorge unexploded bombs from the Second World War. Archaeologists in Denmark recovered thousands of objects going back as far as 4000 BCE from the scree-covered edges of Oppland's melting glaciers, while hunters, hikers and children stumbled on 1500-year-old Viking swords. In 2019, the revelations continued. That August, the Twitter account 'Secrets of the Ice', run by scientists based in Norway, posted new finds: a 1500-year-old arrow and a medieval packhorse, which died wearing custom snowshoes.

In the United Kingdom, over the 2018 summer, the footprints of vanished Roman mansions, Victorian houses, airfields and prehistoric settlements were also manifesting in grassed fields and parks. Straw-yellow, or lush emerald green on lighter green, these weird patterns were 'parch marks': ghostly scars of human activity that revealed themselves as the land dried and grasses died off. In one haunting image, taken above farmland in Eynsham, Oxfordshire, a 'harvest' of darkly outlined Neolithic barrow graves and paths and walls sprawls across two vast fields, the inscrutable ceremonial structures of a lost society dwarfing a modern farmhouse tucked into its tiny patch of garden. The dark green circles, lines and smooth-edged squares make the yellowing fields look disconcertingly like the pages of Leonardo da Vinci's notebooks, as if a giant hand has made busy calculations across the Earth itself.

Other parts of the Earth also seemed to be trying to communicate with us in some way. In the Batagaika Crater – a 'megaslump' in the Siberian wilderness a kilometre long and almost 800 metres wide – the sound of running water and chunks of frozen ice thumping down the cliffs from the unstable rim announces the rapid melting of ground frozen for thousands of years. 'As you stand inside the slump on soft piles of soil ...', one ecologist told the *Siberian Times*, 'you hear it "talking to you", with the cracking sound of ice and a non-stop monotonous gurgling of little springs and rivers of water.' Recently, the United Nations Framework Convention on Climate Change (UNFCCC) has been backing a project in which musicians mix compositions from recordings made by scientists from the Alfred Wegener Institute of melting icebergs in the Antarctic Weddell Sea, to raise consciousness of global warming. These sounds are 'excruciating', like 'animals in pain', according to UNFCCC spokesman Nick Nuttall. Meanwhile scientists from California's Scripps Institution of Oceanography and the Polish Academy of Sciences in Warsaw have been using underwater recordings of air bubbles continuously exploding in the water – 'like rain hitting the surface of the lake' – to try to predict the speed at which glaciers are melting. The higher the melt rate, the more intense the noise. 'These tiny air bubbles are singing songs', said the study's lead author Oskar Glowacki, 'and these songs are the songs of the changing climate.' In their disturbing power, these descriptions remind me of Edgar Allan Poe's story 'A Descent into the Maelstrom', in which a sailor recounts being sucked into a mighty whirlpool; he escapes death, but his hair turns white from his exposure to its 'general burst of terrific grandeur'.

Not so long ago, it would have been possible to dismiss these observations as instances of 'the uncanny', defined by Sigmund Freud in his 1919 essay of the same name as a dread and creeping horror that occurs when the hidden or secret seems to become visible and something once very familiar acquires an eerie sensation of animation. This experience, Freud wrote, 'forces upon us the idea of something fateful and inescapable when otherwise we would have spoken of "chance" only'. For Freud, the uncanny was not 'real' but rather a result of not having fully banished 'animism' from our modern souls. A belief in the return of the dead or the animation of the inanimate was also related to infantile impulses towards wish fulfilment that adults should normally overcome.

Yet now, French philosopher Bruno Latour argues, the Earth really *is* speaking. The Earth is no longer the distant, objective foundation to our lives. Because it is now so entangled with us, it is unstable and 'trembling'. Once we begin to see that our human activity is present everywhere, Latour writes, the world becomes 'an active, local, limited, sensitive, fragile, quaking, and easily tickled envelope'.

If we accept Latour's claim that the Earth is in fact addressing us – that the uncanny is real – then the apparent 'wonders' in our feeds become horrors. Take Russian deep-sea fisherman Roman Fedortsov's popular Twitter account, in which he posts photographs of bizarre bycatch, which have been trawled up from the mesopelagic or 'twilight' zone of the Norwegian and Barents seas. We have only explored less than 0.05 per cent of this zone, whose creatures scientists believe may 'pump' carbon from the surface to the seabed, but fishing nations are exploiting its immense masses of pelagic shrimp as feed for farm-raised fish. The ratfish and ghost sharks Fedortsov photographs are 'relics' of life that preceded human existence. As we penetrate further into a dying ocean, and the conditions of their existence fall away, they appear now at their most vivid and strange. One of the reasons that these fish are so spectacularly 'ugly', disturbingly shapeless with faces contorted into almost human grimaces, is because they are designed to live in high-pressure environments. Their fat cells 'melt' as they are hauled to the surface. What we are seeing is a ghastly distorting mirror of our own human activities, just as the Batagaika Crater is the ghastly spectre of our dependence on fossil fuels. Those fossil fuels are themselves the ghosts of 650-million-year-old forests, which have returned to life in the form of global heating that is splitting the permafrost and churning methane into the atmosphere to heat it further. Yet the reason Fedortsov is able to post these images of distorted fish goes unremarked on the numerous aggregator sites and newspaper websites which re-post these images, in turn, in sections dedicated to the weird or curious. I have not been able to find any that note that deep-sea trawling, which dates from the 1980s, is listed by the World Wildlife Fund as one of the three main threats to deep-sea biodiversity. Instead these fish appear as objects of idle entertainment, even amusement. 'Something about this reminds us of *The Shape of Water*', jokes an anonymous writer on a CBS photo gallery in response to a 'crazy-looking fish' in Fedortsov's feed. 'This looks like my sister', an Instagram user says of another.

Messages written by human hands also appeared in the unprecedented heat of the 2018 northern hemisphere summer, in the form of a dozen 'hunger stones', which emerged from the drought-stricken Elbe River, near Decin, in the Czech Republic. Recording low water levels caused by 'megadroughts' dating back as far as 1417, their inscriptions, in German, were intended to act as warning signs for future generations. '*Wenn du mich siehst, dann wiene*', one from 1616 read: 'If you see me, weep'. 'If you see me, weep', seems like pertinent advice in the face of the many emerging signs of the Anthropocene: this new geological era in which human activity has become the dominant influence on climate and species loss is occurring, fifty years into the 'great acceleration', at a thousand times the normal background rate. These days, the infantile impulse towards wish fulfilment that Freud described seems to lie not in our experience of the uncanny, but in our determination to dismiss the stories of ruin these phenomena express.

Yet we continue to refuse to see these phenomena, isolated in their own strangeness and stripped of their complexity, as signals of distress. In the *New Yorker*'s piece on the English parch marks, after a paragraph paying lip service to the weird awfulness of the unusual hot weather, the writer quickly shifted his attention to the bonanza these marks represented for aerial archaeologists. 'It's a bit like kids in a candy shop', one said, as the author went on to speak to other excited beneficiaries of these 'freak conditions'. Faced with evidence of a dying river system, the *Daily Mail* chose instead to mock Jeremy Buckingham's vomiting, triggered by the stench of rotting fish, as a 'bizarre moment'. Having 'already amassed 2000 views' this story was consigned to the newspaper's bank of other bizarre vomiting stories, alongside the father who threw up eight times a day and the regurgitating vultures that overran a couple's Florida holiday home.

Even when these 'wonders' appear in a more critical context, they still retain their bewitching glamour. 'Secrets of the Ice' retweets tweets about global heating, but it is its latest excited 'finds', photographed in close-up, that are constantly retweeted. Another account on Twitter, 'Lego Lost at Sea', has since 2014 been tracking the five million pieces of Lego lost overboard, when a giant wave washed sixty-two shipping containers off the *Tokio Express* in 1997, as they turn up on the beaches of Cornwall. Although it also reports on plastic pollution, the account's images of plastic sea creatures and mythical beasts flattened into collages by the camera are so beautiful and addictive that, as they are re-posted, it is easy to forget that they represent our literal haunting by plastic pollution, which is predicted to outnumber fish in the oceans by 2050. 'Lego Lost at Sea' finds have now become collectors' items, especially the octopuses and dragons, which are often photographed posed against a natural landscape.

Scattered, gilded with enchantment or dismissed as curiosities, these wonders appear to us as numbing diversions, sapped of their prophetic agency as signs. And yet, both signs and wonders are trying to tell us, with a terrible animation, that we can no longer depend on the stable patterns of the Holocene. We are now seeing 'once in a hundred year' events almost daily, along with news of irrevocable loss. Most recently, Iceland has placed a plaque to mark the loss of the iconic Ok (Okjökull) glacier as arctic ice melts at much faster than predicted rates and prehistoric forest burns. They are telling us that a door is closing, that the past is returning to engulf our future, like Edgar Allan Poe's maelstrom. We should be attending to their warning with rage and urgency. In 2018, the Intergovernmental Panel on Climate Change report gave us a scant twelve years to limit global heating to levels which still threatened frighteningly unpredictable effects. More recently, some scientists have revised down the critical window for action to the next eighteen months.

AND STILL – IT'S HARD TO KNOW QUITE HOW TO FEEL. LIFE IS often, in harbourside Sydney at least, still very beautiful. When I walk with my seven-year-old twins through the park on a winter evening so balmy that it is full of families in light tops and shorts, I wonder if this is a lucky warm weather system – and certainly, the mood in the park is joyful – although my heart knows it is a sign of global heating. 'Is it true that everyone in the world is going to die soon?' my daughter asks me on the way to school. My heart stops. 'Everything dies eventually', I tell her – 'but hopefully not soon.' For the time being that's enough of an answer and she and her brother race ahead, past basking cats and terraces with brightly painted doors, in the unseasonably humid autumn morning.

Time itself seems to have become unreal. On the one hand, I fill in my work plan at university. I book our accommodation for Christmas holidays on the south coast. I talk with my children about their plans for what they will do when they grow up – although I do this with a strange detachment, with no genuine sense that any of the familiar pathways will lie ahead of them in even ten years. Instead of awe or even rage, most often I feel pervasive dread. I have lost my belief in futurity. I recall Brian Dillon, in *Essayism*: 'Depression, among other things, has always felt to me like a drying up of one's reservoir of symbols and figures for a continued and perhaps even improved life'.

In an essay on his family history for the *New Yorker*, Nathan Heller writes that, long before the founding of Rome, the Etruscans measured time by something called a *saeculum*. 'A saeculum spanned from a given moment until the last people who lived through that moment had died.' What moment will my children date time from? From the time they went to their first climate change school strike? From the time orangutans or koalas are declared extinct? From the first water wars? Or from a time when it was still possible – just – to imagine a future anything like the past?

On another walk, along parkland reclaimed from the sea at the beginning of last century, grass and soil laid down over old marsh and sand, it suddenly strikes me that if, or more likely when, the water rises – and these timelines and heights are being redrawn drastically as I write – not only will it rise up the hill to our apartment but every sandy beach and every tidal swamp with all their unique life will also go under the water. I find my mind playing with other what ifs. Once the glaciers melt away – once the insects die off – once our coral systems collapse – how can anything survive? Then I return to a present in which to think about catastrophe seems unhinged. 'I have absolutely no belief that we're going to be threatened by rising water or warming anytime soon', a father at my children's school tells me. 'I think things are going to be pretty much the same, forty or fifty years in the future, where we'll be fretting over the same small worries.' And yet. 'Have you started to feel guilty about having children yet?' a colleague at work asks me in the corridor. 'Yes', I say. But we keep our voices to hushed whispers beneath the fluorescent lights.

Although we are surrounded by clear signals of distress, exact cause and effect are difficult to pinpoint: the chain of events bringing us to this point is complex and hazy, and overwhelming. Sometimes I think all I can do is to just record these signs. Sometimes I think it is no bad thing to be more like those ancients in their alertness, their willingness to link the small to the enormous; to return to the concept of hubris.

One night not long ago, my children's godmother is reading to my daughter from a book about elements, in which tiny samples of gold leaf and zirconium are folded into envelopes between the pages. Do you know, my friend says to my daughter, that we are all made out of stars? The universe was originally only hydrogen and helium, she explains. Everything else that makes up life on Earth – the carbon, nitrogen, oxygen, and all the heavier elements – was created over billions of years in the cores of stars, which exploded, sending their dust through interstellar space. And so almost every atom in our body, every unique animal and bird and plant on Earth, is made of stardust. From the kitchen, over my daughter's head, I hold her gaze for a moment, and feel the tears start. 'I know', her eyes say back.

Readings

Brian Dillon, *Essayism: On Form, Feeling, and Nonfiction*, New York Review Books, New York, 2018.

'Disturbing Melody of Melting Permafrost in "Crater" Called "Gateway to Hell"', *Siberian Times*, 10 March 2017, <bit.ly/siberian-crater>.

Hannah Ellis-Petersen, 'Dead Whale Washed Up in Philippines Had 40kg of Plastic Bags in its Stomach', *Guardian*, 18 March 2019, <bit.ly/guardian-ellis-petersen>.

Sigmund Freud, 'The Uncanny' [1919], in J Strachey (ed.), *The Standard Edition of the Complete Psychological Works of Sigmund Freud, Volume XVIII (1917–1919)*:

An Infantile Neurosis and Other Works, The Hogarth Press and the Institute of Psychoanalysis, London, 1955, pp. 217–56.

Oskar Glowacki, 'These Tiny Air Bubbles Are Singing Songs', *Bulletin of the American Meteorological Society*, September 2018, p. 1739. *Gale Academic Onefile*.

Jeremy Hance, 'How Humans Are Driving the Sixth Mass Extinction', *Guardian*, 20 October 2015, <bit.ly/guardian-hance>.

Nathan Heller, 'Private Dreams and Public Ideals in San Francisco', *The New Yorker*, 30 July 2018, <bit.ly/newyorker-heller>.

Rebecca Hersher, 'Massive Starfish Die-Off Is Tied to Global Warming', NPR website, 30 January 2019, <bit.ly/npr-hersher>.

Brooke Jarvis, 'The Insect Apocalypse Is Here', *New York Times*, 27 November 2018, <bit.ly/nytimes-jarvis>.

Chris Jordan, 'Artworks for Change', online photographic folio, <www.artworksforchange.org/portfolio/chris-jordan/>.

Sam Knight, 'The British Heat Wave and Aerial Archaeology', *The New Yorker*, 5 August 2018, <bit.ly/newyorker-knight>.

Anthea Lacchea, 'Spectacular Ice Age Wolf Pup and Caribou Dug Up in Canada', *Guardian*, 15 September, 2018, <bit.ly/guardian-lacchea>.

Bruno Latour, 'Agency at the Time of the Anthropocene', *New Literary History*, 2014, vol. 45, pp. 1–18.

Michael McCarthy, *The Moth Snowstorm: Nature and Joy*, Hachette, London, 2015.

Richard McLellan, 'State of the Planet', in Richard McLellan, et al. (eds), *Living Planet Report 2014: Species and Spaces, People and Places*, WWF, Gland, Switzerland, 2014, <bit.ly/wwf-mclellan>.

Valeria Masson-Delmotte, et al. (eds), *Global Warming of 1.5°. An IPCC Special Report on the Impacts of Global Warming of 1.5° Above Pre-industrial Levels and Related Global Greenhouse Gas Emission Pathways in the Context of Strengthening the Global Response to the Threat of Climate Change, Sustainable Development, and Efforts to Eradicate Poverty*, World Meteorological Organization, Geneva, Switzerland, 2018, <www.ipcc.ch/sr15/>.

Cameron Muir, 'Ghost Species and Shadow Places,' *Griffith Review*, edition 63, 2019, <bit.ly/griffith-muir>.

Edgar Allan Poe, 'A Descent into the Maelstrom', *Complete Stories and Poems of Edgar Allan Poe*, Doubleday, New York, 1966.

Graham Readfearn, 'Decline in Bogong Numbers Leaves Mountain Pygmy Possums Starving', *Guardian*, 25 February 2019, <bit.ly/guardian-readfearn>.

Meilan Solly, 'Scientists Extracted Liquid Blood From 42,000-Year-Old Foal Found in Siberian Permafrost', *Smithsonian Magazine* website, April 2019, <bit.ly/smithsonian-solly>.

UNFCC, 'Sounds of Melting Icebergs Inspire Climate Action', UNFCC website, <bit.ly/unfcc-sounds>.

Craig Welch, 'Half of All Species Are on the Move – And We're Feeling It', *National Geographic* website, 27 April 2017, <bit.ly/natgeo-welch>.

COLOURS PURPLE

Ashley Hay

Brisbane, Queensland

There's a tibouchina tree on the street that leads from my son's school
to the railway station. I pass it once or twice a week, the brilliant
flare of its colour pressing hard against my eyes when it's in bloom.
Tibouchina lepidota: its flowers blaze with one of the least subtle purples in the world. There was a tibouchina tree at my grandparents'
house in Thirroul on the NSW south coast; it grew at the bottom of
their front stairs. I can't remember now if those stairs were wooden or
if they were concrete. What I can remember is the colour of the flowers on that tree; my grandmother would pluck two petals and stick
one on each lens of her glasses, transforming her vision, and mine,
into a crazy, psychedelic sight.

Whenever I see that brilliant purple, I think of my grandmother.
I think of altered vision. I think of something that made me laugh
when I was three or four, and that now makes me smile.

IN 1856, A BRIGHT YOUNG ENGLISH CHEMIST CALLED WILLIAM Perkin 'invented' the first synthetic dye. He gave it the grand name of Tyrian purple at first, to speak to the history of regal Roman robes, before renaming it mauve – a lesser-used word for purple that came from the French word for a mallow flower. With this name, it became so fashionable that one colour historian thought it would have been impossible to step onto London's streets without 'thinking there was something wrong with your eyes'.

The colour began, unprepossessingly, as a pretty-coloured by-product of Perkin's attempts to make synthetic quinine to combat malaria. But there was soon a recipe that would produce it reliably: take a hundred pounds of coal, Perkin began, and refine it through coal tar, coal-tar naphtha and aniline. At the end of this process, a hundred pounds of coal – roughly my body-weight – would have yielded a quarter of an ounce (about 28 grams) of pure mauve. You'd need about four times that to match the purported weight of a soul.

In 1881, the French artist Edouard Manet declared that he had 'finally discovered the true colour of the atmosphere'. This true colour, he said, was violet. Years later, the great Impressionist Claude Monet spoke also of the air around the trees, the buildings – these 'motifs', as he called them – that most artists made the objects of their paintings. 'I want to paint the air in which the bridge, the house, and the boat are to be found – the beauty of the air around them', he said in 1895. His shadows were thick with indigos made possible by new pigments of cobalt and manganese violet. In fact, the Impressionists used so much violet tint that some of their contemporaries thought they really must have seen the world in a different way.

Monet had one ocular lens removed in 1923, years after the first violet wash of his own Impressionism, and this is thought to have given him more purple-skewed vision in one eye compared to the muddied yellow-reds that his other clouded eye saw. He painted one of his most famous canvases – one of his waterlilies – three years after that. That most beautiful, ultraviolet floral thing.

The world's first UV index was created by Canadian scientists in 1992 and adopted and standardised by the World Health Organization and World Meteorological Organization two years later. In Australia, Brisbane endured 105 days of extreme UV (a reading of 11 or more on the scale) in 2004 and again in 2013. Sydney's highest annual tally was 57 in 2004; Melbourne's was 50 in 2009. Stay in the shade, the advice says. Wear some sunscreen and a hat. Or stay indoors altogether.

When I think about these things in combination, I see a purple light between them – a brighter relative of the violet of Manet's and Monet's air; a darker relative of Perkin's mauve. The shimmer of a tibouchina's hue.

It is also the colour added to the Bureau of Meteorology's (BoM) maps to indicate temperatures above and beyond 50°C. When it was first introduced, in January 2013, the *Guardian* framed it in the context of an imminent temperature forecast – of more than 52°C – and called it 'a suitably incandescent purple'.

That 52°C didn't arrive – we're still inching towards its benchmark, washing in the reds and Tyrian tones that mark the forties-temperatures and nudge towards black. The 2018–19 summer was the hottest ever recorded, with a mean temperature across the nation in January of 30.8°C, which was 2.9°C higher than the average for that month. In February 2019, a BoM map showed areas destined for temperatures of 40°C, with a vast shape that covered more than a third of Australia's mainland. In March 2019, south-east Queensland recorded its first 40°C day for that month, with the BoM noting some locations were experiencing temperatures '10 degrees above the March average'.

WHEN PANTONE CHOSE 'ULTRA VIOLET' AS THEIR COLOUR OF the year for 2018, they spoke of the colour's ability to communicate 'originality, ingenuity, and visionary thinking that points us toward the future'. Painting the air between the objects; marking the rising, rising heat.

I watch the colours swirl across the night-time weather forecasts and wrap-ups: the reds giving into purples that stain darker and darker still. I watch the way this darkness flows out across the familiar shape of the continent, leaching and staining that notional space, unremarked. I wait for the first blaze of that tibouchina flare on the nation's weather charts – perhaps it will be almost a relief when it arrives.

A later purple puzzle: as Rudi Hendra and Paul A Keller documented in their phytochemical study of the Illawarra flame tree (*Journal of Chemistry*, 2016), Australia's first tibouchinas were introduced from South America to Alstonville, in northern New South Wales, in 1978. My grandmother's tree lit up my childhood at least five years before that. But then perhaps it's always hard to keep track of where things are and how they're moving. Perhaps it's as hard to unravel the provenance of things as it is to see how they'll change or how they'll spread.

My grandmother's tree is long gone now, along with her house, her garden. The disruption of progress and change. Perhaps that's why I register the echoes of that colour, mementoes of a version of the world that's disappeared.

Here we are, a species that can acknowledge beauty – this flower; that beautiful tree – but does not have the vision to see ultraviolet light. A species that can create its own colours – after mauve, a whole rainbow of synthetic dyes – and wear them now, day after day, as if they were no remarkable thing. A species that can tilt temperature into a whole new normal and wait for summer to stain our meteorological maps that dark and inky purple shade.

And still not really see what's going on.

THE SUPER PIT

Ruth A Morgan

The Super Pit was just four years old when I visited Kalgoorlie with my parents in 1993. It was the Easter school holidays and we'd gone to see where Mum's family had come from. We had set out from Perth on the Great Eastern Highway, and seven hours and 600 kilometres later we arrived on the edge of what is known as the richest square mile of earth on the planet. Back then, the Super Pit was the largest open-pit mine in the country, over 3 kilometres long, a kilometre wide, and 500 metres deep. It's so big you can see it from space – a dark grey crater in a red landscape. The rockface is etched with terraces like enormous steps leading down into the earth.

The Fimiston Open Pit, or 'Super Pit', was the brainchild of Western Australia's golden boy, Alan Bond. The bubble of WA Inc. had yet to burst in 1988 when Bondy bought the mile that Midas touched with the plan to amalgamate dozens of old leases into a single big pit with a single owner. Many scoffed at his idea. Thirty years later, the Super Pit has produced over 20 million ounces (566 tonnes) of gold, and looks set to continue production until at least 2025.

Over 60 million ounces (1700 tonnes) of gold have been poured from the Golden Mile since the prospectors Paddy Hannan, Tom Flanagan and Dan Shea struck it lucky at Mount Charlotte in 1893.

Their discovery drew thousands of people to the West in search of the latest El Dorado, and my great-grandparents were among them. There, they had to separate gold from the dirt and dust using a technique called 'dryblowing', since water was in such short supply on the fringe of the desert. But relatively little gold lay at the surface; the real riches were to be found in the quartz dolerite greenstone. Getting to it was an expensive undertaking and London-based speculators were only too happy to oblige. By Federation in 1901, the first of Western Australia's mining booms was well underway.

With the low-hanging fruit long gone, gold's siren song still lures mining companies to drill ever deeper into the Earth's crust, gouging the Yilgarn Craton for the lodes that formed there nearly three billion years ago. In 2015, at the southern end of the Super Pit, the miners set an Australian record when they drilled over 3 kilometres deep. Drilling, blasting and hauling rock, the Super Pit is awake 24/7, 365 days a year. Each day, some forty Caterpillar 793 haul trucks lug 240 000 tonnes of earth to the surface on a round trip that can take up to forty minutes. From every eight trucks, about a golf-ball-size amount of gold is extracted. It's not much, but it's enough to keep the Super Pit going.

A LOUPE AND A
FORGOTTEN KINGDOM

Alison Pouliot

Ecologist EO Wilson famously reminded us that it is the 'little guys' that run the world. Invertebrates, fungi and various micro-organisms are those 'little guys' that drive ecosystem processes. Fungi, for example, build architecture in soils and influence hydrology. They recycle organic matter and sequester carbon. They form relationships with most plants and provide food and habitats for animals. They engineer atmospheric and geospheric chemistry. They are most definitely not just lying around on the forest floor.

Yet for all their industriousness, conservation efforts tend to focus on the bigger stuff, often colourful birds and 'attractive' mammals. It seems that size does matter after all. To be endowed with chlorophyll or a backbone is to be charismatic. Such organisms are assigned greater value and deemed worthy of conservation. Our emotions and empathies usually extend to other organisms relative to their resemblance to ourselves. Hence we tend not to identify with slime moulds, stinkhorns or sucking lice. Well, most of us don't, anyway.

The invention of the microscope in the seventeenth century radically changed the way the world is understood. Previously unseen micro-worlds of life were revealed. Many remain undescribed today. But a hand magnifier or loupe (or 'flea glass' as it was originally called) can also take us to amazing new places. When I was seven I was given one. It changed my life. I still have it today and experience that same thrill of its small and satisfying form nestled in my hand – smooth and cold and somehow perfect in its simple engineering, the lens pivoting neatly out from its snug metal housing. And then the process of bringing it to my eye and the sense of anticipation of what it might reveal. It cost $15 – the same as it costs today. Fifteen bucks to open worlds of wonder and discovery.

My loupe has also alerted me to environmental changes: often slow and insidious changes, undetected; happening secretly, out of sight. Small changes with potentially large consequences. Fungi occupy the subterrain. They occupy litter and dirt. These places aren't well regarded. Nor are their inhabitants. They require close observation. That's what my loupe is for.

Today, fungi remain largely absent from an ecological consciousness that incorporates other life forms, as well as places inhabited by fungi – even though almost all environmental issues also involve fungi. But how do we draw attention to the unnoticed, the unimagined, the unregarded? Fungi only usually gain media attention when they cause harm (for example human poisonings or crop destruction) rather than for being casualties of environmental calamity themselves. They are rarely considered part of environmental issues such as climate change, species extinction or wildfire, all of which affect fungi. If a fungus species or a thousand fungus species succumb to extinction in the subterrains of the soil, would anybody notice?

Some of my most revelatory moments in the forest have been shared with others as we've ventured into its microcosms; witnessing the delight of life magnified times ten. I recently passed my loupe to a friend and pointed to a fruiting lichen on an overhanging blackwood branch. I watched as her head and the loupe moved in and away trying to find focus. Then a great whoop signalled success. Bent double, with her nose jammed into the wet branch, my friend's exclamations of discovery continued. Something captured her curiosity and imagination. Something precious. Something not describable in words.

So much of the beauty and wonder of nature is in the detail, in the cracks and crevices and in its nuances and subtleties. As well as keeping us in touch with environmental change, closer observation of the less-seen corners can reveal unimaginable treasures. All we need is curiosity, imagination and fifteen bucks.

LISTENING TO BIRDS
IN A CHANGING WORLD

Saskia Beudel

The Birds are singing in the tender Rain, as if it were the rain of
April, & the decaying Foliage were Flowers & Blossoms.

Samuel Taylor Coleridge, Coleridge's Notebooks

A bird chuckled outside. 'A nightingale?' asked Mrs. Haines.
No, nightingales didn't come so far north. It was a daylight bird,
chuckling over the substance and succulence of the day, over
worms, snails, grit, even in sleep.

Virginia Woolf, Between the Acts

I am fortunate to be able to return to a garden I have known since
childhood. It belongs to my 86-year-old mother who lives in bayside
Melbourne. Over more than five decades she has been shaping and
reshaping this one garden – long and narrow and built upon flu-
vial sand-belts that underlie the suburbs. When I visit my mother
from interstate, what strikes me most through my long familiarity

with this place is a shift in sound. Currawongs have arrived for the first time (in my experience) in Melbourne, with their looping, vivid calls. Two sets of crows are nesting in a eucalypt my mother planted when I was in primary school; we have never had crows in our garden before. Along the nature strips, colonies of noisy miners and flocks of rainbow lorikeets squabble and dispute. They too are newcomers and theirs have become the dominant bird calls in the neighbourhood. This is an entirely altered avian soundscape. Most unnerving is the absence of small native birds once common here: the silvereyes and small honeyeaters called greenies. Even the (much larger) supposedly common blackbirds, where have they gone? In the summer of 2019, I walked along the Yarra in Richmond with a friend and her dog. She too noted the loss of small birds in her suburb. 'The silvereyes were my favourite', she said.

Anthropologist Andrew Whitehouse writes in his article 'Listening to Birds in the Anthropocene: The Anxious Semiotics of Sound in a Human-dominated World' about one of the legacies of biologist Rachel Carson's *Silent Spring*. In her opening chapter, 'A Fable for Tomorrow', she painted futuristic scenes marked by a 'strange stillness' wrought by synthetic pesticides. 'The birds, for example – where had they gone?' Carson asked. 'Many people spoke of them, puzzled and disturbed.' Her haunting prospect – spring no longer announced through birdsong – was formed, in part, through conversations with other people equally concerned about the indiscriminate use of DDT, dieldrin and other chemicals in America in the mid-twentieth century. One of Carson's many correspondents wrote her a letter, quoted in the book:

Our place has been a veritable bird sanctuary for over half a century. Last July we all remarked, 'There are more birds than ever.' Then, suddenly, in the second week of August, they all disappeared … There was not a sound of the song of a bird.

It was eerie, terrifying … Finally, five months later a blue jay appeared and a wren.

Something deeply appreciated but also common enough to have once been taken for granted – birdsong, birds in backyards, local parks and city streets – was thrown into relief. 'Listening to birds, Carson implied, was no longer something conceivable as straightforward or inevitable', writes Whitehouse. And ever since, many people 'have been listening carefully and often anxiously to birds' – a process that has only become more heightened in our own times of great human-induced environmental transformation. In this era, Whitehouse says, we listen with a sense of our own culpability; we listen for change and loss, and for reassurance that all is still well with the world around us. It is a heightened listening, rich with ambivalence and uncertainty.

Like the weather, birdsong is something we can no longer take as straightforward.

My mother's garden is not so much silent as morphed and altered. Species jostle. They shift geographic and climatic zones. Some, like the silvereyes and greenies, have disappeared altogether. A photograph my father took of a greenie (*Lichenostomus penicillatus*) feeding from a grevillea in the back garden attests to their presence and absence. He died in 2001 and didn't date his photos, but this one, we think, was taken around the mid-1990s. When did these small birds stop feeding in my mother's garden? Did it happen gradually or suddenly?

My father was a passionate bird photographer. In a corner of the spare room we keep meaning to sort is a cabinet full of his slides, prints, undeveloped negatives. He never went digital. His slanted, almost geometrical, handwriting in permanent marker on the yellow plastic lids of dozens upon dozens of slide boxes spells out favoured bird-watching locations: salt marshes at Point Wilson where migratory waterbirds arrive from Siberia, the You Yangs, Tooradin, Walkerville, Cranbourne, Werribee, under the Westgate Bridge. Less often, he photographed birds in his own backyard. We have framed very few of his images, but the one of the small greenish honeyeater – with a fine tapering white streak beneath its cheek, perched at the mouth of an ornate red grevillea blossom – graces a sideboard. At the time, this sight would have been commonplace. But something about it arrested him. And now the photograph marks an absence. Not just the augury of death or memorial to the individual observed by Roland Barthes in *Camera Lucida* as he contemplated photographs of his recently deceased mother, but the absence of an entire species at this location.

My father's photograph marks an absence, too, one that's more complicated (if that's possible) than extinction or placement of a species on a critically endangered list. It is complicated by global warming and what I've come to think of as the uncertainty of attribution. One of the great impacts of living during this period of mass attritions and transformation of Earth systems – of atmosphere, water, land, ice – is an uncertainty about what we're seeing, noting, experiencing as change in our own local surroundings: is this 'normal' change? Ecological systems are, after all, dynamic, they flex, shifting and adapting (although debate surrounds the extent to which any given system can alter before it 'flips' into another state). And in a settler nation like Australia, environmental change wrought by colonisation is a kind of bedrock in the contemporary landscapes we inhabit. We live, always, with the legacies of the drastic change meted out over the past two centuries. Or could this be climate-change-driven change? Some climate change impacts are large, dramatic and easy to see (melting glaciers, wildfires in the Arctic circle, bushfires in Australia burning in usually damp Gondwana rainforests); but others are subtle, incremental and perhaps difficult to read.

AS IS WELL KNOWN, SOME ANIMALS AND PLANTS WILL SHIFT their range with global warming. Some will be pushed, retreating to ever-higher altitudes or latitudes to stay within the temperature range they require. Others will gravitate towards new opportunities opened up by increasing heat. In some cases these relocations are already occurring. A recent vivid example is the particular species of blue-green algae that flourished on the Murray River during the last major El Niño. *Chrysosporium ovalisporum* usually blooms in warm tropical waters when they reach a temperature of 26°C, but in the summer of 2016 it formed a 1700-kilometre plume of green along the suppos-edly temperate waterway of the Murray. As global ecology and Earth system scientist Pep Canadell said to me when we were discussing this and other changes that occurred during the same El Niño, whose usual increased temperatures were amplified by the underlying global average increase of 1°C (heat on top of heat):

> Algal blooms are a normal thing when waters get too hot. Then you cannot use the water for irrigation or livestock so it's a big deal even economically let alone for other reasons. But the El Niño we had then was so big and so hot that the algae involved was not one that even belonged to the region. It came from hotter adapted places up in Queensland.

When he told me about this and other changes that occurred during the same period – hundreds of kilometres of dead mangroves in the Northern Territory, dying kelp beds, storm surges, fires in the alpine peatlands of Tasmania where the archaeological record contains no evidence of burning over the past 8000 years, bleaching coral – his voice held a tone of surprised wonderment even though he has worked as a leading international scientist in the field since the 1990s, steeped in modelling of global carbon levels, the projections, the troubling, foreseeable futures. 'It brought home to me', he said with tears in his voice, 'that these are not fictions we're talking about.'

HAVE THE SMALL BIRDS DISAPPEARED IN MY MOTHER'S neighbourhood for a highly specific and also consequential climate-related reason? Something that I, as an ordinary resident, cannot necessarily observe or recognise?

When I visit my mother the background patterning of bird-song and bird calls is entirely different from the one I recall from childhood and early adulthood. What I remember: the call of the common dove with its speckled necklet, which my father translated as 'the paw paw is cooked'; blackbirds advancing and retreating into undergrowth ('note-blurt, clear, airy ... Blackbird, practising his scale', runs an early Irish poem I came across hung on a wall at the University of Edinburgh); the silvery, whipping call of the greenie honeyeater; the sudden, scrambled but clear notes of the silvereyes; raucous wattlebirds; a willy-wagtail down on the street corner calling 'sweet pretty little creature', so my grandmother told me; sparrows; the occasional visiting New Holland honeyeater; peewees with their emphatic 'peewee, peewee'. On my most recent visit over summer I kept an informal logbook of birdsong in my mother's backyard, just to see: was I imagining these changes? Admittedly, the eucalypts were in flower and so were particularly attractive to the noisy miners and lorikeets feeding on their nectar, but often for hours these were the only birds I heard, interspersed with the occasional dry caws of the crows, now and then a dove, and once the sudden, bold, explosive, uplifting melody of a butcher bird.

There are other changes too – for the first time, over the past several years, flocks of fruit bats descend into my mother's garden to feed on her figs. At night, there is the new sound of their high-pitched screeches, the leathery flap of wings as they settle and resettle among foliage. When they first began visiting, I had a strange dream: my childhood doll was hanging from a tree against a dusk sky of sinister greys and pinks. Behind her, a squadron of bats winged through the air, large, powerful, purposeful. During a recent visit to Papua New Guinea, I was reminded of this dream. I was standing in a friend's guest room looking out over the waters of Port Moresby. Dark shapes appeared, more and more of them, winging across the sky. As they drew closer, passing right by my window, I saw they were large bats. It was mid-afternoon, full daylight, and during an unseasonably hot and wet winter, these usually nocturnal creatures filling the city skies in broad daylight seemed the portent of some great calamity.

IN AN ESSAY IN STEPHEN GILL'S BOOK OF BIRD PHOTOGRAPHS, *The Pillar*, novelist Karl Ove Knausgård captures something of both the ubiquity and elusiveness of birds:

> What was shocking about it was that I already felt familiar
> with birds, as I imagine most people do, since we can hardly
> go anywhere without being surrounded by them in one way or
> another. Here, where I'm sitting, in London, if I turn my head
> and look out of the glass doors, two, perhaps three seconds will
> go by before a bird passes over the trees and rooftops. But this
> is precisely why they evade us. Either we fail to see them fully,
> because they are merely birds, or else we see them in certain
> preconceived ways – the majestic eagle, the wise owl, the crafty
> magpie.

Bird voices interject among our conversations. They are deeply meshed with a sense of place, season and time. The nightingale belongs, or it did once, unquestionably, in Virginia Woolf's times, to a particular geographic range; Coleridge's birds sing in different ways in different seasons – the distinctive song of spring heard uncannily during the 'tender Rain' of late autumn; bird calls mark the rising and setting of the sun, the passage of day and night. Birds attend and intuit human tragedies and upheavals. During a lull in writing this essay, I picked up *A Woman in Berlin*, an anonymous memoir of the arrival of Russian troops in Berlin in April 1945. On her first page, describing the distant roar and rumble of guns and war drawing ever closer amid a lilac-perfumed spring, the author writes: 'Only the birds seem suspicious of this particular April: there's not a single sparrow nesting in the gutters of our roof'. Birds attract, too, associations that differ across cultures and places. On my recent visit to Papua New Guinea I noticed an abundance of willy-wagtails (*Rhipidura leucophrys*) (whose call my grandmother likened to 'sweet pretty little creature'). In Goroka, I asked one of the men we were travelling with: 'What do you call that bird?' 'That one', he said and thought for a moment. 'We call it toilet cleaner. Because it is always hanging around the toilets.' We all laughed. In Warlpiri culture in Central Australia the *jintirr-jintirrpa* (the willy-wagtail) is a messenger bird, telling people when rain is coming.

During these times of profound environmental change, what are bird voices heralding? What does their song tell us? What does the composition of species indicate?

As I write before dawn back in Canberra, waking early to escape a run of heat-saturated days above 40°C, one of the first morning calls comes from the koel. The koel is a large, black bird, a species of cuckoo often perched high in the canopies of the tallest trees over summer, retreating northward for winter. I first heard this bird in India while on a writer's residency in Delhi. Before I arrived, the woman running the office warned me that I would be landing in the middle of the monsoon, when Delhi was unpleasantly hot, and that there would be no other international visitors to keep me company. The date worked for other reasons so I went anyway. For the first couple of weeks my partner kept me company and after that I was indeed alone – in a complex of understated architect-designed living quarters, double-storey with a balcony, ochre on the outside and tiled inside with cool, green slate. I ate in a dining hall alone apart from the staff who laid out my carefully prepared Jain meals. At first it was peaceful and then it became intense. I could barely stand to eat in the hall, attended by staff with whom I quickly ran out of small talk, the only sound my own chewing. The nights became ever hotter until at 2 am the temperature still hadn't dropped below 35°C. I lay beneath a ceiling fan, draped in wet towels whose moisture evaporated even at that hour. I would get up, re-dampen the towels, then try again to sleep. Well before dawn, the koel began with its distinctive call: a single whooping note ascending, repeated over and again. It was a call I became fond of – it seemed so much of this place.

So I was startled to hear it again during a stint living in Sydney years later. It was unmistakeable. A Google search told me that the species was making its way down the eastern seaboard of Australia, travelling from the tropics and Papua New Guinea where it usually resides. A couple of years later, I heard its call for the first time in Canberra – heralding its arrival, having made its way this far south. Now it is part of the dawn chorus, often an outlier, beginning earlier even than the magpie. Apart from the repetitive ascending whoop, koels have another call, made when they're disputing. I hear them squabble with currawongs and other birds, a bright burst of contending sound among the trees outside our windows. Has the koel made it this far south due to opportunism? An abundance of a particular fruiting tree? Some other reason? Climate change? Some studies suggest the latter is the case.

DECADES AGO I LIVED IN A SHARE HOUSE WITH AN OCEAN-
ographer. While I was at art school, he disappeared for weeks on end
to Antarctica. His bedroom lay empty, unused during his absences.
One afternoon, when he had just returned, we talked a little of his
research. He explained how, in Antarctica, he and his colleagues were
collecting ice cores within which were trapped bubbles of air that
showed increasing levels of carbon dioxide in the atmosphere over
time. With hindsight, I now know he was at the cutting edge of climate change research. These days, scientists refer to the field as Earth
system science, or global environmental change science (because it
is the whole interlocking system that is changing, not climate on its
own). Back then in the late 1980s, the field was in its earliest years.
This conversation gave me my first inkling of a world profoundly
altered by human activity, by the burning of fossil fuels. A globally
warming climate, with its cascade of impacts, seemed remote then,
at a scale so large and historically deep that it was of great but not
pressing interest. Its consequences, I imagined back then in youth
and naivety, would be felt in hundreds or thousands of years if at all.

In the early 2000s, I was sitting at the botanic gardens café in
Canberra with a friend of a friend, an art historian. 'What do you
think of all this talk about climate change?' he asked at our outdoor
table, upon which alighted the boldest species: magpies, currawongs,
apostle birds, even a single male bower bird with blue-sheened black
plumage, hustling for crumbs. 'Do we only care because of selfish-
ness?' I asked. The world will go on, but altered from the way we
know it, it will alter into new forms as it has across deep time, across
its geological past. Do we only care, I wondered back then, because
our own way of life will be impinged upon?

But now, as the impacts of global warming and evidence of the
Sixth Great Extinction become ever more tangible, they prompt an

anxious listening and looking. In Canberra, I find myself examining trees: is this canopy thinner, has that tree died, are swathes of local open woodland suffering because of a heating world? Simple local things – birds and trees – are both an index of change and harbingers of worse to come. I have recurrent periods of imagining a world in which trees cannot survive, like the one in Frank Herbert's *Dune* series that I read as a teenager. During the worst of the summer heat, birds in my garden and on the streets keep their beaks fixed open in a kind of permanent avian panting. Will there come a day when they expire from heat exhaustion, I wonder, and drop from trees and skies like the flying foxes in Queensland and Victoria, unable to cool their systems? In Canberra over the summer of 2019 we experience four days in a row when temperatures sit at and above 40°C. The possum in our garden emerges, dazed, from its box, wanders blindly across the neighbour's roof in broad daylight. I ask myself whether my daughter will experience food and water shortage and major social disruption in her lifetime. She asks, 'Can we visit the Great Barrier Reef before it's gone?' Who could have imagined such a question even two decades ago?

We visit the south coast of New South Wales for the weekend, walk along the beach. At one small headland a sign tells us to keep away from the nesting area of a single pair of hooded plovers. There are fewer than fifty of these birds left in New South Wales, it tells us. Hooded plovers with their fine, wild, wheeling, plaintive cry, dashing across wet sand so fast their legs can barely be seen. My father photographed them. They too are marked for demise. And the pied oystercatcher, less than 200 pairs left in New South Wales, diminishing along with the pipis upon which they feed, abundant during my childhood, splayed open in pinks and purples like a pair of butterfly wings on the sand, now hardly ever seen.

When I learn of the bogong moths, their numbers reduced from billions to a handful over a single spring and summer, I am profoundly shocked. Each year the moths pass over Canberra on their migratory route to the mountains. There, they are crucial food for the endangered mountain pygmy possum, now struggling more than ever. With this news it seems to me as though the world has already reached a tipping point, crossed a threshold. Not only because of the crisis affecting the possums and moths but as an indicator and forewarning of the deep ecological strife within which we are bound. For days, I carry with me this dark shock at having crossed over into catastrophe.

IN MY OWN GARDEN IN CANBERRA, WHICH I'VE BEEN WORKING on for over a decade, I have set up two shallow terracotta birdbaths, and they attract a plethora of birds: silvereyes, wrens, pardalotes, eastern spinebills, peewees, thornbills, rosellas, corellas, gang gangs, king parrots, magpies, currawongs, white-winged choughs, crested pigeons. Once a hawk descended into the garden and spent the best part of a day dismembering and consuming a pigeon. Once a king-fisher perched on the clothesline. Sometimes, during summer, the small birds drink together in mingled interspecies flocks, great groups of them taking it in turns to bathe in threes, fours, fives, then rear-ranging their damp feathers in the branches above, while the next lot take their turn. A friend who lives around the corner dropped in one day just as one of these flocks was drinking. She too is a gardener but she noted in surprise that these birds never visited her garden. There's something about the combination of shallow water, storeys of vege-tation, and sections of 'messy' garden (tangles of old creepers, dense bushes, an array of indigenous species) that attracts and protects these smaller birds.

During heatwave and drought, the flocks of small species are drawn to the water throughout the day, returning again and again to drink. One of the birdbaths is just outside the room where I write, and I can hear the soft, melodic *thunk* when their tiny bodies hit the bottom of the bath, chiming against terracotta during particularly vigorous bathing. Some days I take photos on my phone of the silvereyes, thornbills, pardalotes, wrens all bathing together. Proof they were here? Future ghosts? Refilling their water has become one of my favourite daily rituals – it is comforting to make this small offering to the birds.

MORE AND MORE, WITH THE RELEASE OF EACH FRESH SET OF evidence of loss, damage, carnage, catastrophic crashes of species, the question is how to respond, how to listen more carefully to a radically transforming world.

With this question in mind, in 2017 my daughter and I volunteered for a citizen science project called Frogwatch, which monitors the impact of a warming climate on frogs and their seasonal behaviour. I wanted to do something tangible. I imagined my daughter, then twelve, looking back on this period in adulthood and asking: what did we do during this crisis? What action did we take? At least this was one small thing. The project has lost its funding now, but for two years it took us out into the local landscape to listen and record. Weekly, in early evening darkness from winter through to spring, we sat by two small dams, first one then the other, in a piece of clapped-out Canberra bush. We switched my phone to Voice Memos and recorded frogs for a three-minute period – along with any other incidental sound: the distant call of a mopoke, hushed traffic, a plane taking off from the nearby airport. These recordings, accompanied by field notes observing water levels, weather conditions, ambient and water temperatures, were later uploaded onto a database that contains, overall, decades of such information.

Ecologists on the project estimate that some frog species are calling up to four weeks earlier than they did when records first began in the 1980s. The males' mating calls are triggered in large part by temperature.

Several years ago, I had a series of conversations with anthropologist and philosopher Deborah Bird Rose. I was writing about Central Australia and she recommended books and articles to read, quite eclectic in their range. 'Reading is like casting a handful of seeds', she said. 'Some will sprout, some won't.' She was seated in her office with her signature waist-length grey plait draped over one shoulder. Around the same time, at a social event, she told of how she'd found a bird nest in her backyard lined with strands of her long, grey hair, woven into the nest's fabric. For someone whose work revolved around interrelationships between people, other creatures and much larger 'forces of nature' (I'm struggling to think of a better abbreviating term for things as varied as seasons, stars, earth, mud, stone), what could be more fitting than this improvisation with and repurposing of her hair – by birds.

During that period of reading, which Debbie likened to broadcasting seed, I came across her counterintuitive exploration of the idea of 'the wild', which she encountered through Daly Pulkara, one of her Aboriginal teachers in the Northern Territory:

> We stopped because I wanted to film some of the most spectacular erosion in the Victoria River District. I asked Daly what he called this country. He looked at it long and heavily before he said: 'It's the wild. Just the wild.' Daly went on to speak of quiet country – the country in which all the care of generations of people is evident to those who know how to see it. Quiet country stands in contrast to the wild: we were looking at a wilderness, man-made and cattle-made. This 'wild' was a place where the life of the country was falling into the gullies and washing away with rains.

Rather than romantic untamed wilderness, this wild is marked by a lack of human *care* and attentive presence (the right kind of stringently learned intergenerational practices, which cannot, as Tony Birch notes, simply be 'cherry-picked' by non-Indigenous people). Daly's concept of the wild, puzzling and provocative, has returned to me on and off over the years.

When I began volunteering for the Frogwatch program, making my way in twilight up a gravel fire trail into the bush behind the Canberra suburb of Hackett, I was reminded again of Daly's haunting notion of unquiet country. Historian John Dargavel captures the state and mood of this landscape in his essay 'The Fence of Sorrow and Hope' (included in this collection) reflecting on Mulligans Flat Reserve, also on the outskirts of Canberra. 'I see it as sad, battered land now', he writes, wrested from its traditional owners, 'the trees ringbarked and burnt, the native grasses gone, weeds everywhere, the soil trampled and eroded, the small animals driven out by sheep and rabbits, or killed by foxes and cats'. Bordering on the suburbs, *this is what it has come to*, he writes.

On Frogwatch nights, my daughter and I walked among eroded gullies, trampled soil, weeds, absences where other life forms once thrived. Last year, too, there was a kind of bone dryness, surface gravel on the dirt trails and footworn paths skidding about like ball-bearings underfoot. Canopies of eucalypt trees were sparse and dying back. Dead trees littered the landscape, dim, pale shapes like a forearm and hand splayed upward in the dusk. The country looked exhausted. *Just the wild*. But there are moments, too, when life pulses in this place: on three evenings we were startled then thrilled by a sugar glider. This didn't occur until our second year into the project. The first time we were sitting on the edge of the upper dam in darkness, making the evening's audio recording. It was a windless night, quiet, and there came a sudden rustling and movement above us. I switched on my head-torch and there it was: a glider perched on a bough, peering down at us then scrambling higher. The second time a glider leaped upward through the tree canopies and out of sight as we reached the lower dam. The final time, as we walked along a narrow dirt path in torchlight, scuffing up dust – velvety in texture, clinging to our boots, grasses, fallen branches, stone – there was again a great rustle and movement. A small, dark shape reached the upper edge of a eucalypt canopy by our side, paused and launched, gliding as if suspended in time across an interval of empty space several metres wide to reach the next tree. This image stayed with me, the possum splayed in the air in slow motion, a silhouette against the faintest trace of light in the evening sky. Something of life itself pulsing and flaring in this sad, battered land.

Other times as we sat silently by the water a night bird winged by, its flight marked by a small creaking noise in the hinges of its wings. Or a pair of ducks passed, emitting a rapid, subdued quacking as if their exertions through the air were forcing an involuntary sound keeping perfect pace with their movements. Some evenings microbats flitted out, circling above the waters, weaving their complex flight lines that dart, make abrupt shifts in direction, circle back on themselves. I tried to keep track of them, imagining what kind of drawings these passages would make if inscribed on paper. Once, one of the tiny bats swooped within centimetres of our faces, passing by in a silence so utter it almost seemed to suck sound in towards it. Perhaps we had stirred up something edible, tiny insects, drawing the bat towards us.

And I wondered, was this a small act of care in this landscape: pacing up the slopes, filling out our field data sheets, recording the calls of frogs so they can accumulate in a much larger database compiled by other volunteers, like ourselves also out and about in the local evening landscape. Together we were making a composite picture over time. Does this constitute care? Or action? I'm not sure.

However you look at it, it's a small act set against the scale of planetary crisis. Over the years, my family and I have done and continue to do other small things, as do many other people around us – things on an everyday scale that we hope will make a difference to emissions reduction.

But I can't help thinking of more dire, angry, punitive responses, especially now that new science is emerging that suggests that if Australia follows a business-as-usual scenario its average temperature is likely to heat by 4°C by the end of this century – within my daughter's lifetime. Life on Earth is difficult to imagine under these conditions. I think of a passage from *A Woman in Berlin* just a few pages from the book's close. 'Our German calamity has a bitter taste – of repulsion, sickness, insanity, unlike anything in history', the author writes. Now we seem to be in the midst of another but quite different period of unprecedented sickness and insanity: oil companies revel in new sources exposed by melting ice in the Arctic region; Australia, unable to shift out of its wealth-extracted-from-natural-resources mindset, remains one of the largest exporters of fossil fuels in the world. Australia, like the Amazon, is a land-clearance hotspot. Will so-called business and political leaders, who put their own economic and political interests before the interests of others and before the physical world upon which we are all entirely reliant, one day be brought to trial? For crimes against humanity and crimes against a global environmental commons – the wellbeing of which should belong to all? Is this a simplistic thought? I'm not sure. But why should the self-interest of a few create so much ruin for so many?

Of course the situation is far more complex than this, it also requires mass willingness to support change, but still I can't help wondering. Historian, author and activist Keith Hancock wrote in 1973, 'What we do here and now is making the future or wrecking it'. This idea, deceptive in its simplicity, seems truer and more acute than ever.

Readings

Anonymous, *A Woman in Berlin*, Virago, London, 2006.

Australian National University Archives: Sir Keith Hancock Research Papers, AU NBAC P96-31-14, 'Odd Lectures' file, correspondence between Hancock and DF McMichael, Department of Environment and Conservation, 3 October 1973.

Tony Birch, 'Climate Change, Mining and Traditional Indigenous Knowledge in Australia', *Social Inclusion*, vol. 4, no. 1, 2016, p. 6.

Rachel Carson, *Silent Spring*, Penguin Books, London, 1962, pp. 100–01.

Samuel Taylor Coleridge, *Coleridge's Notebooks: A Selection*, edited by Seamus Perry, Oxford University Press, Oxford, 2002, p. 40.

Joëlle Gergis, 'Grief, Anger and Climate Change', *7am*, Schwartz Media 2019, <bit.ly/podcast-gergis-2019>.

Karl Ove Knausgård, 'To Be A Bird', *The New Yorker*, 2 May 2019. (The *New Yorker* piece is drawn from Knausgård's essay in Stephen Gill (ed.), *The Pillar*, Nobody Books, UK, 2019, <bit.ly/newyorker-knausgaard>.)

Deborah Bird Rose, *Nourishing Terrains: Australian Aboriginal Views of Landscape and Wilderness*, Australian Heritage Commission, Canberra, 1996, p. 19.

UNEP, *Emissions Gap Report 2019: Executive Summary*, United Nations Environment Programme, Nairobi, 2019, <bit.ly/unep-emissionsgap>.

Andrew Whitehouse, 'Listening to Birds in the Anthropocene: The Anxious Semiotics of Sound in a Human-dominated World', *Environmental Humanities*, 6, 2015, pp. 53–71.

Virginia Woolf, *Between the Acts*, 1941. A Project Gutenberg of Australia eBook, <gutenberg.net.au/ebooks03/0301171h.html>.

GEOLOCATOR BROOCH

Annalise Rees

Pinned to the lapel of my coat is the cut-out silhouette of a bird, wings spread in full flight. Dangling from its leg is a geolocator, a small device used for tracking marine predator species called a geolocator. Geolocators record ambient light levels, water temperature and time. The data they collect reveals the foraging movements of marine top predators, allowing scientists to identify regions of the ocean that are of high ecological significance.

This specific geolocator, hanging from my brooch, was attached to the leg of a light-mantled albatross (*Phoebetria palpebrata*) on South Georgia Island and tracked for 759 days. It travelled an incredible 89 019 kilometres. The geolocator was given to me by albatross researcher Jaimie Cleeland. She explained geolocation to me and how the information collected helps us to better understand the impacts of changing climate and human activities upon marine predator species. By gaining an understanding of how marine predators use their ocean habitats, more effective management strategies can be put in place for their protection.

I was intrigued as I listened to Jaimie, turning the small device over in my hand, revelling in the stories held in its tiny componentry. Through the geolocator I glimpsed a view of the world through the eyes of an albatross soaring above the waves. Jaimie told me that once the batteries in the geolocator go flat it can no longer be used. It sparked an idea that has turned into a project called *Geolocation Journeys*, supporting marine predator research <www.geolocation-journeys.com>.

Jaimie and I repurpose these 'retired' geolocators, transforming them into wearable art. With each piece comes a printed map of the track and the unique identifying number of the animal. The brooches have the silhouette of the animal (in this case an albatross) cut from an old metal sign from Casey Station in Antarctica. My brooch signifies the beginning of my friendship with Jaimie and our collaboration. It also presents an alternative approach to communicating scientific data in a meaningful and engaging way. Pinned onto coats and jackets the geolocators go on new journeys, opening up our eyes, minds and hearts to help share the amazing stories of these unique species and their habitat. It is my hope that through this small object I, too, can help Jaimie and her research colleagues to better understand how we can make positive changes to protect these animals and the environment of which we are all custodians.

THYLACINE BUGGY RUG

Katrina Schlunke

This is the thing I can't get over. That the most practised, ordinary intimacy between the now-extinct thylacine and humans may have happened with this rug. The casual touching of the skin as hands pulled the rug over cold human knees. The absentminded stroking by adults. The intense, curious engagement from children until they too accepted and assumed the warmth of multiple thylacine skins stitched into a rug. This makes me frightened for other species. As if humans knowing them and even loving one part of them always require a catastrophic distinction from them. Knowing the thylacine 'scientifically' rendered it a subject of zoo and museum collections, as a specimen of study or Antipodean curiosity. Knowing the thylacine in the shared space of a farm made it into the 'Tasmanian tiger', to be hunted and trapped. All this white human knowing leading to its destruction. The thylacine is recorded in rock art dated on mainland Australia to at least 1000 BCE, and sightings are recorded by European visitors to Tasmania from the late 1700s. In 133 short years that vivid life lived across the island of Tasmania was progressively annihilated to leave only stilled remains, including this rug.

What to feel about this rug? It is carefully made. Eight different thylacine skins have had their distinctive, beautiful striped backs removed and then sewn together in an elegant mosaic with a scalloped edge and red baize backing. Robert Stevenson, circa 1903, is credited with the making of the buggy rug, but I suspect a woman's work. A buggy was an open, horse-drawn vehicle, so when one buggy passed another, the buggy rug would have been on prominent display. So was this rug a calculated bid for status? A mark of hunting and needlework skill?

Most of the animals killed to provide the pelts to make this rug came from the Upper Blessington area in northern Tasmania. From the comfort of my car it is easy to marvel at the sharp crags and rocky river crossings that break into the lush rolling hills of good-looking farmland. But there is also a sense of anxiousness that the rich pasture and cropped hills are intimately entwined with the caught and killed thylacines.

Just beyond the shot-up sign announcing Upper Blessington we choose a path that, according to the topographic map my partner and I are consulting, should take us over the hill and back to the highway (we can't check with Google Maps as there is no reception). But what begins as a well-marked road is undone by the constant criss-crossing of logging tracks. The landscape shifts from tree-fern-filled, subtropical rainforest to the monocultural world of plantation pines and eucalypts. The dirt road develops wheel ruts with a higher and higher, loose-sided middle ridge, as if made only for trucks with elevated clearance, or for bulldozers. Finally, we come to a kind of cul-de-sac with walls of stripped and cut logs, and although we see that the track continues down the very steep side of this hill we no longer trust it.

We slowly fight our way back to bitumen and highway via another set of rough tracks. Losing our tracks to the demands of commercial logging makes me wonder how quickly the thylacines lost their way. For so long their tracks would have worked – until their paths of belonging, their everyday foraging, did not end up anywhere at all. Or nowhere useful. And with nowhere to go back to. The buggy meanwhile would have been making tracks. Tracks that shaped the land into 'settled' blocks connected by 'communication' lines.

Did any other thylacine see, smell that rug on those human knees? Did it figure for even a second that something familiar but terribly monstrous was moving across its land? Did that watching, near final, thylacine learn to take a different path? Not realising that the policies of eradication would be too pervasive, the promised price on its head too powerful, to enable it to arrive anywhere and remain alive for too long. Taken from animals killed as a frightening pest, sewn together to warm the knees of the killers – now the skins are too precious for human eyes. Too easily damaged, even by our gaze. As if we could ever see, really see, what we did.

On display in this Tasmanian museum, the Queen Victoria Museum and Art Gallery, the rug can only be seen as a whole in glimpses. The display light is on a timer to help preserve the colour and quality of the rug. The seemingly casual excessiveness of eight (eight!) now-extinct thylacine skins cut and organised by human hands for human comfort makes the seeing of this rug a deeply unsettling experience. So, too, is knowing the role of the museum in the killing and capturing of thylacines for collection and exchange with other museums.

The thylacine, dead and alive, became a currency of curiosity that built the standing of individual collectors, members of the Royal Society and directors of museums, and the quality of this museum's collection. The museum harvested the diverse values of the living thylacines and now preserves the remains. Remains made precious, even prestigious, through extinction. The on-again, off-again lighting draws you closer to the rug, the flickering light perhaps bringing forth some underlying anxiety that somewhere a lightbulb will blow.

The texture is alluring. Like any fur or hide there is a call to touch, which is accentuated by the stripes – as if their figuration matches in some way the tips of the human hand that could sketch out each stripe. But so many skins, so much death standing in for the ultimate death of all thylacines, is also sickening.

It confronts our assumptions about the natural good of making use of available animals. It challenges the idea that if we kill an animal we should eat every bit of it, use every part of it. For these skins stripped of their bodies do not confirm that thinking. They suggest ghastly unclothed ghosts walking the forests. They cry, I think, to go back.

Robert Stevenson of 'Aplico', who killed all these thylacines (and many more), appears in the correspondence pages of newspapers in the 1890s agitating against the ban on 'opossum' hunting. And by the 1900s he places notices in the public announcement sections of the newspapers warning people off hunting on his property. We don't know whether the signs were to preserve the animals on his property for his own hunting or because he wanted to save the animals themselves. By the time he dies in 1947 the last thylacine is already dead. The rug remains.

AN ENCOUNTER WITH
BRINE SHRIMP AND DEEP TIME

Emily O'Gorman

Julie and I walked carefully along the stark white sand of the banks of the Coorong. I was undertaking an interview for research on the histories of wetlands in the Murray-Darling Basin. Julie is a long-time resident of a small settlement located about a third of the way south from the mouth of the Murray River, along the Coorong lagoon in South Australia (to protect her identity as a research participant, her actual name has been withheld). This lagoon, known particularly for its birdlife, is one of the icon sites for The Living Murray initiative and is listed on the Ramsar Convention on Wetlands of International Importance.

It was summer and the water was low, exposing a wide shoreline with such a small incline that it looked almost flat; a sign of the shallowness of this part of the lagoon. In the distance, across the water, were the Hummocks, the sand dunes of Younghusband Peninsula running parallel to the thin stretch of water. The name 'Coorong' is supposedly from the term *Karangk* in the local Aboriginal languages of the Tanganekald, meaning 'long neck'. This peninsula was the setting of Colin Thiele's novel *Storm Boy*, a coming-of-age story centred on the friendship between a boy and a pelican, which takes place against a national context of the Aboriginal land rights and environmental movements of the 1960s. From the opposite shore, and half a century later, we find ourselves at another, related, possible turning point in the Anthropocene.

From the moment we stepped on to the sand, Julie told me to be careful, that the shore was slippery. I began slowly, warily, but found the sand was firm and had a rough friction. I started to walk more confidently. We discussed the changes Julie had seen on the Coorong over the last fifteen years. The most recent drought, the Millennium Drought, infused our discussion. It had lasted longer here than elsewhere, from at least 2000 to 2011. Julie told me how the humans and non-humans reliant on the waters of the Coorong had suffered. Water managers had not let fresh water through the barrages, built in the 1930s to protect irrigation interests. This meant that the Coorong did not receive freshwater inflows and became, in places, saltier than sea water. The pelicans that frequently caught our attention as we walked had for a time stopped breeding on the nearby islands in the lagoon; other birds had also stopped breeding here, fish had reduced in number, and some people left the area because certain industries could not function without more fresh water.

Julie turned to the positive changes that had occurred since the drought broke. *Ruppia tuberosa*, an aquatic plant that provided food for many waterbirds, was gradually repopulating the shoreline. The pelicans were back. As we began to return to the grassy bank I suddenly slipped in the sand. Julie said, 'Look, that's the briny shrimp.' I looked where my shoe had scraped back what I now saw was just a thin layer of white sand. Underneath was what appeared to be black clay. This is what had been slippery. I asked Julie: 'The black stuff, is ... shrimp?' 'Yes!' She explained that during the drought the water in the southern lagoon of the Coorong had reached a level so salty that large numbers of the dormant brine shrimp had hatched. Others have said that a reduction in the number of fish predators meant the shrimp had thrived. The decayed bodies of the shrimp formed a layer of black matter. They had been there waiting for just the right conditions. So many hatched that banded stilts – birds that normally feed on these creatures after floods in ephemeral, arid lakes – descended on the area in a feeding frenzy. Some, then, had flourished during the drought. Yet many people on the Coorong had seen this burst of life as the death knell for the wetland. Julie had not. Clearly, Julie explained, while this was in some ways an unusual event for the Coorong, it must have happened before. But there was something different about this drought, too.

While Australia is, in the words of Dorothea Mackellar, a land of 'droughts and flooding rains', the Bureau of Meteorology declared the Millennium Drought had been linked to climate change. This, together with significant changes to the Murray River system caused by large dams and more intensive agriculture in the twentieth century, along with the diversion of local inflows into the southern lagoon, had opened up an uncertain future for many in the area. In light of expected permanent changes, how could these sorts of events now be interpreted? Droughts and shrimp hatchings resonated with the deep rhythms of this continent, recognised only relatively recently by western science. In the Anthropocene they take on a new significance, rendered both familiar and unfamiliar. The decomposed bodies of the shrimp that formed such a distinct black layer brought us into the multiple temporalities and scales of this continent's history and of the Anthropocene, of deep time and upstream-downstream Murray River politics, of international environmental conventions and local industry, of expected and unexpected consequences, of possible winners and losers in the Anthropocene. New layers of black will be laid down over time, part of the strata of the Coorong that echoes the dynamic and changing relationships between water, salt, plants and animals.

The shrimp, intricately integrated into these waxing and waning systems, will be in the Coorong lagoon, waiting, perhaps playing the long game in a new epoch.

HOLDING
ON

THE END OF ABUNDANCE

Justine Hyde

Suburban Sydney, 1980s. Primary-school-day summers in the shade of the playground's row of Moreton Bay fig trees. Their wide, leathery leaves create a canopy against the heat of the sun. The smell of over-ripe fruit. Each tree's meandering root system rises from the ground like the half-buried hip bones of some prehistoric beast. With my friends, I construct dams from sticks and leaves in the buttressed landscape. We bank the dams together by pressing dirt into the gaps with our small hands, fill them with water from our plastic drink bottles, and watch to see whose dam will hold fast, whose will breach, and where the water will flow; it dissolves into the earth, etching fine muddy trails.

Other days we hunt for the cast-off skins of cicadas. I pick the crisp brown casings from the branches of eucalyptus trees, hook their spiky legs onto the chest of my school uniform and chase my friends, who let out high squeals of feigned horror. Some trees are thick with exoskeletons moulted onto their bark, as if the tree has sprouted them. Often, the shells are beyond the height that I can reach. I stretch my arm up as far as I can; being one of the tallest kids is an advantage.

Some summers bring bumper seasons of cicadas. Over an hour-long school lunchtime, I can easily fill a large OMO washing-powder box with cicada shells. They pile up inside, becoming coated in the dregs of washing powder, ghost insects. When I get home from school I line them up in my bedroom, the shells accumulating over the summer into an army. Over autumn, the cicada shells begin to gather dust and disintegrate, get knocked over, trodden on, and are eventually thrown out by my mother, forgotten until the next summer arrives.

KATHERINE GORGE, IN THE NORTHERN TERRITORY, IS CALLED 'Nitmiluk' in Jawoyn, the local Indigenous language. It literally means 'cicada place'. A Dreaming story tells that this name was given by Nabilil the crocodile, an important figure of the creation time. In his travels through the country, Nabilil arrived at the gorge. He heard the cicadas singing, 'Nit, Nit, Nit!' and named it Nitmiluk. Indigenous Australians consider cicadas a symbol of vitality. Their song heralds summer, the arrival of new life and abundance.

THE EXACT DETAILS OF THE LIFE OF A CICADA ARE ELUSIVE. Most research about these insects is by citizen scientists and PhD students, whose tenure of study is shorter than the average cicada's life cycle. We know that cicadas live most of their lives as nymphs, underground – in some species for up to seventeen years – where they feed off the sap of tree roots until they reach adult size. Around nightfall in late spring or early summer, zombie-like, the nymphs dig themselves out of the ground, settle on a tree branch, and begin shedding their exoskeleton. First the skin splits down the centre of the nymph's back and then the cicada slowly emerges, spreading its still-papery wings. Once above ground, the adults live for only a few weeks.

Australia is home to more species of cicada than any other continent. Of the estimated 800 species, only around 280 have been named. Many were christened by children: greengrocer, cherry nose, double drummer, black prince, floury baker, golden emperor and masked devil. Essentially tropical insects, cicadas can be found all over the country in diverse ecosystems, from coastal bushland to suburban gardens to alpine snowfields.

The cicada is the loudest insect on Earth. At 120 decibels, the greengrocer's song edges close to the pain threshold of the human ear. The male cicada's mating call is the quintessential Australian summer soundtrack. During the heat of the day, the cicadas' deafening chorus protects them against birds, which are repelled by the volume of their song. With their stocky bodies, broad, flat heads and multiple eyes, cicadas are slightly monstrous-looking. Their two pairs of delicate, translucent-vein-laced wings are folded by their side when not in flight.

'A frog with wings and a horrible voice, is in my room,' a scared girl new from England cried, rushing out to her mother, in a suburban garden. The 'frog' was a cicada, but our goggle-eyed insect, and its 'song,' are mysterious to many immigrants. Cicadas – 'Locusts,' most people call them – have invaded Melbourne district in millions, and daylong and after sunset their shrilling music is heard. Plane trees in city streets, and the parks and gardens are sheltering the big green insects, which fiddle ceaselessly. Only the male cicadas play on 'fairy fiddles.' The ancients knew this, and one of their bards wrote the famous couplet:

HOLDING ON

'Happy the cicadas' lives,
Since they all have voiceless wives.'

The Richmond River Express and Casino Kyogle Advertiser,
Friday 21 December 1923

SUBURBAN MELBOURNE, 2010s. MY TWO SONS ARE OF AN AGE when they are fascinated by insects. We go to the Melbourne Museum and spend most of our time in the 'Bugs Alive!' exhibition exploring the rows of metallic beetles and colourful butterflies pinned in glass cases, sliding magnifying lenses over specimens of bed bugs, searching a backlit web for an orb weaver spider, and watching an army of ants make their way around a maze of dirt tunnels. One of my sons' favourite displays is a tiny replica of a suburban kitchen, crawling with cockroaches which look gigantic in their scaled-down world. At the library we borrow illustrated books about bugs and in the two-dollar shop we buy oversized plastic toy replicas of spiders. We hunt under rocks in our garden for slaters, uncurl leaves to find spiders, and follow ant trails across a terrain of grass and brick paving.

One year, hundreds of ladybirds descend on our backyard vegetable garden. We turn over the leaves of our zucchini plants; the underside is thick with black-spotted yellow bugs. My four-year-old son collects them, patiently allowing them to crawl onto his fingers – they trail all over his hands and arms. One by one, they take flight, a tiny squadron of beetles. His smile is wide in the photos I take on my phone. Days later, just a few remain. Then they vanish completely. With my son, we study illustrations of ladybirds that reveal their two layers of wings, their hard casing and, underneath, the delicate, veil-like wings that spread out in flight.

I tell my sons about the cicadas I collected as a child. We have a pronunciation debate about the word: cic-ah-da if you're from

Sydney like me or cic-ay-da if you're a Melbourne native like my children. I refuse to acquiesce. I assume that I'm relating a childhood memory unique to Sydney, that my sons' experience of insects diverges from mine because they are growing up in a different ecosystem. We go to the local park with its Melbourne-typical mix of European plane and oak trees, interrupted by the occasional eucalyptus. We search the branches for cicada shells, only turning up two smallish specimens after several hours of intensive looking. We all leave a little disappointed.

Back at home, I show my sons photos online of cicadas. We watch YouTube videos of them shedding their skins and we listen to recordings of their song. This is nature intermediated by the internet. I feel nostalgic and a little sad that I can't recreate my childhood memory for my sons, but don't dwell on it. It's not the first or last time I will try to conjure nostalgia as if it can be inherited. Cicadas are just another tugging ghost-memory I have left behind in Sydney, like the earth-scent of frangipani trees and the feel of salt-crusted skin after a swim in the ocean.

With summer ahead the dawns and dusks will soon be made merry by the song of the locusts. Our Yellow Mondays, Floury Bakers and others are in no way related to the true locusts of the Middle East and Africa – the locusts that devour every green herb of Egypt. Our locusts are not destructive. Their correct name is cicada. The hotter the day, the louder their chorus. Asked by a stranger on what they fed, a country lad pointing to one of their cast-off shells, replied: 'Nothing, mister. They just sings and sings until they busts!'

Western Grazier, Friday 1 January 1943

IN GERMANY, A GROUP OF CITIZEN SCIENTISTS DILIGENTLY trap and collect flying insects from grasslands, swamps, sand dunes, wastelands and shrubland across the country between the years 1989 and 2016. On weighing the insects' biomass the amateur entomologists discover an alarming decline: over twenty-seven years, the numbers of insects decrease by a seasonal average of 76 per cent. Publication of the German study opens the floodgates; suddenly the media is interested in the fate of insects. A Google search throws up panicked headlines that seek answers: 'Where Have All the Ladybugs Gone?', 'What Happened to All the Bugs?', 'Where Have All Our Insects Gone?' And then the big one. The *New York Times* declares, 'The Insect Apocalypse Is Here': Seattle-based writer Brooke Jarvis turns the question into a definitive statement. 'Insectaggedon' has arrived.

Insects aerate soils, they pollinate plants and crops, and they clean up the environment, disposing of dung and dead bodies. Losing insect abundance and diversity will have devastating effects on ecosystems and consequently on humans. The obvious metaphor is one of dominoes falling. First their predators will disappear: birds, bats, spiders, amphibians. The food chain will collapse, kick-starting a chain of events: landscapes changing, whole ecosystems disappearing, mass starvation, and for the humans who are left, wars over precious, diminishing resources.

Jarvis gives numbers for measuring the loss of individual species. Over a twenty-year period in the United States, 900 million – 90 per cent – of monarch butterflies were lost and the population of rusty patched bumblebees dropped by 87 per cent.

Our ignorance is quantified in the millions of species of insects we will never even know existed before they vanish. With such an abundance of insects, hardly anyone has thought to study their volume, and no funding body would support this kind of longitudinal research. The German study is the only one of its kind in the world. So we have no baseline measures of insect populations, just a haunting, gut feeling that something is missing.

'Windshield phenomenon' – the absence of squashed insects on car windshields – has become shorthand for anecdotal evidence of disappearing insects. And there are other signs and symbols: declines in populations of species of birds and fish, suggesting a correlation to insect loss. We have hypotheses, but without data we might as well be reading tea leaves or tarot cards.

The reasons for insect decline are multifaceted, making them complex to pin down: light pollution, climate change, habitat destruction, monocultures. The common factor is that they are all caused by humans.

I can't help thinking about cicadas. It is possible that their absence is not so easily explained away by my living in a new ecosystem. Perhaps it is, more frighteningly, a new epoch: one in which the insects around us are vanishing. I want to understand more about what is happening to insect populations, so I go in search of an expert to ask.

I MEET DR KEN WALKER, SENIOR CURATOR OF ENTOMOLOGY at the Melbourne Museum. He greets me with a warm smile and handshake. I ask him about the German study and its application to Australia. 'The evidence is there, but Germany is quite different to Australia', Ken says. Germany is heavily populated, has intensive agriculture and uses lots of pesticides, whereas 70–75 per cent of land in Australia is arid or semiarid, giving plenty of space for insects to thrive away from human populations. 'The great deficiency of that study is that no one ever looked at what insects were missing', he says,

'It was a huge failing ... was it across all groups? Was it the beetles that were missing? Was it all the wasps or the flies?'

Ken tells me that there are no comparable studies in Australia. 'You would never get funding to run a project over twenty-seven years', he says. 'We don't have that kind of evidence ... but it made us all – scientists – sit up and pay attention.'

Since the German study was published, Ken has been asked repeatedly about the insect 'Armageddon'. 'Without seeing the evidence I can't say that there's been a loss in the biomass of insects in Australia', he says. He takes issue with terms such as 'Armageddon' and 'apocalypse'; words that, he says, are highly emotive and make catchy headlines rather than reflect scientific evidence.

And what of the anecdotal evidence? Ken recites all the usual observations: fewer insects splattered on car windscreens, and not as many bugs buzzing around lights at night-time. He explains these conjectures away: more aerodynamic cars that allow insects to disappear over the windscreen rather than sticking to it, many more lights than there used to be, and more lights with low wattage making them less appealing to insects – which are attracted to incandescent light.

Ken peppers his conversation with laughter and anecdotes; he doesn't seem like someone who is anxious about the fate of his favourite creatures. While it is his job as a scientist to look to the evidence to prove a hypothesis, Ken's rationalisation and optimism unsettle me.

There is simply not enough peer-reviewed evidence to prove a decline in insects, Ken says. To illustrate his point: 'If the insects have been decimated and 70 per cent of our food is pollinated by insects, why aren't we seeing famines? Why aren't we hearing of crop losses?'

They are fair questions, but even with its flaws, publication of the German study prompted many entomologists to express their concerns for the fate of insects in the face of known pressures such as habitat loss, pesticide use and climate change.

Ken says, 'There's got to be a consequence.' What is certain is that because we lack evidence and longitudinal research, most likely the first warning of insect collapse will not be seen in observing the insects themselves, but will be borne out in witnessing those consequences. Ken points to crop collapse, followed by a rapid crash in the human population due to famine and breakdown of the food chain. And by then, he says, it will be too late, the insects will already be gone. Ken adds, 'Everyone loves the vertebrates, the furry cuddly things', but insects are 'the little things that run the world' – a phrase coined by American entomologist EO Wilson.

Insects are incredibly resilient creatures and many species are adaptable to their environment. Their populations vary widely from season to season, going through repeated boom and bust cycles. Ken traces a sine curve in the air to illustrate. Insect numbers can be close to decimation, he says, then rise again when environmental conditions change. For example, Christmas beetle larvae feed on rotting wood. During prolonged droughts – like those we've experienced in Australia over the past decade – the wood simply isn't available, so there will be fewer beetles and they will appear later in the season.

I think about my childhood summers and the proliferation of Christmas beetles, their rainbow-metallic exoskeletons hitting like pellets against my bare skin, or landing in ice-filled drinks and barbecue dinners. I remember their hard bodies crunching underfoot on sun-warmed concrete footpaths where they lay upturned, legs waving. I have never seen a Christmas beetle as an adult.

Ken says, 'It's very hard to say whether an insect has become extinct' because they are so elusive and little-understood. The Melbourne Museum's exhibition 'Extinction Is Forever' featured the Lord Howe Island stick insect. Two weeks after the exhibition opened in 1980, Ken chuckles, the insects were rediscovered in the wild on Balls Pyramid, a remote sea stack just over 20 kilometres south of the island.

Native bees are Ken's area of expertise. He relies on his own research, that of other experts and the work of citizen scientists. He describes 'the first bee for the season' – the instance of where and when an insect first appears – as being critical information for understanding the health of an insect population. It sounds ominously like the canary in the coalmine. I wonder if there will be a season when the first bee simply never appears, and how long we might wait for it in hope.

We talk about global honeybee colony collapse. Ken says that 50 per cent of honeybee stocks around the world have been lost to the varroa mite. We don't yet have the pest in Australia – our biosecurity controls around it are tight, but not infallible. Should the mite enter Australia, it will be devastating. Ken estimates that we will lose 70–80 per cent of our honeybee stock, with massive consequences for crop pollination. We already rely on imported honeybees to support our agricultural export industries, such as almond crops. In China, cheap human labour does the job of bees by hand-pollinating crops.

Ken leads me into what he jokingly refers to as 'the morgue', the basement rooms packed with the 2.5 million dead insects that make up the museum's collection. The oldest specimen is a butterfly collected in China in 1742. Ken pulls out drawer after drawer of native cicadas from ancient wooden cabinets; it is an insect *wunderkammer*.

I ask Ken if I'm not seeing cicadas in Melbourne because their numbers are declining. When I tell him that I live in the inner-northern suburb of Coburg, he tells me that it is very urbanised, has a dense population, and most of the native trees have been chopped down and replaced with exotics. 'Go down to St Kilda where the cicadas are deafening', he says.

Ken leads me back to the museum entrance. We part, agreeing to be 'alert, not alarmed' about the fate of insects. Yet when I step out into the bright Melbourne summer sunlight, I feel troubled. What if he is wrong?

A plague of cicadas covering the national station 4RK's mast at Gracemere is interrupting transmission and defying the efforts of staff to smoke them away. The cicadas first appeared on the mast at mid-day on Wednesday and each time one of them is electrocuted the station goes off the air. The divisional engineer (Mr. N. Scott) said to-day that there must be millions of the insects on the mast and feeder lines from the transmitter to the mast which were covered from one end to the other. Each time a cicada was caught between the lines or on the lightning arrestors a short circuit was caused. The insect was burnt to death and an overload circuit breaker automatically switched the power output off.

Townsville Daily Bulletin, Friday 10 December 1954

SOME WEEKS AFTER MY CONVERSATION WITH KEN, THE *Guardian* declares, 'Plummeting insect numbers threaten collapse of nature', with the prediction that all insects could disappear within a century. The piece is based on a 'global scientific review' published in the journal *Biological Conservation*. I email Ken.

'In my view the authors are really over-stretching the data they have', he replies, and that data set is flawed. The study's authors have used managed honeybee colonies in China and Australia as models for native insect fauna in those countries. 'That's a stretch', he says. They used this data set to conclude that 80 per cent of biomass of insects has disappeared. The researchers developed world-wide trends based on single-location studies.

Of their methodology Ken says, 'They did a Google search for a few variables and weeded 653 articles down to 73 studies' then used only the data sets that showed change, rejecting those that didn't. 'Is that good science?' he asks. Ken dismisses the study and its conclusions: 'As I said to you when we met, show me the data'.

Ken's dissection of the scientific credibility of the study does nothing to relieve my anxiety. My search for understanding – prompted by my childhood nostalgia about cicadas – is still unresolved and it is beginning to feel like I'm jumping at shadows.

A FEW WEEKS PASS, AN EMAIL FROM KEN LANDS IN MY INBOX. It's a link to an *Atlantic* piece, 'Is the Insect Apocalypse Really Upon Us?' with the note: 'For a bit of balance on this issue, read this recent article'. Science writer Ed Yong's conclusions mirror Ken's: there's just not enough data to make the hyperbolic claims about insect annihilation that are being reported in the media. Yong does stress, however, that while the evidence may be lacking, the underlying concern is real. This view balances out Ken's breezy optimism; we have to pay close attention to this 'wake-up call' about insect populations.

In his article, Yong asks: 'How, then, should we act on that imperfect knowledge? It's a question that goes beyond the fate of insects: How do we preserve our rapidly changing world when the unknowns are vast and the cost of inaction is potentially high?'

Yong's questions are central dilemmas in the Anthropocene. In a market-driven world, when even proven scientific facts are contested by deniers who stand to lose their power and capital, how do we wrestle with ambiguity? When we cannot quantify precisely what we are losing, or exactly why that is important, how do we act on these unanswerable questions and make an argument to stem the loss?

To keep searching for evidence before we act is – to grasp at clichés – sleepwalking over a cliff. I turn my feelings over to examine them; they are prismatic, faceted with grief, despair, anger. And if I'm honest, denial too. Some days I can't bring myself to read the articles on melting glaciers and rising ocean temperatures and species extinction that appear in my social media feed; I scroll past them and watch a funny cat video instead. Non-human life is in peril and with it follows human fate. We are the first of our kind to contemplate the possibility of our own extinction, but it is impossible to live with this knowledge always front of mind.

Philosophers such as Ernest Becker have written about the elaborate belief systems we construct to guard against the knowledge of our own mortality. It is our survival mechanism. As a species, we seem not to be very adept at noticing gradual change. Indian writer Amitav Ghosh calls it 'the great derangement', our inability to process and engage with loss. Canadian nature writer JB MacKinnon calls it the 'great forgetting'. He says:

> Memory conspires against nature. The forgetting can begin in the instant that a change takes place: the human mind did not evolve to see its surroundings – what we now so clinically refer to as 'the environment' – as the focus of our attention, but rather as the backdrop against which more interesting things take place.

My sons' fascination with insects coalesced with my childhood nostalgia about long, hot summers punctuated by the song of cicadas and the pleasure of collecting their sloughed juvenile skins. Their absence prompted me to search for answers about the fate of insects, the most abundant creatures on Earth. While expert views are contradictory, what is certain is that many millions of insect species will disappear without us ever knowing they existed. The scale of loss cannot be quantified.

In a secular society, where religion no longer provides the symbolic scaffold to construct our immortality, and where we increasingly turn to science for absolutes that it can't provide, we have to instead look in the mirror to understand that the way we live is antithetical to our long-term viability. We are facing the looming finale of our species and taking the lives of many others with us. There won't be any applause when we draw the curtains on our performance.

Readings

Australian Museum, *Cicadas: Superfamily Cicadoidea*, updated 12 October 2018, <bit.ly/am-cicadas>.

Damian Carrington, 'Plummeting Insect Numbers "Threaten Collapse of Nature"', *Guardian*, 11 February 2019, <bit.ly/guardian-carrington>.

Amitav Ghosh, *The Great Derangement: Climate Change and the Unthinkable*, University of Chicago Press, Chicago, 2016.

Brooke Jarvis, 'The Insect Apocalypse Is Here', *New York Times*, 27 November 2018, <bit.ly/nytimes-jarvis>.

JB MacKinnon, *The Once and Future World: Nature As It Was, As It Is, As It Could Be*, Random House Canada, Toronto, 2013.

Ed Yong, 'Is the Insect Apocalypse Really Upon Us?', *Atlantic*, 19 February 2019, <bit.ly/atlantic-yong>.

FOR THE LOVE OF LARVAE

Kate Phillips

We all start out as babies, small, soft and utterly dependent on the care of others. But what if we were not looked after by our kin, but raised by aliens, by members of another species who were very different from us? This is the case for many species of butterflies which, when they are young, are cared for by ants. I have witnessed this strange and wonderful synergy in action.

I first took part in the Eltham copper butterfly larvae count in 1998, when a colleague invited me to help during one of the annual surveys at the butterfly reserves in suburban Eltham; on an early spring night a small band of people combed the bushland plots, counting larvae. Since then I've joined the count several times as part of the monitoring effort to keep track of the population. Larvae counts occur in spring, when the larvae are tended by ants, kept in the ants' nest underground during the day, then at dusk escorted up the stem of their food plant, the sweet bursaria. The larvae are highly efficient leaf-eaters, and in return for their care by the ants, they produce a sweet substance that the ants drink. When the larvae have grown sufficiently large, they pupate and emerge as adults – butterflies – in early summer. The butterfly species (*Paralucia pyrodiscus lucida*) requires both the ants (*Notoncus* sp.) and their food plant (*Bursaria spinosa*) to survive, and they are only known to live in a few places: some sites in the Eltham/Greensborough area in Melbourne, and others around Victoria at Bendigo, Castlemaine and in the Kiata/Salisbury area. In 1991 the subspecies was listed as 'threatened' under the *Flora and Fauna Guarantee Act 1988*.

There are six reserves in Eltham, and when I helped in a survey in 2012, the numbers of larvae across these sites had dropped to very low levels. I remember the general disappointment when we found only a dozen larvae at a reserve where they had been plentiful in previous years. The people managing the population embarked on a major process of bush regeneration, weeding and restructuring to create ideal conditions for the larvae and butterflies, and a few years later this appeared to be working. I was curious to see how the numbers were tracking when I joined the count at the Eltham reserves in 2018.

Stumbling through dark bushland looking for tiny invertebrates could be a scene from a nightmare for many people, but for me it has an element of magic. Like waiting to see a little penguin waddle out of the inky black surf towards its beach-side burrow, I am here in hopes of glimpsing a ritual that is part of this animal's survival. It requires patience and I might not see anything, but when I do, it is a real thrill.

That night the tiny larvae were difficult to spot. I found myself staring at a bush for some time and not seeing anything. I was just about to give up when the movement of ants alerted me to look more closely. Then I saw a larva in plain sight that somehow I had missed before. I watched the ants patrolling back and forth around the larva, deterring potential predators such as spiders which were also active at night, looking for a meal.

It turned out to be a good night. On almost every bush we found larvae, so our progress through the reserve was slow. It was after midnight by the time we finished, tired but triumphant. In total we found more than 200 larvae.

My companion larva-counter was Julia Davis – an eighty-year-old, highly experienced nature volunteer – and she told me a little of the species in Eltham over time. She knew Michael Braby, who as a young man rediscovered the species in 1987 at sites in Eltham where it had been presumed extinct. That was the good news, but the bad news was that the area was set for development as a housing estate. A community campaign began. The local council and the state government put up some of the money required to buy the land. The community donated and fundraised to generate the rest. From well-known artists such as Clifton Pugh donating artworks, to locals baking butterfly-shaped cakes, it took a collective effort to buy the land for conservation reserves.

Today these reserves flanked by suburbia are precious protection for the Eltham copper butterfly and other native species. Precarious? Yes, but also an example of survival, successful interdependence and the power of collective action in a time of great change. Ongoing care by land managers, Friends groups, and the Eltham Copper Butterfly Working Group will give them the best chance of surviving in a world that continues to change.

The Eltham copper butterfly is a reminder of the amazing business of life that happens right under our noses that we mostly ignore or just don't see. Thanks to people who work to understand and protect these interconnected species, I was able to see the beautiful, otherworldly sight of butterfly larvae feasting on sweet bursaria, guarded by ants, all just a short distance from my own backyard.

THE FENCE OF SORROW AND HOPE

John Dargavel

Mulligans Flat Woodland Sanctuary, Australian Capital Territory

I think it an ugly thing. Punched through a patch of scruffy bush outside Canberra, its steel gates and electric wire look like a prison of sorts, which it is. It jars me to find it in a nature reserve and it tells me of a sad history. But it is also a story of recovery. Heroic or forlorn? I don't know.

It skewers a remnant scrap of grassy woodland that once stretched far and wide; a land of sustenance with plants for every purpose, kangaroos and possums for feast and skin, and with quolls, bettongs and echidnas scuttering about. A hard land, but it had homes for all and grew its people for millennia.

New people came with sheep, disease and guns. Only a few in the 1820s, but enough by the 1840s to settle and breed at Mulligans Flat. Its long-nurtured grassy woodland made good sheep country, but no longer for the sickened, chased Ngunnawal. Shepherds tended

158

the sheep on the open land until they became too expensive or scarce to employ, wire became cheaper and rights to the land became secure. We don't know when our old fence was built, possibly in the 1880s, but old fences have lost histories of wooden posts and rusty wires replaced; ours no less, no doubt.

I see it as sad, battered land now; the trees ringbarked and burnt, the native grasses gone, weeds everywhere, the soil trampled and eroded, the small animals driven out by sheep and rabbits, or killed by foxes and cats. A new suburb next door, a great city nearby, but this is what it has come to.

There were a few patches of grassy box-gum woodland left. Little enough on Ngunnawal Country, but ideas changed and they were kept. In 1994 a tattered block on a stony ridge was made the Mulligans Flat Nature Reserve. The sheep went, the kangaroos flourished. With care, further deterioration can be halted, but can the land be repaired? Could the bettongs and quolls return? Could the ecosystem, as they call it now, be recreated? There was goodwill, knowledgeable environmentalists, government funding and ecologists keen to experiment. Nobody knew, but they could hope and try.

They burned patches as the Ngunnawal people had done to renew the land and they stacked piles of old logs for animal homes, but they had to get rid of the weeds and rabbits before the plants could recover, and they had to get rid of the foxes, dogs and cats before the native animals could breed safely again. They built the great fence – 11 kilometres of it – too hard for cats to climb over, too deep for foxes to dig under. It went up in 2009 and the ecologists swarmed in to find out how to restore the birds and animals – even the reptiles and invertebrates – that had once lived there.

A few echidnas had survived on this scrap of land, but ecologists needed to bring bettongs and quolls from Tasmania as there were none left here. Once in the sanctuary both species started to breed, and so successful were the bettongs that eighty-seven animals were released into the hills. Now as I write in 2019 there is the news that they have had their own babies, the first to be born in the wild on the mainland in a century. Their future is assured in the sanctuary and possibly outside, if foxes don't gobble them up.

The sanctuary offers hope, but of what? The ecologists can show results in scientific papers, but restoring an ecosystem will be an endless, perhaps impossible, task. The government can show that its community and scientific partnership works, but the sanctuary is expensive to run. The environmentalists are heartened that their arguments have at last borne fruit, but only locally. Perhaps it will lead on to broader restitutions, not just in sanctuaries and local hills.

I can see the hope in the fence, but I feel its sadness.

THE REGISTER OF
SIGNIFICANT TREES

Nadia Bailey

The University of Sydney jacaranda
(*Jacaranda mimosifolia*)

The jacaranda, for our purposes, refers to *Jacaranda mimosifolia*. Its flowers are not mauve or lavender or lilac. They are bluer than that. But they are not the blue of cornflowers, of hydrangeas, of salvia. This colour resists categorisation. Not a true colour at all but a tint; pale indigo filtered through sunlight; sometimes luminously purple, sometimes indistinctly blue. Each individual bloom marked slightly with pure white inside, elaborately scalloped around the edges. Each like a curved trumpet, a cornucopia, an open mouth. They grow in *panicles*, a word that brings to my mind the swaying of bishop's robes but means a many-branched cluster of flowers. An elaborate word. Like blossoms collapsing with the weight of their own inflorescence. A tree in full bloom against the clear deep sky of late spring makes the sky seem somehow purple and the jacarandas blue. Don't ask me how this works. I can only guess at some kind of transference.

Seen from a distance among the green of nearby trees, the jacaranda seems shrouded in a hazy blue cloud. On closer inspection, this resolves into myriad delicate violet-blue blossoms. The ground below takes on the same tint, first as a scattering of stars, then later a brilliant constellation. Native to Brazil, the jacaranda dislikes frost. Warmth, humidity, long summers: these things suit it. The flowering season of jacarandas moves down the eastern edge of the country: first in temperate Queensland, then the glory of Sydney, then onward down the coast to Victoria. It's impossible not to stop at the sight of a jacaranda in full flower. For a few weeks every year, my phone is full of nothing but purple.

The jacaranda I loved died in bloom. It grew in the south-east corner of the University of Sydney's Quadrangle, where normally it didn't reach full flower until early November. But every year spring comes earlier and summer lasts longer, burns hotter. It was late October. The jacaranda was already hazy with purple.

An almost spring evening, turning to night. The last of the sun gilding the sandstone. In the library, students worked under fluorescent lights, curled over computers or propped up against the stacks. Bats circling the sky over the Port Jackson figs. No one witnesses the moment of passing. The Quadrangle is still. The grass holds its secrets. The sandstone is golden, even at night. If there is a crack – the sound of a grey-brown trunk breaking, of something suddenly split – then no one is there to hear it.

The next day is sunny; the city seems to shimmer. Bright blue skies overhead, the kind that makes everything incandescent. A light particular to Sydney. Beyond the sandstone cliffs, the ocean inhales and returns, inhales and returns. The news spreads as news of a death does, as quickly as contagion. The tree has collapsed, eaten through by a wood-decaying fungus – *Ganoderma applanatum*, a parasite with a name meaning 'shining skin'. It comes slow, felt in the heartwood. Once a tree is infected, death is inevitable.

The strength of my grief surprises me. I feel guilty for caring too much. Embarrassed even. When the news reaches me, I can't stop crying.

The jacaranda was planted in 1928 by Professor Eben Gowrie Waterhouse, a German linguist and horticulturist who was tasked with beautifying the University of Sydney's grounds. His lasting obsession was with camellias, but I think he must have loved jacarandas too. He was instrumental in their planting across Sydney, in Newcastle, in Brisbane. At the university, he planted several as seedlings in the Quadrangle; when they kept getting ripped out by vandals, he had more mature specimens brought in. Of the Quadrangle's four original trees, only one survived. That jacaranda flourished. It eventually grew to stand 12 metres tall and the tips of its branches stretched 18 metres wide. My jacaranda. At the time of its death, the tree was eighty-eight years old.

There's a photo, taken on the morning of 29 October 2016, that shows the tree where it fell. It's shot from the south-eastern quadrant. The Gothic Revival architecture of MacLaurin Hall looms in the background; to the right, a rope hung with orange flags, meant to warn people away from walking on the grass, looks like tape cordoning off a crime scene. The jacaranda is broken at the base of its trunk, its canopy toppled, branches spread over the grass in surrender. Its flowers appear purple – a true, deep purple – against the gold of the sandstone, the green of the grass. You can intuit where the branches once reached by the halo of blossoms ghosting the ground.

Today, looking up the Quadrangle on Google Maps yields a strange piece of technological dissonance. Go to Street View. Depending on what area of the Quadrangle you choose as your anchor, you can see the jacaranda at different points in its lifespan. Pick one, and it's September 2013: a few puffs of green clothe its otherwise bare branches. Another: October 2014, a cloudless day and the jacaranda is in full, glorious bloom. February 2017: the corner stands empty. If you look at the university on Aerial View, you can see the tree at the height of its verdancy. It must be December. The jacaranda is beautifully green.

The coda to the story is this: knowing that it would one day die, the university engaged specialists to take cuttings from the jacaranda tree. The cuttings were taken to the Central Coast, where they were grafted to the roots of other jacarandas. After about two dozen attempts, the specialists succeeded in creating four genetically identical clones. Of the four clones, two remain in waiting, just in case they're one day needed. One has been planted in the grounds of the university's nursing school. And one now grows in the Quadrangle in the same spot as its predecessor. It shares the Quadrangle with an Illawarra flame tree – a tree endemic to Australia's east coast – which will bloom red each year at the same time the jacaranda flowers.

I read somewhere that in the 1920s a colour cure of blue-violet was prescribed to treat headaches, fever or insanity. It's perhaps no coincidence that jacarandas were often planted on the grounds of Australia's early mental hospitals. While I can't speak as to the scientific validity of colour therapy, something about this theory rings true. The jacaranda's colour calms. Its blues soothe the blues. At the Queensland Art Gallery, a painting called *Under the Jacaranda* depicts a man and two women dwarfed beneath an ecstatic, bluish impression of a full-flower jacaranda tree. During jacaranda season, visitors sometimes bring handfuls of flowers with them to scatter on the floor beneath, and it's as if the painting itself has burst into bloom.

The Kalatha Giant mountain ash
(*Eucalyptus regnans*)

It's hard not to see it as a doorway. Like the entrance to a cathedral. Arched, open-mouthed. Rust-coloured leaf litter trailing a pathway into darkness. The trunk is so large you can step all the way inside. Look up: its hollowness soars skyward. At the top, a tiny solar flare. A pinpoint of light in the distance. Inside, cobwebs are tatted over ancient wood. That camphoraceous scent, cineole, fills the air. What you feel when you stand inside is what churches can only aspire to. Made tiny. Made humble. The obliterative effect of awe. To feel the potential for rapture; the possibility of communion. With your neck craned all the way back, you assume the position of supplicant, of someone asking for mercy. Even standing, you are on your knees.

This is what I think about days later, when I watch the footage of the Notre-Dame Cathedral in flames. Its spire in slow, terrible collapse. I remember the burnt-out architecture of this mountain ash, the *Eucalyptus regnans*, the Kalatha Giant. How, long ago, a fire roared uphill, consuming the leaf litter and herbaceous understorey, burning faster and faster; how it reached the fluted trunk of this tree and tore through the rough basal bark, right into the heartwood, where it smouldered and finally died, leaving the tree hollow.

The doorway is a memory of fire.

Land and architecture are both powerful holders of memory. The only real difference is that we ascribe more value to what human hands have built. Another difference: architecture, once burnt, cannot regenerate itself.

The work of the mountain ash is to self-destruct and be reborn by fire. It takes root in powdery clay loam over which broken fern fronds, fallen leaves and long strips of bark ferment in dank layers. On the forest floor, decomposition is slow, allowing detritus to build up; to become deep and loose, a bed for brushwood and bracken. The presence of eucalyptus alters the very atmosphere. You can feel the air change as you enter the forest. Wetter. Bluer. It's the isoprene and cineole that give the grove its blue haze, its distinctive, pungent scent. Here, the air is woody-sweet over base notes of earth and damp mulch. The light is indirect; the air cool and alive with moisture. There is a sense that a brighter, warmer environment exists somewhere beyond the canopy, but it is distant to this place of shadows and wet leaves.

In spite of the damp, the leaf litter and understorey lend themselves to fire. The oil in eucalyptus leaves is volatile, combustive. This is important. When a fire comes, the leaf litter goes first, fuelling the flames with its oil-rich leaves. The understorey goes next, kindling the fire as it catches the woody trunks, licking branches higher and higher, until long strips of bark turn to burning streamers. When it reaches the canopy, it's called a crown fire. Something antediluvian about it: each tree alight, bright as a saint's halo. Once the crown is on fire, there's no stopping it. Vast tracts of forest will be razed. The trees burn. Branches drop. Embers lilt for miles on the wind. The smoke, you imagine, is blue.

One thing you should know about the mountain ash is that it can only grow from seed. Imagine that: this giant of the forest, so tall you must look at it crick-necked to see its top, grew from something no bigger than a pinhead. In summer, amid its leaves, the tree sprouts fleshy buds – little clusters, growing tight with flower. They burst into inflorescence: fluffy stamen, rings of white filament. Each one a little nimbus. When the flower is spent, its base thickens, becomes hard. Outer armour for the tiny seeds inside. A gumnut won't unloose its seeds until the conditions are right: at the end of summer, when the air is hot and dry. Bushfire season.

Bushfire kills these trees. And yet it is only in the aftermath of wildfire that its seed germinates and grows. Anywhere a mountain ash forest exists, there must be a history of fire. It is there, in the crucible of wildfire, that its pods open, releasing the tiny seeds to be buoyed on the wind, to scatter and fall to the scorched earth. Where the soil is dark and rich with ash. There, the seeds hum into life, germinate in the sunlight, sprout readily. Put out tender shoots; tiny, tiny. They grow quickly, anticipating future height. In the end, the tree endures its own death so that it might regenerate: fire as salvation.

The Toolangi State Forest grows on the land of the Kulin Nation, of the Taungurung and the Wurundjeri peoples. Fire flares through its history, part of the Indigenous understanding of landscape. Their fires were deliberate, slow burns catching only the lowest strata of understorey. Afterwards: a flowering and seeding, a flush of new green shoots.

The Kalatha Giant lived through the fires of 1851. The fires of 1939. Now, we experience a far more frequent cycle. There were forest fires in 2003, 2007, 2009, 2013 and 2014. During the devastating days of the Black Saturday fires, two-thirds of the state forest turned to ash. It was only luck that the Kalatha Giant survived. The fire stopped just short of where it stands.

No event, however significant, leaves an everlasting imprint on the world. Not the loss of a cathedral. Not the incineration of a forest. Erasure is the condition of existence. And yet: how small we feel in the face of that which outlasts us. Envision a tree so old that it remembers the landscape of 400 years ago. So tall that looking up induces a feeling of vertigo. Without fire, the mountain ash would not survive. Look up. High above, the sunlight glances in its long leaves. It is flowering, its blossoms testing the air.

Punt Road golden wych elm
(*Ulmus glabra* 'Lutescens')

In Melbourne, some years back, the council mapped every tree growing on the city's public land and assigned each one with an identifying code and email address. The thinking was that, armed with the relevant identification number, members of the public could report a fallen branch, a tree in need of pruning. But soon, rather than writing to the council, people began writing to the trees themselves. Letters of thanks. Notes of appreciation. Fan mail. Some wrote asking for advice. Others for forgiveness. It should be noted this happened organically. No one meant for the trees to take on lives of their own.

The council reports that of all the trees in Melbourne, the one that receives the most email is a large golden wych elm, an *Ulmus glabra* 'Lutescens', on the corner of Punt Road and Alexandra Avenue. The *wych* in wych elm comes from Old English *wice* meaning 'pliant', or from Middle English *wyche* meaning 'tree', rather than from witches, who were said to prefer elders (*Sambucus nigra*). Driving down Punt Road, this golden wych elm appears quite suddenly, rising over a carpet of dry fallen leaves in a dramatic canopy of green and shadow and light and gold and movement. Its branches are the colour of wet soil; in winter, stripped bare, they resemble blackened bones. In spring, if you walk through the cascade of yellow-green leaves and into the filtered light beneath, the air seems green, like the green oceanic light of underwater. Within that bell jar, the roar of traffic seems very far away.

It's easy to understand why this tree inspires such devotion. It has a particularity to it. An identification number and an email address somehow affirm this, shifting the tree from being part of the scenery to a state of almost-personhood. You might see a hundred thousand trees in your lifetime, but you will only really look at a handful of them. Maybe that's the problem. None of us are really looking.

But over the last few years, in courts of law around the world, there have been debates as to whether culturally or spiritually significant sites of nature should be afforded the same rights as human beings. A river in New Zealand and a lake in Ohio are now legal entities. Legal personhood has also been granted to New Zealand's Te Urewera forest, rivers in Colombia and India, the Amazon rainforest, and a particular species of wild rice, native to North America, called *manoomin*. It's easy to dismiss the rights of a forest or a lake when we think of them as something inherently different from ourselves. Less so when they are, in the eyes of the law, people.

If you walk certain old-growth forests in Thailand, you might encounter a tree draped in orange robes – a sudden flare of fire amid swampy, sweat-damp green. The robes are wound around its trunk like bandages or flutter wing-like from branches. Orange, the colour of caution. The robes warn that the tree is no longer only a tree. It has been elevated. Ordained. It happens this way: a group of monks gather around the tree, recite Buddhist scripture and then clothe it in orange-dyed robes, just as is done in the same ceremony for a novice human monk. Once ordained, the tree and the land around it became sacred. God-touched. *Human.* These Buddhist monks began this practice in an effort to discourage loggers from razing the forests. In Thailand, almost 94 per cent of the population is Buddhist. No one would dare harm a monk, even when that monk happens to be a tree. Humanness, it turns out, is mutable. Its edges are fuzzy.

When I was young, I went through a phase of what I can only describe as solemn animism. My concept of god was cobbled together from the instructions of a secular Jewish father, an omnivorously New Age mother, and from books on ancient Greek mythology borrowed from my primary school library. Formal religion meant little to me, but ritual mattered. In our backyard, beneath the fragmented shade of a native fig tree, I built a rudimentary shrine from grey concrete blocks, arranged in a kind of stepped pyramid. On it, I arranged displays of whatever was blooming: fronds of native mint, wattle and lemon myrtle. Handfuls of densely petalled camellia flowers, the kind that turned milky crushed between the fingers. Scribbles of jasmine, its flowers bright, fragrant stars. I tasted everything; nature as communion wafer. Rose petals have a delicate quality. The stalk of the oxalis is so sour it triggers an involuntary rush of saliva in the back of the throat. Honeysuckle blossoms hold within them a drop of sweetness. I think about my childhood self, performing daily devotions to the more-than-human world. If I prayed, it was to something almost but not quite abstract. Something *tree-like*.

What do these stories tell us? That our empathy runs towards those things that most closely resemble ourselves. And yet: when we project ourselves onto nature, we also take nature into ourselves. The boundaries blur a little more. A lake becomes a person. A tree becomes a monk. The specifics are different but maybe the idea is the same. I no longer pray to trees, but I am charmed by the idea of correspondence with them. When I emailed the golden wych elm with a brief note of appreciation, I received a personalised response. *Thank you for your lovely message*, it read. *I hope you like the bluebells under my trunks.* It's possible, with some magical thinking, to believe it came from the tree itself.

Readings

Robert Macfarlane, *Underland: A Deep Time Journey*, Hamish Hamilton, London, 2019.

Mark Tredinnick, *The Blue Plateau: A Landscape Memoir*, University of Queensland Press, Brisbane, 2009.

Peter Wohlleben, *The Hidden Life of Trees: What They Feel, How They Communicate – Discoveries from a Secret World*, trans. from the German by Jane Billinghurst, Greystone Books, Vancouver and Berkeley, 2016.

RAPTURE, RUPTURE
AND ERUPTION

Josh Wodak

I'm sitting on the shore of Pemuteran Bay in Bali, where I've travelled to learn about Biorock: a life-support system for coral. A patented technology developed by an architect and a marine biologist in the 1980s, Biorock is a system of plastic, metal and electricity that provides coral with a more tolerable biophysical environment than the open ocean offers at the advent of the Anthropocene. Life buoys float in the waters of the bay, topped by solar-panel arrays that supply low-voltage current to metallic scaffolding underneath. Wires that extend from the underside of each buoy to the scaffold resting on the sea floor supply a kind of lifeline to coral, whose existence is propped up by the electrical current, which induces beneficial changes to the chemistry of the immediately surrounding water. Just as a life buoy is employed as an emergency measure for refugees lost at sea, the artificial reef forms a *refugium* for coral that can no longer survive out there 'in the wild'.

A great deal of marine life depends on the survival of coral. Once coral get established on the metal scaffolding, they form reefs, which offer refuge for smaller fish who need nooks and crannies in which to hide from larger fish. Coral reefs then offer two kinds of life support: the various forms of marine life drawn to it are food for one another, and the coral itself is food for other marine life. The complexity of relations grows in orders of magnitude to upwards of thousands of species that all trace their core dependency back to coral. And this is replicated the ocean over – with coral occupying 0.1 per cent of the ocean floor, but supporting 25 per cent of all marine life. Little wonder that if you want to throw a lifeline to the marine, you would start and end with coral itself. While 'we live submerged at the bottom of an ocean of air', as Renaissance mathematician Evangelista Torricelli revealed, our attention should not stop at the bottom of the terrestrial realm, but rather go from terrestrial to marine realms. We live at the boundary between two oceans, one above, one below.

Biorock is a guide to my journey across such boundaries, between 'volatile worlds' and 'vulnerable bodies', which human geographer Nigel Clark positions at the heart of 'confronting abrupt climate change'. Clark writes:

> A tiny nudge may be all it takes to unleash a set of cascading, self-reinforcing changes in the climate system. Conversely, a major impetus to change might lie dormant in the system for centuries or millennia before its impact is manifest … global climate might already be 'naturally' close to a tipping point, thus dramatically amplifying the significance of human forcing, while there is also the possibility that human impacts have taken climate systems closer to a threshold, for which the final push could turn out to be an unforeseeable nonhuman forcing – such as a large-scale volcanic eruption.

If desperate times call for desperate measures, how can they be measured against their true correlate – the cosmos? Technoscientific conservation, such as Biorock, may seem self-evidently essential. But such radical conservation practices need to enter into dialogue with the radical asymmetry and radical contingency of all earthly life. Hence the title of the article from which the above quote is taken: 'Volatile Worlds, Vulnerable Bodies: Confronting Abrupt Climate Change'.

To immerse my body in this ocean of water, I visit the largest and longest-running Biorock site in the world: Pemuteran Bay on the island of Bali. It is 2018 and three successive global coral bleaching events have occurred since the first event of 1997. The global mass coral bleaching event of 2016 was unprecedented in both severity and extent. This was followed by the first-ever back-to-back global bleaching event the next year, bringing into sharp relief how the current velocity of environmental change already exceeds forecast rates. Little wonder, then, that experimental conservation such as Biorock is of such growing interest among scientists, environmentalists, conservationists and engineers. What *should* be done – a dramatic and sustained decrease in greenhouse gas emissions, alongside all other human-induced environmental change – faces the stark reality of what *is* being done, which is a dramatic increase in all forms of human-induced environmental change. Time is running out if we are to contemplate 'saving' nature by throwing it a lifeline through technoscience.

The artificial reef calls into question notions of the wild and the natural world. Once coral life comes to depend on such support and human interventions, can coral survive without it? Say a wave turns the life buoy upside down; or the length of cable cannot extend far enough to accommodate a king tide, causing the life buoy to sink; or the slack in the length of cable gets wrapped around itself during a low tide; or the cable itself breaks from the sustained pressure of waves constantly pushing and pulling the buoy in different directions; or a sustained period of cloud cover reduces the volume of electricity generated – the list of contingencies is without end. With each variable comes another design consideration focused on providing life support that is self-perpetuating. Yet the laws of entropy will never be outrun – and once rendered dependent on means of metal, electricity and plastic, life forms become the living dead.

Why should people intentionally intervene in an ecosystem? Can the ends ever justify the means when intervention only begets more intervention? Picture the cascading interventions that would ensue in order to make this life support as perpetually self-perpetuating as possible: from barriers around the buoy to reduce waves during storms, to catering for coral spawned from the metal framework, many of which will be carried by ocean currents to other places where they won't receive the life support provided by the artificial reef. The list of interventions begot by the initial intervention is endless.

The answer to the question of why intentionally intervene in an ecosystem is, in some ways, dead simple. Radical conservation experiments are necessary because much of what is presently alive at the advent of the Anthropocene will go extinct over the coming decades. However, the more vexing question speaks greater volumes for what is at stake: to what extent will humans 'remake' nature in order to 'save' it? Biorock is a portal into these delusions of grandeur, as they are currently being applied from cell to sky, and atom to atmosphere.

The solar panel supplying this conservation experiment measures a rough metre squared. Due to its darker colour, sea water absorbs even more heat relative to the global average for the surface of the Earth. This solar panel is stopping solar radiation being absorbed into the ocean, by shading the water and absorbing the heat in the photovoltaic panels. Yet its influence is limited to the area under the solar panel – the entire surface of the tropics won't be covered in solar panels.

To add greater life support to coral struggling the world over, we would need to dissipate all the excess heat that has built up in the atmosphere since the Earth went into net positive energy balance in 1971. Proposals for this intervention operate at the scale of the planet,

through climate engineering. Seeking either carbon dioxide reduction or solar radiation management, such proposed interventions
would create a contract between the biosphere and a technoscientific
life-support system. And, just like all the variables that threaten the
buoy–solar–metal–wiring array, climate engineering is orders of magnitude more uncertain, complex and contingent. The most intensively
pursued proposal is to spray sulphur particles into the stratosphere, in
mimicry of what volcanoes do. This would form a 'sunshade' over the
planet, to slow global warming. It'd be like going to the beach during
summer, without sunscreen, and putting up a beach umbrella: the
people under the shade of the umbrella would have little chance of
getting sunburnt. But should it blow away, they would quickly burn
up, in the absence of shade, umbrella or sunscreen. There are more
technological barriers between life forms and oblivion than we would
generally like to let on.

As I dive through the Pemuteran artificial reef site I see the chalk-
versus-cheese difference between ecosystems on artificial life support
and those fending for themselves. A brilliant, iridescent kaleidoscope
of colours belonging to coral and their ancillary sea creatures, surrounded by dull and muddied coral that are of relatively little interest
to marine life that makes its living off coral. The Biorock reefs come
in inorganic shapes – strict cubes, distorted prisms and spheres; and,
more recently, in the shape of sea creatures, to make Pemuteran's artificial reef more visually appealing, as this has become the town's main
tourist attraction. I follow the network of criss-crossing pipes, going
along the beach under the parasails, across the wading area and out
into the bay. Back to the boxed-in converters and inverters humming
away, with their flashing lights. Out to the floating pontoon with its
solar array, and the other with its micro wind turbine. I follow fish
back and forth between so-called artificial and so-called natural ecosystems. I follow the bubbles that emanate from the metallic structures – a concoction of oxygen as a result of the chemical catalysis

brought about by the electricity–metal–mineral interaction. Boarding a boat, I follow the line of underwater mountains a kilometre out to a nearby offshore reef, and a further 20 kilometres away to the most protected reef in all of Bali, within the island's sole national park.

I read through the technical reports, patents and scholarly articles by the scientists behind Biorock. Their unambiguous call to arms with capital letter headings like 'BIOROCK ARKS: THE LAST HOPE FOR CORAL REEFS'. I interview Biorock co-inventor Dr Goreau and the local staff on site. I read through the blog posts and forums of curious lay citizens, such as myself. And the promotional websites of local businesses with a vested stake in the continuance and success of Biorock. And the international websites hailing Biorock as the future of marine conservation …

I visited Pemuteran in January 2018 during an especially dynamic time. A few weeks before I am due to depart for Bali, Mount Agung erupts and my trip looks to be off. One hundred and fifty thousand Balinese are relocated to shelters outside the anticipated eruption zone, leaving their animals and farms untended, in an overwhelmingly subsistence-based economy. For locals, this is a matter of life and death – and not just in terms of volcanic eruptions raining down from above. For tourists such as myself this is a matter of inconvenience and insurance – airports closed due to ash clouds, and travel insurance companies voiding any coverage of such *force majeure*. It is no coincidence that there is an unprecedented number of humans on the move, seeking refuge from intolerable conditions owing to calamities political, religious, military, economic or climatic.

Indonesia has the largest concentration of active volcanoes on Earth, some 130, and of these Mount Agung is one of only seven in the world rated at the top of the Volcanic Explosivity Index for its eruption potential. In the lead-up to the November 2017 eruption, scientists the world over had been studying Agung in detail, modelling the anticipated amount by which it would cool global temperatures with a full-scale eruption, as a kind of surrogate experiment for improving estimates of the efficacy of the climate engineering proposal to spray sulphur particles into the atmosphere. Locally, soil scientists were studying the volcano, to estimate how much soil fertility the ash would provide. In other words, this is the story of how to fall in lava with volcanoes …

Mount Agung appears to pull back from the brink of another eruption, and so I board the flight from Sydney to Bali. It is now the first week of the new year, 2018: the International Year of the Reef. On the way to Pemuteran, I climb Mount Batur, the active volcano neighbouring Agung. Much of Bali is relatively empty of tourists due to fears around Agung erupting. It is also the middle of the monsoon, meaning tourist numbers would already be relatively low. I make for the trailhead on a trusty scooter that now doubles as an off-road all-terrain vehicle. Being next to Agung, or as close as I can go to the exclusion zone, all the tea shops and snack stalls are closed. So I hike to the Batur crater, passing only a trio of locals who quiz me on why I am walking alone up the volcano in the rain. Our actions need not always have a rationale. Mine are to experience the dynamism of an active volcano that has devastated the region twice in the past century alone, and to get as close as possible to Agung, with its possibility of imminent eruption.

In the midst of the unfolding Sixth Mass Extinction event, and in light of the manifest failure to implement any meaningful reform of the political and economic orthodoxy which is conducting ecocide on the very systems that support life on Earth, it is difficult to imagine a force that can actually throw a spanner in the works. Earthquakes and their associated forces of tsunamis and fires are unequivocally destructive. You end up with a city buried in the same materials used in Biorock – plastic, metal and glass – charred, or mixed with sludge rolled in from the ocean. On the other hand, the indiscriminate effluence of volcanoes is as close to a *tabula rasa* as you can get from sources intrinsic to Earth (rather than extrinsic, such as asteroids). Volcanoes can destroy much of life on an island, or even an entire bioregion of Earth, only to provide it with markedly more fertile soils that enable an even greater abundance of life to return decades later.

When I visit the Biorock site at Pemuteran Bay these issues percolate within my body, coursing as it is with microplastic, protected by my membrane of skin, shiny with the grease of an 'eco-friendly organic' sunscreen. One must get out of one's head to fathom even the remotest depths here at play. The absurdity of *Alice in Wonderland* rolls out before me. The sand of the bay, only about 50 kilometres from Agung, is already black from the volcano's last eruption in 1963. After all, this is a region whose marine and terrestrial biomes boast dynamism of the highest order on Earth. Back then, the bay received no net benefit from the eruption – instead coral was decimated by the sediment raining down, and by the inability of zooxanthellae (the algae that live within coral tissue) to photosynthesise. After the recovery, coral then faced an increase in local fishing following population growth. Fishing methods changed too – from rod to net to dynamite. Then, with the rise of tourism around snorkelling and scuba diving, the local economy changed to favour interest in the protection of marine ecosystems.

This combination of proximal pressures prompted Biorock to make Pemuteran their main site of experimentation. Before the catastrophic global bleaching of 2016, Biorock had offered the longest-running baseline for comparing artificial coral reefs to their notionally natural counterparts. The array of dozens of metallic structures is supplied with electricity from one experimental solar array and one micro wind turbine, with the vast majority of electricity being supplied by three local businesses – two hotels and one scuba diving shop. The power, while low voltage, adds to the bills for the businesses. During the peak of the 2016 bleaching the businesses interrupted their supply of electricity to the reefs, in a bid to save on bills.

Without the assistance of altered ocean chemistry, the scale of the underwater heatwave was greater than the tolerance threshold for many of the artificial reefs. While a large number of coral became sick or died, their mortality levels were much lower than those of the decimated natural reefs nearby.

After all of this I am no less muddled as to how on earth there is a compelling case for such interventions, or for the consequences of holding the moral high ground against such interventions. The chalk-versus-cheese difference between artificial coral reefs and their natural neighbours does not scale up to the entirety of the planet. Nor should it. Nor does it scale up to the *long durée* of the emergency that is the twenty-first century. Nor should it.

Returning to the vexing question of what is at stake: to what extent will we attempt to 'remake' nature in order to 'save' it? Climate engineering, assisted evolution and synthetic biology are emerging technologies. They claim a grand future but, as yet, their feasibility is unsubstantiated. Moreover, profound debates are now emerging as to whether the belief that we can control climates and direct evolution is an expression of technical progress or the reflection of a dangerous hubris based on delusions of human grandeur.

Neither do the dilemmas allow for a moral high ground, when the ground is so clearly going underwater and drowning species in the act of rising up. Shakespeare's adage, 'all the world's a stage, and all the men and women merely players', needs to be updated, to reflect our present tense. All the world's a sinking stage, and some disproportionately powerful men and women are no longer 'merely players' – they are active agents in reconfiguring how much of the world's stage will sink. Or, conversely and perversely, how much of the world will rise.

The dilemma recalls Gary Larson's cartoon where the devil is impatiently prodding an indecisive inmate to make him enter one of two doors. One is labelled: DAMNED if you do. The other:

DAMNED if you don't. On first glance it appears that there is no difference between the options. Why even choose if both just lead to damnation? However, there is an important difference: one option is the act of actually doing, of making the effort, however empty the gesture. In our 'present tense' that pertains to mitigating and advocating for the more-than-human, while challenging the small percentage of *Homo sapiens* who are so hell-bent on continuing a fossil-fuel-based brand of industrial capitalism. The other option is to not do. To throw up one's hands and let the devil make the decision, as though that would somehow absolve us from taking responsibility for having wound up with only these two vying contenders for a course of action.

Larson's cartoon is set in the fiery depths of Earth's mantle. Home to magma and micro-organisms that sought *refugia* in Earth's crust when their fellow organisms breathed toxic oxygen into the previously oxygenless atmosphere 2.5 billion years ago. Down here there is a third possibility, part of the deep historical trajectory of Earth and the solar system to which it belongs. This third possibility lies in the forces at work under the Earth, from earthquakes to volcanoes to plate tectonics, which hold the prospect of bringing everything to a grinding halt (from industry to the continued existence of much that is living in the biosphere at present). Having already been partially woken by the completed melting of the Holocene and the advent of the Anthropocene, this third possibility could throw our two equally unpalatable options into stark relief. This is the true measure for the desperate times facing down conservation in the Anthropocene. To confront abrupt climate change with one's volatile body is to become open to the volatility of the world itself. So be it for whatever lifelines we attempt to extend to life forms that are otherwise denied any refuge.

Readings

Nigel Clark, 'Volatile Worlds, Vulnerable Bodies: Confronting Abrupt Climate Change', *Theory, Culture & Society*, vol. 22, no. 5, 2010, p. 42.

Global Coral Reef Alliance, 'Biorock Arks: The Last Hope for Coral Reefs', <bit.ly/Globalcoral>.

Ursula Heise, *Imagining Extinction: The Cultural Meanings of Endangered Species*, Chicago University Press, Chicago, 2016.

Christopher Preston, *The Synthetic Age: Outdesigning Evolution, Resurrecting Species, and Reengineering Our World*, Massachusetts Institute of Technology Press, Massachusetts, 2018.

Evangelista Torricelli, 1644, quoted in Gabrielle Walker, *An Ocean of Air: A Natural History of the Atmosphere*, Bloomsbury, London, 2010, p. 24.

SUN SMART

Lauren Rickards

As a kid, sunscreen was about a slash of white zinc across the nose and cheeks, a kind of war paint that signalled serious playtime in the sun. Being zinced up was a licence for my brother and me to race worry-free into the water off Nuns Beach at the mouth of Port Phillip Bay. The water was clear, the sand clean, the waves booming. Even the last remaining nuns would come out on their boogie boards.

As I got older, SPF sunscreens came on the market, sold to us by the cheeky face of America's Coppertone Girl. Finely regulating the distribution of tan across one's body became an art: SPF 4 on the legs, SPF 6 on the arms, SPF 10 on the face, etc. Sun protection was a concept, but being tanned was cool. No longer just working class, like my grandfathers' farmer arms, a deep tan was a sign of the beach, relaxation, health. It was about being a (white) Aussie.

But then Australia's relationship with the sun began to change. The planet's own skin was in trouble. Something had happened to the sky and the sun was no longer friendly. A future Nobel Prize winner, Paul Crutzen, and other atmospheric chemists explained that a giant gash had opened up above our heads. There was a 'hole' in the ozone layer and invisible killer rays were now raining down. More bizarrely, the cause of this dramatic shift lay in our hands: it was our aerosol sprays. The answer, they seemed to be saying, was to use less deodorant. Then Sid the Seagull arrived to teach us to Slip, Slop, Slap. So, it seemed we were to use less deodorant, but more sunscreen. But I knew in the back of my mind that this was not just about ablutions. Our bodies, the sky and the sun had entered some kind of conflict. Nature had been split and my childhood bubble had been pricked, leaking its comfortable assumptions into space.

Our relationship with the sky and the sun has continued to change. We now know that not just the ozone layer but the whole atmosphere is in trouble. There might be too few ozone molecules in the stratosphere, but there are too many in the troposphere, along with a cacophony of other greenhouse gases. Yet the issue is more than a matter of reorganising the distribution of molecules. Climate change and ozone depletion are increasingly entwined in complex feedbacks, wrapping us tighter and tighter into the Earth system – the functional whole of all the planet's interconnecting components, including oceans, winds and clouds, plants, animals and rocks. Climate scientist Will Steffen and colleagues now tell us we are transitioning into the Anthropocene, as the collective effects of our impacts shift the Earth system into a new state.

My brother and I still go to Nuns Beach, with our own small children in tow now. With hotter weather, so do many others. Most of us are now 'sun smart': not in the sense that we use 'smart' real-environmental monitoring to calculate our UV exposure (though that is on its way). We have just been well schooled in the need for rashies, hats and SPF 50. Despite some recalcitrants, Australia's uptake of sunscreen is trumpeted around the world as a public health success. Sid the Seagull is a hero.

But on the beach, the real birds and many critters underwater may be less sure. It turns out the sunscreen I vigilantly slather on the family is not so smart after all. It might be good for us, but it's not good for phytoplankton, seaweed, corals or anything that relies on them, particularly given the fact their surrounding water is also warmer, more turbulent and more acidic. Increasingly, in other countries with tropical coral reefs – such as Hawaii – sunscreen is being banned. Not only does it disrupt coral reproduction – it also blocks the sun's *good* rays from the plant cells that need it. More care is needed.

No one really knows what the effects are on temperate marine ecologies such as that in Port Phillip Bay. Reefs here don't attract the same sort of research funding. But the signs aren't good. Our collective experiment in compensating the planet's defunct solar radiation protection mechanism with our own body-scale replica is likely to have spawned more than a few side effects, local as well as global.

The sun continues to shine its admixture of radiation, and the sea continues to beckon physical and psychic relief. But like Paul Crutzen, my thinking is now of the Anthropocene and the dark futures layered within it. From my own damaged dermis and the kelp beds in the bay, to the stratosphere above and the sun's rays close and far, to my sun-kissed childhood and the impatient child in my arms – all shimmer within the sunscreen lying quietly in my hand.

TREADING
WATER

KELP

John Charles Ryan

Included in Joseph Hooker's *Flora Antarctica* from 1844, botanical artist Walter Hood Fitch's plate is one of the earliest scientific drawings of giant kelp. A translucent sash swerves across the yellowing page. I gaze over its symmetries of olive and chestnut. At the top of the solitary frond, a pear-shaped bladder clings to a tendinous stipe. Known as a pneumatocyst, the gas-filled float allows the submerged blades of the seaweed to lift towards the ocean's surface and the promise of sunlight. Scrutinising the illustration, I suddenly understand why, in the late eighteenth century, Linnaeus chose the name *pyrifera* – Latin for 'bearing pears' – for this species.

Known as string kelp in Australia, *Macrocystis pyrifera* is a miraculous macroalga – a bearer of many gifts. It is among the quickest-growing organisms on Earth. Plants can elongate 30 centimetres per day and reach 60 metres in height. Likened to biological engines by ecologists, kelp forests are eminently productive and biodiverse. Dense mats of kelp provide nursery grounds for abalone, rock lobster and myriad fish. Along the shoreline – where beachs trolling humans encounter it – kelp serves as vital habitat for birds and other littoral creatures. The expeditious build-up of biomass by kelp signifies its global importance in sequestering carbon and mitigating climate change.

Imperilled by rising ocean temperatures, however, giant kelp has become a bellwether of ecological disruption and a victim of climate change. In Tasmania, according to the Institute for Marine and Antarctic Studies, warmer water with lower nutrient levels has precipitated a 95 per cent loss of kelp forests. With fewer lobsters and keystone predators, dark purple urchins settle in, overgraze the weakened kelp beds and create what are known ominously as urchin barrens. Lacking primary producers, these preternatural zones become underwater wastelands unable to support urchins, starfishes, brittle stars and other spiny opportunists. Exhausting the environment, the colonisers swiftly move on.

I write this from a place of personal uncertainty that, perhaps, echoes the broader precarities of the Anthropocene. I am not sure how to grieve the demise of the kelp forests of south-east Australia. Neither a marine biologist nor a scuba diver, I am more comfortable on land than sea – more at home in the terrestrial forests of Australia than their aquatic counterparts, more conversant with she-oaks than seaweeds. As a landlubber with unfulfilled maritime ambitions, I fear deep water and become queasy even when standing quayside. My scattered memories of kelp are of pungent, decaying, sand-speckled tangles on Tasmanian beaches.

Though I might have little basis for grieving, I feel compelled to do so. For as long as I can remember, kelp forests have entranced me. I close my eyes and see otherworldly undulations of blades, bladders and stipes reaching towards the diffuse light streaming in from the surface. I envisage schools of iridescent fish zipping in and out of the canopy in synchronised bouts. I sense the clammy, textured gelatin of kelp skin on the back of my hand as it sways to the subtidal rhythm. What does it mean to mourn the loss of something not encountered in situ but which, nevertheless, saturates the imagination?

With this question in mind, I look towards what I call *archives of loss* – the written accounts and visual depictions of kelp forests from past to present. These archives intertwine the *phycological* and the *psychological*. They remind us that grieving the disappearance of kelp is a lesson in grieving the loss of more-than-human lives in the Anthropocene. To be certain, the scale of ecological transformation nowadays tests the limits of human understanding and empathy. Global in extent, climate change registers most tangibly within places and bodies. Yet, responding to planetary change requires attention to the local inflected by – and within – the planetary.

DISTRIBUTED FROM TASMANIA AND NEW ZEALAND TO ALASKA and South America, *M. pyrifera* is a widespread – though not cosmopolitan – brown alga. In Tierra del Fuego, Charles Darwin marvelled at the ecological richness of kelp beds. In *The Voyage of the Beagle*, appearing in 1839, he effused that 'the number of living creatures of all Orders, whose existence intimately depends on the kelp, is wonderful. A great volume might be written, describing the inhabitants of one of these beds of seaweed'. He observed kelp fronds 'incrusted with corallines'. Along the 'exquisitely delicate structures' of the seaweed were found 'innumerable crustacea'.

Shaking the 'great entangled roots' of one kelp specimen, the naturalist delighted in the small agglomeration of fish, sea stars, crabs and shells that tumbled forth. Notwithstanding this palpable tenor of wonder, Darwin acknowledged the far-reaching implications of losing kelp. His conservation message strikes me as eerily prescient: 'Yet if in any country a forest was destroyed, I do not believe nearly so many species of animals would perish as would here, from the destruction of the kelp'. He speculated that the demise of piscine diversity within kelp ecosystems would instigate the decline of cormorants, otters, seals and porpoises.

The Anthropocene is a time of pervasive loss and also of profound loneliness. I am reminded of this duality in viewing a sketch of *M. pyrifera* by artist Robert Taylor Pritchett for an 1890 edition of Darwin's *Voyage*. Labelled 'Magellan kelp', the black-and-white illustration features the tentacular holdfast, air bladders and falcate blades of the species arranged vertically against a stark white background. An aura of incompleteness haunts the image – of the kelp extracted from its habitat and suspended in barren space. Indeed, to grieve the disappearance of kelp is to mourn the rupturing of its intricate relations.

Moving further into these archives of loss, I return to Hooker's monumental *Flora Antarctica*, the last part of which covers the plants of Tasmania. During his journey in the southern hemisphere, the explorer-botanist wrote lucidly – and, at times, lovingly – of kelp as 'a remarkable gigantic seaweed' that formed 'large vegetating floating patches'. *M. pyrifera* energised Hooker's ability to imagine the planet as a whole living system. He noted the distribution of kelp 'from the Antarctic to the Arctic circle' and praised its adaptation 'to the calmest or most tempestuous situations'. Facing the demands of climate, temperature and exposure, kelp flourishes.

For me, kelp embodies the idea of *resilience*, literally, the act of rebounding. This term recurs in discussions of the future of life on Earth and the need for hope in the Anthropocene. Hooker understood that resilience becomes possible only where lives interweave. He thus observed the sea creatures 'through whose agency the plant increases and the floating island it forms dilates'. The astute naturalist also saw this quality in a beached *Macrocystis* with 'entangled cables [...] much thicker than the human body, and twined of innumerable strands of stems coiled together by the rolling action of the surf'.

Kelp is a liminal being – a threshold organism – twisting with tide and surf in the tempestuous zone where land meets sea. Its opaque grace limns possibilities in a world weathered by despair and isolation. Hooker mused that kelp's 'relation to other vegetables and to the myriads of living creatures which depend on it for food, attachment, shelter and means of transport, constitute so extensive a field of research that the mind of a philosopher might shrink from the task of describing them'. Rather than becoming weighted with the *wreck* of the Anthropocene (and the recklessness of the human), we might instead immerse ourselves in the wondrous workings of *wrack*, as Hooker did.

Yet, my mind, indeed, shrinks from the task. The interrelations of kelp are as colossal as Hooker's treatise. For a split second, I forget the pains of language and plunge to the forest floor. Jaundiced light stipples kelp ribbons. Descending further, I reach out to grasp the mucilaginous fronds but instead slide further into the vastness. The bristly edge of one blade leaves a red track on my leg. Sharks surveil the seaweed tangles with eyes steeled for small fish. An octopus lies disguised on the sandy bottom. My feet bend downward, anticipating landfall. I am exposed.

GIANT KELP LIVES A LIFE OF EXPOSURE SO THAT OTHER creatures, such as the charismatic leafy seadragon, may find shelter. Masterful illusionists, these diaphanous enchanters are endemic to coastal temperate areas from south-west Australia to South Australia. Sporadic sightings have been reported in northern Tasmania. Tinted olive, their elongated appendages mimic seaweed, presenting a convincing kind of camouflage. But leafy seadragons also play the part well, imitating the elegant gestures of the forest. Their graceful movements within kelp habitats represent their evolution in close relation to these macroalgal ecosystems. The calamitous decline of kelp, though, raises concerns about the future of seadragons.

Sifting through the archive for images and impressions – for indices of a threatened terrain I might never experience firsthand, except in an aquarium – I come across William Henry Harvey's *Phycologia Australica*. This landmark work of nineteenth-century phycology resulted from his three years of collecting seaweeds in Australia. Harvey describes *M. pyrifera* as prevalent 'throughout the Southern Ocean, south of the tropic'. As with other botanists, he was captivated by the physical presence of giant kelp, 'the *longest* (though not the *largest*) vegetable in the world. The cord-like stems, when the plant grows in deep water, have been estimated variously at 500 and at 1500 feet'.

Natural science involves the visual categorisation of life. Even so, early Australian narratives of seaweed disclose the sensuous responses of naturalists to their subjects of study. Craving textured appreciation – derived from touching, tasting, smelling and *being with* – I fear that a world deprived of kelp becomes an impoverished and sense-less barren. As kelp disappears, the tactile possibilities of experience – archived by Harvey and others – narrow and wane. He evokes the frond as coriaceous, or like leather: 'In drying it does not adhere to paper'. The leaves, moreover, are 'buoyed up by their vesicles' and extend across the waves 'for many fathoms horizontally'.

An illustration in Harvey's compendium features two overlap-ping fronds of kelp. The larger one resembles a hazel-coloured scythe sweeping across the page, the smaller a chlorophyll-infused sickle hooking upward. The three taut bladders of the scythe are more pod-than pear-like. On the sickle, new leaves – each with a bladder fas-tened to the stipe – divide off progressively from the apex. Harvey was engrossed by the orderly emergence of kelp fronds, 'formed by the continual splitting of a primary terminal leaf, developed in secund order [on one side only] along the lengthening stem'. The visual effect is one of vegetable origami.

I listen to the archives as they murmur of the time before loss.

Alan Bridson Cribb's detailed 1954 account of *M. pyrifera* in Tasmania, for instance, brims with the bountifulness of kelp: 'On calm days the margins of the blades often project in graceful golden arcs above the surface of the water which in dense beds is completely covered by the mass of floating stipes, bladders and blades. Blue cranes often rest on the bed and small boats find it almost impossible to penetrate'. The botanist reported extensive forests along the east coast of Tasmania from Eddystone Point to Recherche Bay.

Cribb observed how the beds imparted to the water 'a somewhat oily appearance' and moderated the action of surf on the shore. As its decaying bladders grew heavy with water and sank, kelp nourished the littoral environment. His aesthetic attention and ecological appreciation, nevertheless, were subordinate to his interest in kelp as a source of algin – a polysaccharide used in manufacturing textiles and as a thickening agent. In the early nineteenth century, *M. pyrifera* was also harvested for its potash. Eerily absent from the narrative, however, is even the slightest hint at the imminent disappearance of kelp forests as oceans warm.

I find Cribb's outlook rather sanguine. But in the 1950s, eastern Tasmanian kelp was so abundant that the notion of destroying the beds was unthinkable. His account reminds me of what is at stake in the Anthropocene – how what was once taken for granted is now at risk of vanishing entirely. Indeed, Tasmania's underwater forests were so impenetrable that they were included on mariners' charts. And this held true wherever kelp occurred – from California to Chile. To this effect, Hooker invoked an adage common among mid-sixteenth-century mariners: 'If you see beds of weede, take heed of them and keep off from them'.

MORE OFTEN THESE DAYS, THE ARCHIVES COME IN DIGITAL
form. I am inspecting the Atlas of Living Australia occurrence map
for *M. pyrifera*, showing a dense concentration of sightings around
Tasmania and South Australia. Unlike a distribution map – which
would reflect the radical contraction of kelp populations in recent
years – the image is a record of everywhere the seaweed has been
spotted. Photos depict bladders desiccating in sun and stipes strung
like garlands across sand. A kelp mass gyrates with the pounding of
waves. A man lifts a blade – the texture of tripe – to snap its portrait.
I lean down to grasp this errata of beachline, to smell the pungent
rejectamenta of tides.

In the late 1980s, marine ecologist John Craig Sanderson first
documented the collapse of Tasmania's kelp populations. He called
attention to the effects of warmer, nutrient-poor coastal waters on
'sensitive algae such as *M. pyrifera*'. During this time, kelp retreated
entirely from Bicheno in the east and George III Reef in the south:
'It is possible that *Macrocystis pyrifera* in Tasmania may be an early
victim of the Greenhouse effect if it exists'. Sanderson attributed the
warming trend to the East Australian Current, originating in the subtropical gyres of the Coral Sea but flowing farther southward than
usual – and during winter months.

In fact, the rate of ocean warming in south-eastern Australia is
three to four times the global average, making the region a flashpoint
for climate change. Due to 'severe change in integrity' from rising
temperatures, catastrophic storms and land-based pollution, kelp
forests were listed in 2012 as an endangered ecological community
under the *Environmental Protection and Biodiversity Conservation Act
1999*. The designation – the first for a marine environment in Australia – recognises *M. pyrifera* as the only species able to maintain the
composition of the forest from sea floor to surface. Even so, the report
concedes that regeneration is 'unlikely within the near future, even
with positive human intervention'.

The Anthropocene renders experience bereft of sense. As organisms such as kelp, diminish, possibilities of relations between species narrow. Like most others, I am left wondering if such a listing is too little, too late. It is so for Mick Baron, who has led dive tours off the Tasman Peninsula since the 1970s when kelp was 'common as muck' and vessels navigated with difficulty – as Hooker noted in the nineteenth century – through thick canopies. Baron characterises the devastation as 'a national disaster' and regards the *M. pyrifera* communities as 'gone forever'. Recreational dives in the submerged forests are increasingly the relics of a bygone era.

The effects of the loss of kelp, however, are not confined to eastern Tasmania, nor even to south-eastern Australia, but resonate throughout the temperate marine system known as the Great Southern Reef (GSR). Stretching across the coastal areas of five states from Western Australia to Queensland, the GSR is an epicentre of endemism and diversity. Contributing food, detritus and habitat to the reef, kelp and other kinds of seaweed collectively constitute the 'powerhouse' of the GSR. What's more, this extraordinary, though unsung, marine landscape is within proximity to two-thirds of the Australian population, unlike the widely celebrated – and generously funded – Great Barrier Reef.

Craig Johnson has been studying kelp for most of his career as a marine ecologist but doesn't seem deterred by the situation. He remains one of the leading proponents of restoration. A recent collaboration between the Institute for Marine and Antarctic Studies that he directs and the Climate Foundation is investigating the creation of a 'marine permaculture industry'. His group aims to assess whether the few surviving wild individuals of *M. pyrifera* are adapted genetically to warmer oceans. Johnson's work points to the potential for new alliances with marine life on an ever more imperilled planet. Without doubt, kelp's future is our own.

I GLANCE AT AN IMAGE OF A SCUBA DIVER. THE CAPTION reads: 'Warm water events have taken their toll on Tasmania's kelp forests'. Air bubbles escape in a cauliflower plume towards the surface. The dark, prostrate shape of the diver edges laterally into the forest. The kelp fronds resemble corn; the stipes remind me of bean stalks twining upward. In the Anthropocene, though, this otherwise ordinary scene becomes a portrait of mourning. Coauthored by thirty-seven scientists, a 2016 study of changes to kelp beds around the world suggests that 'the capacity of kelp forests to recover from disturbance may be eroding'. Other scientists have referred to 'the new ecological order in the marine Anthropocene'.

How should we grieve the unseen? What is this affection I have for the strange seaweed thing and its unearthly terrain which have haunted the margins of my lived experience yet pulse in the centre of my consciousness? Is it possible to love in absentia? To make sense of this attachment, I have had to rely on others – scuba divers, marine ecologists, botanical illustrators, historical figures. I am left grasping at kelp's material wisdom: of bending with elements, of giving over oneself, of existing with elegance despite the exposure, of holding fast to terra firma so that others may get a grip.

Living in and with the Anthropocene is a practice of witnessing – the visible and invisible, the material and immaterial, the local and biospheric, the personal and collective. I think this is why kelp keeps pulling me in, and under. These archives of loss to which I have turned speak of the human and more-than-human communities of grieving wherever kelp grows, in Australia and elsewhere. Within loss and loneliness, however, inheres the potential for renewal – for regeneration, hope and interrelation – on a planet all the more endangered by catastrophic change. Kelp embodies the resilience we so desperately need, teaching me how to live with grace in the face of uncertainty.

Readings

AB Cribb, '*Macrocystis pyrifera* (L.) AG. In Tasmanian Waters', *Marine and Freshwater Research*, vol. 5, no. 1, 1954, pp. 1–34.

Charles Darwin, *The Voyage of the Beagle*, PF Collier and Son, New York, 1909 [1839].

William Henry Harvey, *Phycologia Australica; Or, A History of Australian Seaweeds*, L Reeve & Co, London, 1862.

Joseph Dalton Hooker, *The Botany of the Antarctic Voyage of H.M. Discovery Ships* Erebus *and* Terror *in the Years 1839–1843*, Reeve Brothers, London, 1844.

Kira Krumhansl, et al., 'Global Patterns of Kelp Forest Change Over the Past Half-Century', *Proceedings of the National Academic Academy of Sciences of the United States of America*, 2016, pp. 1–6.

John Craig Sanderson, 'Subtidal Macroalgal Studies in East and South Eastern Tasmanian Coastal Waters', MSc Research Master thesis, University of Tasmania, 1990.

PLASTIC IN THE PACIFIC

Jennifer Lavers

On Lord Howe Island, 600 kilometres off the east coast of Australia, is a unique forest where seabirds and palm trees have evolved an unexpected and intimate relationship. Nowhere on Lord Howe do the birds exist without the palms, and no stand of palms exists in the absence of the birds. Bird and tree are one. Nature is whole.

As an ecologist born into an era of 'jobs and growth', it's increasingly rare to witness and document such intact ecosystems. And so, every year for the past decade, I have counted down to the month of April to the moment when I can return to the palm forest. My happy place, where I become whole.

So, 'why April?' you ask. My arrival is, oddly enough, synchronised with the departure of the birds I'm there to protect. Over the preceding three months, the adult shearwaters (or 'muttonbirds') on Lord Howe Island have been working hard to raise their chicks on a diet of fish and squid sourced from the adjacent waters of the Tasman Sea. By late April, the chicks are grown and it's time for their first flight out to sea. They do this solo, the parent birds long gone. And they do this never actually having seen the ocean.

Emerging from the depths of their burrows for the first time must be a daunting task, but the chicks are driven by hunger and instinct.

As the sun sets, we meet for the first time, among the palms, so I can record key measures of population health, such as chick body mass. The chicks are sporting some truly remarkable hairdos, as remnants of their fluffy down hang on in a few awkward places. One has a mullet, another a mohawk, and one looks like my grandfather with little tufts coming out his ears.

During my first trip to Lord Howe Island in 2007, I struggled to communicate with my colleague due to the raucous noise of the colony. Each bird screaming 'pick me, pick me' at the top of its tiny lungs. The forest was so full of life we had to stand side-by-side to complete any work. I must have shouted 'huh?' a hundred times that year.

But in April 2017, I did not say that once.

Thick stands of palms still blanket Lord Howe Island. They captivate the soul with sunlight twinkling down between the leaves, shining spotlights onto the empty burrows in the sandy soil below. But the palms are quiet, and alone, now. Bird and tree are no longer one.

Each year, fewer and fewer birds have emerged from their burrows in April. Those that attempted their first flight out to sea have increasingly washed up dead and dying on Lord Howe's beaches. On a good day, I am fortunate to hold life in my hands; healthy, robust and aggressive. A bird will try to bite its way free and I'll find myself saying 'Yes, you get 'em!' Because the majority of birds I now get to hold are small, underweight – the light in their eyes fading. Why?

To answer that question, one can follow a trail of toxic breadcrumbs, leading straight to the burrows. Where once the boundaries of the shearwater colony were demarcated by feathers and footprints, now the sandy substrate is littered with plastic junk. So-called 'disposable' items that society uses once, maybe twice, then discards to a mystical place called 'away'. Bottle caps, clothes pegs, pen lids, balloon clips, dice and Lego, fishing floats, the list goes on and on.

Each item has been carried to Lord Howe Island in the stomach of an adult shearwater, which mistook plastic floating in the Tasman Sea for prey. The hungry chicks wait patiently in their burrows, gradually and lovingly fed to death by their parents on a diet of plastic instead of fish. Our wildlife and remote islands have become repositories for the world's waste. This is 'away'.

Once consumed, plastic contributes to starvation and dehydration, and exposes the birds and other wildlife to an array of toxic chemicals. Demand for plastic products is increasing exponentially in our cities, and with that, so is their presence in our oceans. While we make excuses to justify our plastic addiction, every April the proportion of shearwaters recorded with plastic in their stomachs goes up and up.

Around the globe, seabird populations are declining faster than any other bird group. Seabirds are also widely regarded as reliable sentinels of marine health. The proverbial 'canaries in the [marine] coalmine'. So, as the quantities of plastic skyrocket and forests fall silent, a moment's reflection: a sentinel only works when we heed the warning.

Will you listen?

TINY FISH, BIG PROBLEMS

Adriana Vergés

I still vividly remember the first time I tasted sushi. I was twenty-one, working in San Francisco for the summer. My newly found American friends could not believe that I had never tasted sushi before, and were quietly amused by the situation. I had to explain that in Barcelona, where I was from, I had never even seen sushi, and I had only heard tales about faraway people in Japan eating raw fish. It sounded like a most bizarre custom.

Fast forward twenty years. I'm about to jump into the other side of the Pacific Ocean, in Gordons Bay, in Sydney, Australia. I'm now working as a marine ecologist and I'm about to do some surveys as part of my research on underwater forests. As I step into the water, I have to dodge various pieces of plastic that the swell has brought to shore. Among the debris are little plastic sauce containers in the shape of a fish. They are usually filled with soy sauce, which is used to season the raw fish that was once so exotic to me.

Sushi is, of course, no longer a mysterious food. There is now a sushi bar on most corners of every major city of every single continent on Earth. And wherever there's a sushi bar there are also hundreds of these minute fish-shaped sauce containers, which to me symbolise three of the greatest challenges facing us in the Anthropocene.

Firstly, their omnipresence is for me a symbol of globalisation and the homogenisation of life on Earth, not only in terms of human culture but also in terms of ecology and biodiversity. Everything is starting to look the same, wherever we go.

And with that homogenisation comes an overall loss of 'uniqueness', which fills me with conflicting thoughts. On the one hand, I remember thoroughly enjoying and devouring my first sushi meal and feeling very special indeed to be discovering this millennia-old Japanese custom. But, on the other hand, I realise it's precisely because of global citizens like me, sharing and discovering customs around the world, that we are living on an increasingly uniform planet.

Secondly, in my mind these plastic fish are also a potent symbol for overfishing, undoubtedly one of the greatest impacts we humans have had in the world's oceans. Ninety per cent of our fish stocks are today either fully fished or overfished, and this is obviously simply unsustainable. We need to stop relying on wild fish as a food staple, just like we stopped relying on wild meat from land animals millennia ago. But right now, we are, shamefully, in the position of still relying largely on wild fish to feed the ever-increasing demand for raw fish in sushi bars.

Finally, the little fish-shaped container is a poster child for the increasingly huge plastic problem that is enveloping our world. Although plastic items only started to be mass produced in the 1950s, plastic is so incredibly slow to decompose that nearly all the plastic that has ever been created still exists today. And much of this plastic (about eight million tonnes of it per year) ends up in the world's oceans every year. Making matters worse, the tiny size of these plastic fish makes them particularly tricky to recycle, as they tend to fall in between the cracks of the recycling machines.

Curiously, however, despite these little fish representing such mammoth problems, they are also pretty in their own way, a simple design that is a very good example of the Japanese *kawaii* obsession, which involves making things exceptionally cute. They also represent quite a revolutionary design. Their resealable nose means you can save any unused soy sauce, and their shape and material make them non-drip, dispensing sauce only when squeezed. No wonder they have taken over the world.

And this is how I still find myself smiling, despite having to collect one last bit of plastic rubbish before becoming immersed in my beloved underwater world. The small feat of design ingenuity represented by these containers somehow brings hope to my inner self. It points towards how, in the Anthropocene, we are not only leaving an everlasting mark on planet Earth, but are also coming of age technologically and developing the tools that allow us to fix environmental problems at a meaningful scale. I can't help but think that ours is the generation to start turning things around, to develop the very solutions that will stop the self-destructive trajectory that has so far led us to the Anthropocene. To me, it's clear that this is the only way forward.

REFLECTING ON A PHOTOGRAPH
OF TOURISTS RIDING SEA TURTLES

Suzy Freeman-Greene

He crouches on a sea turtle, knees bent, like a surfer catching a wave. Wearing a white cotton shirt, dark shorts and a crisp, straw hat. It's hard to see his face in this old, black-and-white photo, but he looks trim. The turtle sits in the sand, head raised, front flippers thrust forward. The man leans in, hands pressed flat on the thick, patterned carapace, and I think of a runner on a starting block.

A woman in a halter-neck bathing suit straddles a turtle beside him. Knees clench the sides of the shell. Hands press hard on it, fingers splayed. She looks down at the creature, seemingly willing it to move. Four more people also perch on turtles: kneeling, crouching, sitting side-saddle. Others stroll on the beach or stand with hands on hips.

This photograph, of tourists riding turtles on Queensland's Heron Island, was taken in 1938. I was shocked when I first came across it. The riders seemed so proprietorial: hands gripping shells; bodies poised to 'surf' into the water. Was there any sense of the turtles as creatures with feelings?

Turtle riding was once a popular tourist pastime. The turtles would drag their human loads across the sand into the shallows. Once in water, their bodies – so slow and ungainly on land – became light and fast.

'Our rides were brief and exciting', a *National Geographic* writer explained in 1930. 'We crept upon sleeping turtles and made seats on their carapaces. Thus surprised, they scrambled over the sand, ploughing quaint furrows with their flippers ... Once in fairly deep water, the turtle won the game. A dive unseated the rider, who splashed ashore for another little joyride to the sea.'

I came across other photos. Men and women standing upright on turtles; or kneeling on all fours. One image, taken in Bundaberg in 1930, showed turtles lying on their backs, stranded and unable to right themselves, as holidaymakers looked on. Turning turtles onto their backs overnight was a favourite technique of the hunters who harvested them for the soup industry in the 1920s and 30s. The nesting turtles would clamber onto the beach in the dark to lay eggs. Once flipped they were powerless to move. Sometimes tourists flipped turtles, then turned them over in the morning for a race back to the sea.

These images, and the Heron Island one, seemed to exemplify the hubris that's so characteristic of our present age of the Anthropocene. There was a sense of these turtles existing merely as playthings for humans. But then I came across a 2006 article, 'Tourists Riding Turtles', by a Queensland-based academic, Celmara Pocock, in which she argued that turtle riding could be seen in a positive light. During the 1920s and 30s, turtles were harvested and canned in great quantities. Riding one, she writes, could be seen as a much more benign activity; and 'ultimately, it was the human rider who was humiliated and lost the contest'. Even scientists who went north to study the Great Barrier Reef rode turtles. One photo in the State Library of South Australia shows a group of ornithologists trying their hand at turtle riding circa 1908.

Still, by the 1960s, the sport had come to an end. Ideas about the relationship between humans and animals had changed. And as Pocock writes, the spread of new technologies, such as scuba gear and snorkels, meant tourists could engage with the reef underwater rather than on the land.

I have stared many times at that 1938 photo and it no longer gives me the jolt of shock it once did. When I look at it today, I find myself thinking of our contemporary sport of horseracing. In 2018, once again a horse was put down after competing in the Melbourne Cup. As thousands of racegoers partied, the five-year-old Irish stallion Cliffsofmoher was euthanised on the track. It was the sixth horse to die in the race since 2013.

THE HORROR OF A RUBBLE REEF

Cameron Allan McKean

It's getting dark on the reef. Particles of sunlight scatter in the water column as oranges, pinks and purples fall into the horizon. Looking west, towards the coastline of mainland Australia, the daylight is retreating from farms and mines. Looking east, towards the 900 other islands that make up the 2300-kilometre-long Great Barrier Reef, the blackness is thick and total.

LED beams from our torches cut across the waves as we float on the water's surface. Resisting the drag of our bulky scuba equipment, we are pushing towards an inshore reef near Alma Bay on Magnetic Island, twenty minutes by ferry from the nearby port of Townsville. The corals around this island are some of the most studied on the Great Barrier Reef and have radically advanced our knowledge about life and death in coastal ecosystems. Just around the headland from where we are swimming, at Geoffrey Bay, Peter Harrison and a group of other marine biologists first identified how reef-building species reproduce. Coral had been procreating underwater for millions of years, but curious humans only began to attune to 'sex on the reef' in 1981. Shortly after sunset, following the first full moon in spring, Harrison and his team witnessed a future reef in its newborn state. They watched as thirty-two species synchronously spawned gooey bundles of sperm and eggs, turning the ocean into a blizzard of coral life. A small blue sign on the foreshore commemorates the achievement:

> This is the bay where scientists discovered in 1981 that many coral species reproduce on the same few nights. The discovery revolutionised coral research.

Often forgotten in the retelling is that the finding was so significant that the municipality of Townsville, which includes Magnetic Island, planned to host a festival around the annual coral spawning and even toyed with the idea of calling itself 'Townsville: Where the Celebration of Life Begins'. But today, the reefs around Magnetic Island – including the one we are headed towards – are no longer models of oceanic abundance and life. Corals have become central figures of ecological collapse that reveal the ways anthropogenic climate change will unfold, unevenly, across the ocean. Also transformed are those who study and spend time with corals. American legal scholar and ethnographer Irus Braverman, in one of the first major interrogations of coral scientists themselves, claims that those who study reefs are now 'spokespeople' and 'guides' who might lead us 'through the perils of the Anthropocene'.

Out in the dark, three of us are headed for the drop zone. We talk as we swim on our backs, and during lulls in the conversation hear the rhythmic splashing of fin kicks and watch the stars taking shape above. As we swim further, the calm is threatened by fear of what's beneath. We nervously wait for the moment when our guide, Tom, will instruct us to put on our masks, exhale and slip into the waves. We will sink to the sea floor in a torch-lit cloud of regulator bubbles, and hover among sargassum weeds that grow over the limestone rubble of a collapsed reef.

There's no one else in the bay tonight, no swimmers, boaters or divers – no one we can see, anyway. At the front of our procession,

Tom's silhouette bobs up and down in the swell. He is one of the island's most experienced instructors, who settled here after years working with marine biologists and scuba schools around the world. He now co-owns Pleasure Divers, one of two dive schools on the island, which serves almost as many local researchers as the young European and British backpackers who keep local businesses afloat. Tom has lost count of the dives he has made around 'Maggie', as the locals call it, but he hasn't forgotten any of the routines: 'Let's start heading towards the headland', he says, 'and double-check your backup torches.'

Trailing behind Tom, Naomi and I search the clips and pockets of our buoyancy control vests, the lifejacket/backpack systems that hold our tanks and other equipment close to our bodies. We are novices, with less than fifty dives between us. Today marks three weeks into our eight-week training period, during which Tom will guide us through a maze of increasingly complex certifications: Open Water Diver, Deep Diver, Wreck Diver, Advanced Open Water Diver, Rescue Diver, all the way up to Divemaster, the certification that will officially mark our ascension from recreational to professional diving. This is also the same pathway required of aspiring marine biologists hoping to study corals underwater, the same pathway that must be taken by those who would become future 'guides' to the underwater 'perils of the Anthropocene'. There are many tasks along the way and, in our case, one of those involves guiding a night dive. That is why we are here, kicking ourselves across a darkened patch of the Pacific Ocean.

'I found it.' Naomi switches on her extra torch and our beams shine white-blue against the black-black water. She leans back in the swell and stiffens: 'Too cold, too cold'. She is young and wiry, and ends her dives shivering, despite sometimes wearing two 5-millimetre-thick wetsuits. Her home is Kimbe, a coastal port town in the West New Britain Province of Papua New Guinea. As we kick further out, she tells us stories about her ocean: it is warm and clear, and reefs sink down into deep blue water. Among the reefs, she says, are the coral-covered bones of crashed Japanese 'Zero' warplanes, material traces of the Pacific theatre of war, when the coral-fringed islands of Papua New Guinea became staging grounds during World War II. 'I don't know why they called them "Zeros"', she says. The reefs near Kimbe are remote, but they're still affected by many of the same anthropogenic pressures affecting the rest of the 'Coral Triangle', Earth's most biodiverse marine environment, which stretches from northern Australia to Thailand and almost to the southernmost tip of Japan. Overfishing, agricultural and industrial runoff, displaced sediment (from dredging), rising temperatures and acidification all contribute to the ascendancy of death in the Coral Triangle. Naomi is here, in part, because of that ascendancy. She is one of the Coral Sea Foundation's first 'Sea Women of Melanesia', a burgeoning group of women from across the Pacific who are learning the diving skills necessary to map local reefs and, they hope, create marine reserves.

I am the third diver, an anthropology student researching the cultural reverberations of coral death for my doctoral thesis. On nights like tonight, I would typically be sitting at an old wooden desk inside the State Library of Victoria, reading bleak reports by reef scientists. Sunk deep in banks of knowledge, I imagined I had a clear idea of climate change and how it operates: these changes are anthropogenic, generated by *anthropos*, by humans. But hovering over real reefs affected by changes to ocean chemistry and temperature makes me realise I have very little idea of who that human is. This doubt – not about the cause of the changes, but the nature of the human generating those changes – begins to surface when I see a colourful sticker on the side of a van parked at the terminal for the ferry that would take me to Magnetic Island. It reads, 'Save the reef'. Embedded in the concepts of 'anthropogenic climate change' or 'anthropocene', is the idea that *anthropos* has become planetary and immensely powerful. The human appears to regain primacy as the master controller of Earth's fate: destroyer and, necessarily, saviour. To critics of this concept, such as the art historian and cultural theorist TJ Demos, the vast scales built into a planetary imaginary of *anthropos* 'overshoot the figural, the actual, the experiential'.

Floating out with our small band of night divers, I wonder about the planetary human that turns Earth's reefs to rubble and, potentially, gives life to the dead. I wonder about the experience of encountering the planetary human. What forms of encounter are possible at all?

Above us, light pollution from industries and homes in Townsville dims the stars over the mainland. Docked at the port, and lit by fluorescent orbs, bulk carrier freighters and other transport vessels are waiting to be loaded with minerals and livestock. Weighed down with resources, these ships will pass through the labyrinth of the Great Barrier Reef to ports across Asia, their cargo destined for heavy industries and factories. Tom draws our attention to these ships one day at the dive school as we look out to sea from a window. 'Probably carrying coal', he says, gesturing with his head towards a red-hulled ship bound for Singapore. During the day, the hulking outlines of the vessels mar the horizon. Underwater, on our routine dives, their presence is sensed through the pulsing drone of engine noise. The ocean feels quieter now as we float further from shore. Once we sink beneath the surface, will we hear the sounds of global supply chains grinding into action?

But other things beneath are capturing our attention. As we continue to swim out through the swell, we wonder about the marine life emerging below to feed under the cover of darkness. Flexible carpet sharks, patterned like lace, are hunting. Cowtail rays, with whip-like hairy flags extending from their body, float above the sand. Spotty coral cod share space with schools of skittish parrotfish, and curious hairy crabs take positions on rocks and corals below swarming clouds of tiny polychaete worms with bodies covered in microbristles. Kicking above, we are trying not to think about the larger forms of life also emerging below, trying not to think about how vulnerable we are, and trying not to think about being eaten. 'Yeah, don't talk about that', someone says.

A few hundred metres beyond us, a series of yellow buoys attached to baited drum lines rise and fall in the swell. They are used to catch predatory 'target species', including great hammerhead, tiger and bull sharks, which frequent these waters. The drum lines give a false sense of security. They do little to change attack patterns, but even a false sense of security is seen by some as better than nothing. In a few months they will be removed, and a local newspaper will run an online article about the situation titled, simply, 'Someone Will Die'.

We just swam over the area where the last person was killed by a shark on the island. At 5.30 pm on 27 January 1929, Harold Wetheril was attacked in a few feet of water. The newspaper graphically reported that his 'right arm was taken off at the elbow and his left arm at the wrist and a large hole was made in his back'. He died in hospital. One year after the attack, a shark fence – a series of vertical pylons – was installed across the bay. Within a decade, storms had destroyed most of it, and the fence now lies ruined on the sea floor. We glimpse its dim shape below with our beams as we pass overhead.

In the dark, confronted with the violence of what ecological philosopher Val Plumwood calls 'being prey', and the abstracted violence of ecological collapse, I focus on my equipment. I tighten straps and shift hoses connected to meters and valves, thinking myself into a state of control through the streams of data entering my devices, technologies that turn the ocean into a series of numbers. Time: 6.38 pm; dive number: 27; depth: 0 metres; temperature: 22°C; time since last dive: 4 hours 22 minutes. But the feeling of the surrounding water – cold, dark, surging – makes it hard to shake thoughts of what's below.

We are now far from the beach, past the site of Wetheril's attack, past the ruined shark fence, out where the water is deeper and the waves have become rolling swell. 'We'll drop down here', says Tom. We begin the process: we face each other, don masks, take test breaths through our regulators, signal 'OK', signal 'descend' with down-turned thumbs, check for obstructions immediately beneath us, release air from our buoyancy control vests, and exhale. Torches are pointed towards the sea floor, but it's too distant to make out yet – just a soup of shimmering particulate and bubbles. On my left and right, the dark forms of Tom and Naomi slowly sink, with beams flashing in all directions. We fall into the dark.

It's quiet here. No thudding of bulk carrier engines, no shuddering of jet skis, no chopping of dinghy motors. But any sensory space opened by the absence of humans is doubly reclaimed by the blackness, which seems to exponentially magnify the water pressure, squeezing the totality of our experiences into the shape of LED beams. The lights push back against the thickness of the dark, projecting shadows from the undulating sand on the sea floor. Hovering above, we communicate with hand signals and patterns drawn with light. Tom looks at his compass, setting a heading that will take us out to sea along a headland. 'This way', he indicates, drawing tight circles with his torch in the direction we will travel.

Beside us, a bluespotted ray, previously enjoying the obscurity of a night-time swim, freezes in the light, wingtips bent to touch the sand and body arched defensively. It vanishes in a burst of movement and sediment. Naomi spots something inside a hole: a small moray eel, watching us pass with its mouth agape, pointed teeth flashing in the beams. Beyond the light, in the negative space of the dark, imagined presences of larger things are swimming. And yet, Tom and Naomi will later talk about how meditative and calming the dive was. I sense this calm in the sounds of breathing from their aqua-lung scuba systems. These sounds gradually slow as our movements become relaxed. We're conserving air by inhaling deeper, by moving as little as possible, by reducing stress. This state change, from noisy kicking on the surface to peaceful submerged flying, lulls me into a dream-like state. The dive becomes a kind of parasomnia: a sometimes nightmarish state between waking and sleeping, with reality and unreality shifting positions.

The 'nightmare' is also a question: what is inside the dark? And how will these presences alter us? There is the horror of an apex predator that would turn us from human beings to meat, but there is another figure, equally transformative, in the blackness too. The rubble of a dead reef, now appearing beneath us, begins to draw it out.

We are thirty-four minutes into the dive, floating in a line above the sea floor. My light catches on spires of sargassum weed standing erect and still. They are growing on the mineral rubble of dead coral. We float over a carpet of ruin, one that hides crabs, worms and fish, which watch from in between the limestone fragments.

This carpet was once the skeletons of living corals. Colonies of fleshy, tentacular animals grew these mineral pieces with the energy provided by tiny photosynthesising algae called zooxanthellae that lived inside their skin. Tom tells me later that marine heatwaves in 2016 and 2017 made the shallow waters here so hot that corals became stressed and, in something like panic, ejected their life-giving algal symbionts. This is coral bleaching. If the temperature decreases and zooxanthellae return, bleached corals can survive this event, but if conditions stay skewed for long enough, death is inevitable. In this scenario, fish and other marine life feed on the necrotic tissue of dead and dying corals, and invasive seaweeds claim space on exposed skeletons, which eventually collapse onto the sea floor like ruined buildings.

Anthropologist Anna Tsing calls these sites of ruin 'the world that progress has left to us'. The planetary human is here, somewhere, distributed among the rubble: it is also in the fluid around us; in the traces of chemicals that have washed here from farms far from the ocean; in tiny traces of heavy metals from the port; in the sediment that has been kicked up by machines dredging the nearby channel; and in the changing warmth and acidity of the water. The rubble beneath us testifies to this large and hard-to-track trajectory that links the extracted fossil matter of coal, petroleum or natural gases with modern engines and biogeochemical changes in the ocean. Even lit with a powerful LED beam, the 'world that progress has left to us' is darkened – but that doesn't mean it's empty.

Floating above a rubble reef, I wonder about the identity, location and shape of the planetary human figure inside Tsing's concept of 'progress' or the 'anthropogenic' in climate change. Breathing slowly through my regulator, with bubbles rising past my dive mask, I struggle to hold together the complex scales, states and abstract formations of toxicity, pollution and – most important for corals – rising emissions. How it is possible to capture this figure?

Attempting to make sense of the rubble, I thought again about the fear of 'being prey'. I felt that something else, capable of terrific violence, was beyond the beam. Above the rubble, I feared that I would look ahead and, at the very limits of light, glimpse the dark shape of another diver, a fourth diver, a diver we did not swim out with. How long was it following us? Who was this other that we had not noticed? The absence of the reef seemed to call it out.

Later, while swimming back to shore, someone asks what it would have been like to suddenly encounter a person under the water – a human who should not have been there. 'Just imagine.'

Confronted by the thought of a seemingly out-of-place figure following us above the rubble, just beyond the light, I vaguely recalled seven lines from TS Eliot's 1922 poem, *The Waste Land*:

Who is the third who walks always beside you?
When I count, there are only you and I together

But when I look ahead up the white road
There is always another one walking beside you
Gliding wrapt in a brown mantle, hooded
I do not know whether a man or a woman
– But who is that on the other side of you?

The 'third who walks always beside you' came to Eliot after read-ing British explorer Ernest Henry Shackleton's accounts of a tragic Antarctic expedition. Physically and mentally exhausted, Shackleton was certain that an unknown humanlike entity occasionally joined his group on their journey across the ice. Counting the members of the party, he sometimes noticed an extra walking among them, but it was only glimpsed obliquely, a presence that watched or perhaps stalked the group from the edges of sense. Who was that on the other side, walking beside them?

We are forty-eight minutes into the dive. Tom circles his beam to draw our attention and we see a resident turtle has wedged itself, head-first, into a rock to get some sleep. Shining my torch above, a school of large fish scatters in the beam. To the side, a long carpet shark, hunting just above the sea floor, hurries to escape the light.

Tom gestures for us to come near. It's time to 'turn the dive', to head back towards shore. But first, he points at his torch, bringing a hand close to the light and cutting the beam. 'Turn off your torches', he is saying.

It's dark on the reef, but the darkness isn't empty. As our eyes adjust, the blackness is repopulated with spurts of green biolumines-cence from tiny algae. It's quiet. The only sound is the slow bubbling of breathing through the regulators. It's still, too. The only move-ments are from tiny marine worms brushing against my face and tangling my hair. Naomi waves her arms in front of her, exciting the algae and filling the water around us with a pinprick galaxy of biolu-minescence. Against the glowing dots, I see the outlines of Tom and

Naomi and, behind them, at the very limits of the light, the dim silhouette of a figure that should not be there – a fourth diver, motionless, watching.

This was what we saw as we floated over a patch of ruin in the world that progress has left to us.

Readings

Irus Braverman, *Coral Whisperers*, University of California Press, Berkeley, 2018.

TJ Demos, 'To Save a World: Geoengineering, Conflictual Futurisms, and the Unthinkable', *e-flux*, no. 94, October 2018, <www.e-flux.com/journal/94/221148/>.

TS Eliot, *The Waste Land*, 1922.

Peter L Harrison, Russell C Babcock, et al., 'Mass Spawning in Tropical Reef Corals', *Science*, vol. 223, no. 4641, 16 March 1984, pp. 1186–89, <doi.org/10.1126/science.223.4641.1186>.

Jaws. Universal/Zanuck-Brown Productions, 1975.

Val Plumwood, 'Surviving a Crocodile Attack', *Utne Reader*, July–August 2000, <www.utne.com/arts/being-prey>.

Ernest Shackleton, *South: The Endurance Expedition*, Penguin Press, London, 2008 [1919].

Eugene Thacker, *Tentacles Longer Than Night: Horror of Philosophy*, Zero Books, Winchester, 2015.

Anna Lowenhaupt Tsing, *The Mushroom at the End of the World: On the Possibility of Life in Capitalist Ruins*, Princeton University Press, Princeton, 2015 (reprint edition).

A LANDSCAPE ALREADY LOST

James Bradley

The water is shockingly cold, the first flood of it into my wetsuit making me gasp as I wade over the broken stone into the shallows. Ahead of me my brother Patrick is already underwater, so, adjusting my mask I brace myself against the chill and push off, my scuba rig still only just clearing the rocks.

Despite the low winter sun, visibility beneath the surface is good. As I propel myself forward the bottom gradually drops away, the flat slabs of stone that litter the beach disappearing into delicate fronds of pale brown seaweed. I have just long enough to wonder how long it will take to find them before I see the first ahead of me. It is a male, perhaps half a metre long, the long skirt of the horizontal fin that runs along each side of its body rippling hypnotically as it hovers in place. With a spark of excitement I kick my fins and move towards him, only to see another half-obscured in the weed below, then two more beside them. And a metre or two further on, three more, and beyond them another four, and another, and another, and another.

For a few seconds I stare about myself, exultantly, grinning behind my regulator. I have seen cuttlefish before, of course. Encounters with them in the waters off Sydney and Jervis Bay are, if not common, then certainly not unusual. Yet they have always been solitary specimens, moving quietly through the water or lurking in the weed. Certainly nothing that would have prepared me for the sight of dozens and dozens spread out across the sea floor.

Descending towards the first group I float just in front of them. The nearest – and largest – is perhaps 60 centimetres long. In its basic design it resembles a short-tentacled squid or octopus, albeit one with an unusually large body. From the front, its blunt face and wide-set eyes make it look a little like an earless elephant, or at least an elephant whose trunk has been replaced by a skirt of half-furled, downward-facing tentacles. Yet from the side its torpedo-shaped body resembles nothing so much as some kind of science fictional space-craft suspended above the sea floor.

Although all four of the cuttlefish in front of me are clearly aware of my presence they do not swim away. Instead they simply adjust their positions, their fringing fins rippling with sinuous grace as they reorient themselves. Whether they are genuinely unafraid or simply so focused on their fellows that I am irrelevant is impossible to say: all I know is that as they orbit each other slowly, warily, fins undulating, or move slowly but purposefully towards each other, they seem entirely unbothered by my proximity.

As they perform this dance their bodies pulse with colour, constellations of blue and brown and orange and white chasing across their skin like the shifting patterns of a school of fish or a flock of birds. The exact purpose of this display is unclear: sometimes it seems to be for communication or a form of mating signal, but it is also defensive. On one occasion I watch a male I have been following swim close to a rock and in a fraction of a second transform himself and disappear, his skin perfectly mimicking not just the rock's colour, but also its texture.

Marvellous as they are in themselves, the cuttlefishes' presence here is also marvellous in a larger sense. While most cuttlefish are solitary hunters, encountered only in ones or twos, this small population of giant Australian cuttlefish – or *yayardloo*, as the Barngarla people know them – native to the upper reaches of South Australia's Spencer Gulf, behave differently. For each year, as winter approaches, they abandon their solitary lives and begin to congregate on this small stretch of coastline just north of Whyalla to breed.

This behaviour is unique, not just among giant Australian cuttlefish, but cuttlefish in general. Elsewhere, breeding males scout out particular areas of real estate on the sea floor, which they then vigorously defend from potential rivals. Yet here many thousands of males live at close quarters with one another, often for days or weeks at a time.

For anybody used to the speed with which many marine animals can move, there is something oddly languorous about cuttlefish behaviour. Like alien submarines engaged in a slow-motion battle, they congregate in small groups of three or four, floating unmoving or drifting towards one another. Most of the time these approaches are the precursor to a fight between two males, an oddly formal process in which they come alongside each other and then tilt inward to grapple with their tentacles, almost like two galleons slowing to fire their cannon. Despite the stakes, there is something oddly desultory about this process, which does not usually seem to result in injury or death. Instead most altercations seem to end in the two combatants disentangling themselves and darting off in opposite directions in the quick, twitchy manner of an offended cat, making it difficult to tell what constitutes victory.

Nor is victory necessarily victory, at least in the mating stakes. The Spencer Gulf cuttlefish exhibit two distinct life cycles. In the first, they grow quickly, reaching maturity at a relatively small size within seven to eight months. In the second, they take almost two years to reach maturity but grow much larger in the process.

In the water it is obvious which are which: the larger individuals are half as big or more again than their younger counterparts. And despite the oddly ritualised nature of the struggles I observe, it is clear these smaller individuals would not stand a chance against one of the larger specimens.

To overcome this problem the smaller cuttlefish have developed a series of behaviours to elude the larger males. Some of these involve simple deception. Using their changeable skin and mutable bodies, the smaller males mimic the appearance of females in order to slip past the larger males and approach the females. But they also rely on distraction: on at least one occasion I see a small male glide beneath a pair of larger combatants and mate with the female while his rivals are occupied with fighting one another.

Mating itself is also a curious process. It takes place face to face, the male's tentacles grasping the female's and pulling her close into a kind of handshake so the pair of them form a strange two-bodied organism. This congress is not quick, often lasting two minutes or more (scientists have calculated the average length of the process at 2.4 minutes), but once the male has inseminated the female (using what our Argentinean divemaster refers to as a 'special tentacle', a term that reduces me to helpless schoolboy giggles for days afterwards), they disentangle themselves and move slowly apart.

Once she has mated, the female lays her eggs under rocks, where they hang like pale stalactites. Three to five months from now they will hatch, releasing tiny but fully-formed cuttlefish which disperse back into the Gulf. By then both parents, and indeed every other cuttlefish around me, will be dead. Because once they have mated, the cuttlefishes' bodies begin to break down and decay. Somewhat disconcertingly, they often remain on the breeding site while this happens. More than once I glimpse dying individuals hovering above their vividly coloured fellows like submarine versions of Banquo's ghost, their bodies bleached of colour and flaking apart. There is, I find, something unsettling about their silent, watchful presence, their augury of mortality.

The idea that these extraordinary creatures live such brief lives is astonishing, of a piece with their physical strangeness, alien beauty and the wonder of this fleeting congregation. Yet it is also intriguing. Anthropologist Claude Lévi-Strauss famously said that animals are 'good to think with'. He was making a larger point about structural categories and their uses, but watching the cuttlefish move through the frigid water I find myself wondering about Lévi-Strauss' words once more. We live in a moment of profound change and impossible grief. Although these remarkable creatures are here today, who can say whether they will be here a decade from now, a century from now, whether this extraordinary dance will endure. If we were to try to think with them, what might we discover? What might their alien otherness, lack of fixed form, dance of imitation and vagrant lives tell us about them, about ourselves, about our changing world and our place in it?

CUTTLEFISH ARE CEPHALOPODS, A CLASS OF MOLLUSCS MADE up of two subclasses: the Nautiloidea, comprised of the shelled nautiloids; and the Coleoidea, the soft-bodied octopuses, squids and cuttlefish, together with the argonauts, or paper nautiluses, which despite their shells are not true nautiluses, but a form of shelled octopus.

Although shell-less, cuttlefish are distinguished from the other Coleoidea by the cuttlebone, or cuttle, that gives their torpedo-like bodies its distinctive shape. A familiar sight on Australian beaches, cuttlebones are the result of the slow internalisation of the shells that once surrounded ancestral cephalopods. Yet unlike the hard shells of other molluscs, the brittle, chalky structure of cuttlebones is composed of delicate layers filled with tiny pockets of air. This allows cuttlefish to control their buoyancy, but the fragility of the cuttlebone's internal structure and its vulnerability to pressure also confines them to shallower water than many other species of squid and octopus.

To our mammalian eyes, cuttlefish and other cephalopods are deeply weird. Whereas mammals and almost every other complex animal are arranged head/body/legs, they are arranged body/head/legs (the literal translation of their name is 'head-foot'). This means their mouths sit underneath their arms, and their eyes atop them, while their bodies and the organs they contain extend backward from the head. Unlike mammals, birds, fish, reptiles and even insects, cuttlefish bodies also lack firm structure. They have no spine or spinal column, in place of articulated legs and arms they have tentacles, and even their bodies are soft and malleable – most strikingly in the case of the octopuses, which can not only climb, fight and even walk on land but are also able to deform their bodies so as to slip through holes narrower than one of their tentacles. Even their skin, which is covered with light-sensitive cells known as chromatophores, is utterly unlike ours, capable of changing not only colour but also texture almost instantaneously, whether for camouflage or communication.

Their strangeness is perhaps less surprising when one considers the fact that humans and cephalopods are separated by more than half a billion years of evolution. Although the exact details of the process remain contested, what we do know is that the last time mammals and molluscs shared a common ancestor was 600 million years ago during the Ediacaran. The Earth of the Ediacaran was quite unlike our own. The ancient supercontinent Gondwana had only just begun to form. Most life still lived in the oceans. Animal life – such as it was – had existed for less than 100 million years, and was mostly comprised of sponges, polyps and other creatures that may or may not have been Cnidarians, and a host of strange microbial mats and jellyfish-like creatures. Even the Cambrian Explosion, that mysterious moment of mass evolutionary divergence that gave rise to most modern phyla, lay fifty or sixty million years in the future, as long, almost, as from the disappearance of the dinosaurs until today.

Exactly what that common ancestor was is not known, but it seems likely it was some kind of flat, worm-like creature, perhaps possessing primitive eyes and a few neurons. Yet from that remote ancestor sprang an astonishing diversity of creatures. In a very real sense the 800 or so species of cephalopods alive today are just a shadow of this much more ancient order. For in the oceans of the Ordovician and Devonian, the cephalopods reigned supreme. During the Ordovician, ancient cephalopods such as *Cameroceras* grew to an astonishing 10 metres in length, while some species of ancient ammonoids, shelled cephalopods that resembled the nautiloids that still swim in our oceans, had shells well over a metre in diameter.

Like today's cephalopods, these ancient animals would have been fearsome hunters, protected by shells but fast-moving and possessed of tentacles capable of grasping and immobilising their prey. And while their dominion over the oceans was eventually surrendered to the fish and then the dinosaurs, they continued to thrive until sixty-five million years ago. At this point their shells disappear from the fossil record, suggesting they were wiped out by the same catastrophe that exterminated the dinosaurs.

Because their soft, boneless bodies tended to decompose without trace, evidence for the existence of shell-less cephalopods in the fossil record is harder to come by. Yet fossils of what appear to be ancestral octopuses dating back to the beginning of the Permian, 296 million years ago, have been found, and evidence of cuttlefish survives from as long ago as the Cretaceous (it seems the ancestors of today's octopuses and today's squid diverged first, probably during the Jurassic, while cuttlefish and squid diverged later). While oddly ephemeral, these fossils, usually little more than a ghostly imprint or a petrified cuttlebone, are a reminder of both the ancientness of the cephalopods and their resilience in surviving not one, but five, mass extinctions.

In recent years cephalopods have attracted considerable attention due to the growing evidence of their high intelligence. Long known for their playfulness – Pliny famously referred to their 'mischief and craft' – octopuses have been observed engaging in a wide variety of complex, adaptive behaviour, ranging from the use of coconut shells as armour and raids on fishing boats to steal fish, to acts of highly organised subterfuge and trickery in order to escape aquariums or eliminate unwanted intrusions. (Otto, an octopus in an aquarium in Coburg, worked out how to short-circuit the facility's electrical system by firing jets of water into his lights.) They also exhibit a variety of behaviours that look remarkably like curiosity and play, as well as clear individual personalities. And in more formal, experimental contexts, they have been shown to be able to navigate mazes and solve problems. Similarly, octopuses seem to possess the ability to remember and learn, often very quickly, as well as a capacity to recognise (and react to) individual humans. There is even tantalising evidence they dream. Videos exist of colours and textures moving across the bodies of sleeping octopuses, transforming and morphing as if images and sensations were passing through their unconscious minds.

Evidence for similar abilities in other cephalopods is less clear-cut. In part this reflects the fact that squid and cuttlefish do not thrive in captivity, making systematic observation of their behaviour difficult. But it also reflects differences in behaviour. Whereas octopuses are continually interacting with their environment as they move across the sea floor, cuttlefish and squid are swimmers, whose tentacles are used not to explore and manipulate their environment but to hunt and grapple.

Still, the evidence that does exist is suggestive. The complexity of the visual displays that ripple across the bodies of cuttlefish would be impossible without considerable processing power, and pointless if they did not also possess the capacity to make sense of the displays of other cuttlefish. Likewise, a 2019 study found evidence that cuttlefish experience something like REM sleep, suggesting they too may dream. And in another study, French scientists demonstrated that cuttlefish possess something that resembles our own episodic memory, allowing them to make decisions based on past experiences. Anecdotes also abound of cuttlefish engaging with divers and swimmers in ways that suggest friendly curiosity. Philosopher Peter Godfrey-Smith describes an encounter with an Australian giant cuttlefish while snorkelling off Sydney, in which the cuttlefish repeatedly approached to look at him, as if as interested in him as he was in it.

For Godfrey-Smith, this sense of inquisitiveness, or 'mutual *engagement*' (his italics), was to become a source of continuing fascination and one he was to find repeated many times. 'They watch you closely, usually maintaining some distance, but often not very much', he writes. 'Occasionally, when I've been very close, a giant cuttlefish has reached an arm out, just a few inches, so it touches mine. It's usually one touch, then no more.'

Perhaps because they are absorbed in the drama of their mating rituals, the cuttlefish in the Spencer Gulf display no such behaviours while I am with them. But elsewhere is another matter. More than once I have dived down to observe individual cuttlefish, delighted by their lack of fear at my proximity. On one occasion, at Bondi, I followed one for almost a quarter of an hour, floating face to face with it as it extended its tentacles towards me then moved slowly away, only to pause until I caught up again. This process continued for five or ten minutes until my clumsy surfacing for air finally broke the spell, and it darted away. On such occasions it is difficult not to feel one is genuinely interacting with the cuttlefish, that behind those strange, beautiful eyes – themselves the product of a completely separate evolutionary process from that which shaped our own – there is a presence, something aware and alive, yet whose existence lies at a profound remove from our own.

AFTER OUR FIRST DIVE PATRICK AND I EMERGE FROM THE water surprised by the absence not just of predators, but of other marine animals more generally. Although cold-water corals and marvellous, beaker-like sponges grow among the weed, other than the cuttlefish, a handful of small sweep and some razor clams protruding from the sand, the water seems largely devoid of life.

As we are pulling on our wetsuits on the second day we talk to John, who has recently returned to Port Augusta after several decades working in Kalgoorlie. Retrieving his phone from his bag he shows us photos of the Torana he bought the day before. He says he still can't believe his luck. 'She's beautiful. Doesn't need a thing done to her.'

Pointing northward, he tells us his girlfriend's father used to have a shack just up the coast, which she inherited from her grandfather. 'Back then there were fish everywhere', he tells us. 'Whiting, snapper, squid. You could catch anything you wanted straight off the beach. All gone now, though.'

This emptying of the oceans is not news, although the constant normalisation of environmental change often obscures it from our view. In June, only a few weeks before our visit, a study found snapper numbers in this area of the Spencer Gulf have declined by almost 16 per cent over the past five years, while in the Gulf's southern half they have declined by more than 30 per cent across the same period. To the east, in Gulf St Vincent the declines are even more significant, with numbers dropping 87 per cent, but in both cases these declines come on top of significant declines in the 1990s and before, suggesting fish numbers in the region are now only a fraction of what they once were.

The patch of coast John's father-in-law's shack stood on is now dominated by the spectral structure of Santos' Port Bonython Processing Facility, the featureless white cylinders of the gas tanks straddling the low landscape like an image of a colony on the Martian surface.

Despite its scale the plant itself is almost silent. Initially I assume that is because it is the weekend, but while we are removing our wetsuits after our second dive a klaxon suddenly rings out across the ground separating us from the facility, shattering the quiet, whooping just long enough for me to think there might be a fire, before cutting out again.

A woman seated at one of the tables the council has provided in the car park by the dive site shakes her head in amusement. 'My husband works there. That's the lunch bell.' When I say it sounded like an alarm she laughs.

'Don't hungry men always think it's an emergency?'

Constructed in the early 1980s, the facility is the terminus of one spur of the Moomba to Adelaide Pipeline, which transports gas south from the Cooper Basin. Long promoted as a cleaner alternative to coal, the supposed benefits of gas have come under increased scrutiny in recent years, largely due to growing public concern about the environmental impacts of its production.

For Santos this concern has been heightened by the company's involvement in proposals to drill for oil and gas in the Great Australian Bight, a fact that is borne home to me during a conversation with two young women here from Adelaide to see the cuttlefish. When I tell one of them the jetty is owned by Santos her face darkens. 'Fucking Santos', she says, her voice low and angry. 'They are one of my unfavourite companies.'

No doubt Santos' PR people would be saddened by her attitude. This plant is now solar-powered, a shift in industrial process that is mirrored by similar efforts to move the steelworks visible across the bay in Whyalla over to renewable energy. Yet it is difficult not to share her fury. The science tells us that to have any chance of avoiding catastrophic climate change, we must reach net negative emissions by the middle of the century, with at least half of that reduction taking place over the next decade. But despite the repeated, unequivocal warnings from scientists there is no sign of that happening. Instead global emissions have risen for the past three years, with much of the upward trend driven by increased consumption of coal and gas. Australia and Santos are key players in this process; indeed, as a report released in 2019 shows, Australia is now the world's third largest exporter of fossil fuels, its contribution to global supply only exceeded by those of Russia and Saudi Arabia.

IT IS EASY TO GIVE WAY TO THE FEELING THERE IS SOMEthing ancient about the denuded hills and empty spaces that make this region so striking. And in many ways, there is. Although the broken sheets of stone that form the beach are presumably more recent, much of this region is old even in geological terms, its low lines the remnants of formations that are not just hundreds of millions, but billions of years old. Not far inland from here, in the eroded granite hills of the Hiltaba Suite, geologists have found deposits that date back over three billion years. And to the north, in the Flinders Ranges, lie the Ediacara Hills, the rocks of which contain evidence of some of the earliest multicellular life, and which gave their name to the Ediacaran period (the hills are also central to the culture of the Adnyamathanha people, whose stories describe the origins of the fossils).

Yet in another sense this is a surprisingly new landscape. Unlike the deep water of the Southern Ocean, some 300 kilometres south of here, Spencer Gulf is surprisingly shallow, only rarely exceeding 30 metres in depth. In other words, until sea levels rose at the end of the last Glacial, only 10 000 years ago this region would not have been water but dry land, covered in grass and trees and criss-crossed by rivers.

No doubt there are still traces of that lost landscape somewhere below the sand and rock that now litter the Gulf's seabed. Gulf St Vincent, to the east, has a similar history, and as children growing up in Adelaide, Patrick and I would often find black, sulphurous mud beneath the sand offshore, a legacy of now-submerged wetlands and mangroves. For the most part, though, it has disappeared, erased by the rising waters.

Yet while it has disappeared it is not forgotten. The Nukunu people, whose Country extends north into the Flinders Ranges from the top of Spencer Gulf, tell stories of a time when the Gulf was still dry land. Speaking in Port Germein in the 1960s, Gilbert Bramfield said:

> There was a spring here one time, where there is a sandpit now. They camped there in the old days. They used to go over for fish from here right over to the Red Sea, the Kaaru-thatni according to the history of my old people. They left the children home, but these other people wouldn't let the children drink water out of the well, frightened they might put snot in. Burnt them with firesticks and hunted them away from the water. When the old people came back they got terribly wild. That is how one old man made this kangaroo bone, and made that sea right through this way. The bloke that went this way with his kangaroo bone he broke it at Port Augusta there, and then he was digging with a really short stumpy one and made all these lakes all the way through.

The Narungga people of Yorke Peninsula have similar traditions. Stories recorded in the 1920s describe a time when there was no water but 'only marshy country reaching into the interior of Australia', a description echoed in the stories of the Adnyamathanha, who say the Gulf was once a low valley containing a line of freshwater lagoons, each of which was the exclusive preserve of a species of bird.

The Narungga also have stories that echo Gilbert Bramfield's suggestion that the flooding of the Gulf coincided with a time of territorial conflict and intertribal violence, describing a dispute that arose because the birds of the region prohibited the other animals from drinking at their lagoons, leading to a protracted conflict in which 'many were killed, and large numbers of land-dwellers died of thirst'.

There is something vertiginous about the idea of stories describing events that happened more than 10 000 years ago. Yet even more striking is the fact that Indigenous culture has preserved detailed information about this now-vanished landscape. Jared Thomas, Gilbert Bramfield's great-grandnephew and curator of Aboriginal and Torres Strait Islander Art and Material Culture at the South Australian Museum, describes being told stories of now-submerged freshwater springs in the waters off Port Germein; likewise he speaks of stories describing a time when fresh water flowed through both Spencer Gulf and Gulf St Vincent, before reaching a waterfall where the continental shelf drops away at Kangaroo Island.

This correlation between Dreaming stories, and the landscape, takes many forms. In the northern Flinders Ranges the Adnyamathanha tell stories about the origin of the Ediacaran fossils and their ghostly record of the soft-bodied creatures of that ancient sea, while to the south, Nukunu stories speak to the contours of the landscape in deep and powerful ways. 'Water is central to Nukunu social organisation', explains Thomas:

> We're snake people, and the large carpet python, Wapma, is
> responsible for water. We see ourselves as the embodiment
> of Wapma. Wapma is responsible for the formation of the

landscape, the mountains, the creek beds, the lakes, aspects of the Gulf, but also the rain in the sky and the aquifers beneath the land. That's the reason we know about the springs, because of how closely we're connected to the water, we see its heart and know its veins.

When you look at the Flinders Ranges, they're some of the oldest rock formations in the world. Once they were below water, and the ranges are a combination of sedimentary deposits from when they were beneath the ocean, and uplifts. There are ripples in the rock scattered through the ranges, and in Saltia there's a big escarpment that shows the ripples from an ancient intertidal zone.

Our stories tell us of Wapma being water and forming these places, and the science tells us it actually was water that has formed these landscapes. Science tells us a particular story about the origin of the landscape. Dreaming stories tell us something similar, but there's always a human element embedded within them that supports emotional and social wellbeing, and the protection of flora, fauna, people and Country. Aboriginal people are scientists. Dreaming stories are based in observation.

Yet this knowledge of the landscape also gives rise to deep grief for the way it has been transformed. As Thomas says, 'the farmers graded over the creeks that connected the hills to the estuaries in the Gulf, and they dammed up one of the rivers, so the springs are depleted'.

IN THE LATE 1990s LOCAL FISHERS BEGAN TO TARGET THE cuttlefish congregation, taking advantage of the huge numbers present in the winter months. As the catch increased, concerns about the impact also grew, eventually resulting in a ban on fishing in the area. At first the cuttlefish population seemed to stabilise. But then, in 2005, divers reported a sudden and shocking decline in their numbers. Over the next few years numbers continued to fall until, by 2013, the 150 000 or more cuttlefish that had arrived each year around the turn of the century had dropped to less than 14 000.

Researchers were concerned the population might disappear altogether, but in 2014 numbers began to increase again. As of 2019 the population has yet to recover to the levels observed in the late 1990s, but for now at least, concerns about its imminent collapse have faded.

The cause of this precipitous decline and gradual recovery remains mysterious. Although abnormally warm water has the potential to adversely affect the cuttlefish's breeding cycle there does not seem to be a correlation between changes in water temperature and the fluctuation in numbers. Similarly there seems to be little correlation between the variations in population and factors such as increased turbidity and algal blooms that have the potential to affect the effectiveness of the cuttlefish's visual displays by reducing visibility in the water. Nor do increasing or decreasing populations of either predator or prey species seem to be involved.

It is possible, of course, that the fluctuations in population are cyclical. Animals with short lifespans like the cuttlefish are particularly vulnerable to changes to their environment, so a bad year can cause their numbers to fall with alarming rapidity, only to recover when conditions improve. But our inability to find a cause for these changes is a reminder that our understanding of these extraordinary creatures is far from complete.

What we do know is that the future holds deep uncertainties

for the cuttlefish that congregate in these waters. While the water temperatures in the Gulf are not rising as rapidly as they are on the eastern side of the continent, it seems safe to assume the water in the Gulf will grow warmer in decades to come, possibly placing more pressure on cuttlefish numbers. Ocean acidification driven by rising levels of atmospheric carbon dioxide may also pose a threat. One 2013 study showed more acid waters adversely affected the development of squid larvae and interfered with the development of the aragonite inner ear structures squid use to control their balance and movement. Although similar studies have not been conducted on cuttlefish, it seems likely their cuttlebones will be similarly weakened by more acid oceans.

Yet whatever happens, this landscape is already lost. Even conservative projections now predict sea levels will rise by a metre or more by the end of the century, and many glaciologists believe they will rise much further. This will devastate local mangroves and estuaries. As I stare out across the bay at the smokestacks of Whyalla or look back at the pale structure of Port Bonython, it is difficult not to wonder what pollutants will be released into the water as the sea invades this region and liberates the hidden legacies of a century-and-a-half of heavy industry from the soil.

In one sense this can be understood as simply the latest stage in the process of destruction that began with European invasion almost 200 years ago, a testament to the heedlessness and lack of regard that has destroyed ecosystems and cultures from one end of the continent to the other. Yet it is more than that as well. The backloaded nature of the climate system means this sea-level rise is already unstoppable, inescapable, and so too is the destruction it will bring. And so, just as this landscape bears within itself the memory of other, far older landscapes, it also contains this future landscape.

In this it illustrates the way in which climate change deranges temporality, collapsing geological and human time into each other, and freighting not just the past, but also this now-unavoidable future with grief and loss.

But perhaps there is also something else to be seen here, something more. For these rising waters are also part of a much longer cycle, one that extends back not just into the Pleistocene, but much further again. And just as the low hills and rock faces and ancient fossils that lie inland connect us to the deep past of the Ediacaran, reminding us of the way time inheres in the landscape, the brief lives and annual breeding swarm of the cuttlefish remind us of the ways these natural cycles overlap and interact, of the impossible depth of planetary time.

This process is made tangible in the bodies of the cuttlefish as well. The British writer Caspar Henderson has observed that as nautiloids grow, they add chambers to their shells, building them a little at a time, a process recorded in tiny laminations in their shells. In modern nautiloids there are twenty-eight or twenty-nine such laminations in every chamber, each one corresponding to a day's growth, the whole corresponding to one lunar month.

Yet when we examine the shells of their Palaeozoic ancestors we find only eight or nine laminations in each chamber. This is not because they grew more slowly, but because their shells offer a physical memory of a time when the Moon was much closer to the Earth and a lunar month was little more than a week in length.

The cuttlefish in these waters are a living link to that deep past, their fugitive presence transporting us back to the oceans of another age and suggesting that intelligence – that quality we pride so much about ourselves – is not a recent phenomenon, but has instead existed for hundreds of millions of years. To contemplate those alien minds moving through the seas of the Palaeozoic and the Mesozoic, or the ocean of time that separates us from them, is to come up against the fragility and contingence of human existence. Yet just as the depth of time embodied in the cultures of the Nukunu, Narungga and

Adnyamathanha, and the complex webs of story that connect them to the country offer a glimpse of a different way of being, one attendant to the land and its history, the fact a creature so utterly dissimilar to ourselves might be capable of complex cognition serves as a reminder not just of the extraordinary diversity of life on this planet, but also the degree to which we, and all of it, are connected to each other.

Readings

Peter Godfrey-Smith, *Other Minds: The Octopus and the Evolution of Intelligent Life*, Harper Collins, London, 2017.

Caspar Henderson, *The Book of Barely Imagined Beings: A 21st Century Bestiary*, Granta Books, London, 2013.

Luise A Hercus, *A Nukunu Dictionary*, Australian Institute of Aboriginal Studies, Canberra, 1992.

Patrick Nunn, *The Edge of Memory: Ancient Stories, Oral Tradition and the Post-glacial World*, Bloomsbury, London, 2018.

S Paige-Ogburn, 'Ocean Acidification Hurts Squid, Too', *Scientific American*, 3 June 2013.

MA Steer, S Gaylard and M Loo, *Monitoring the Relative Abundance and Biomass of South Australia's Giant Cuttlefish Breeding Population, Final Report for the Fisheries Research and Development Corporation*, South Australian Research and Development Institute (Aquatic Sciences), Adelaide. SARDI Publication No. F2013/000074-1. SARDI Research Report Series No. 684, 2013.

REGENERATING
COUNTRY

POSE, YOUR FUTURE DESCENDANTS ARE WATCHING

Ellen van Neerven

In 1824, organised theft of land and cultural genocide of First Nations people began on the land now known as south-east Queensland – the land of the Yagera, Turrubal, Jinibara, Yugambeh, Bundjalung, Wakka Wakka, Gubbi Gubbi, Noonuccal, Joondaburri, Ningy Ningy and Ugarapul nations.

In June 1859, Queen Victoria of England authorised the separation of northern lands from New South Wales, establishing the new colony of Queensland.

In February 2019, I move back to live with my parents in my Meanjin (so-called Brisbane) childhood home. I come back from busy years in Naarm (so-called Melbourne). My mum and dad have been living in Mparntwe (so-called Alice Springs) for the last six years, and have just started their retirement. At first, being back is strange for all of us, but we slowly settle in.

My parents give me the room underneath the house, where I have a view of the bush out the back. The sun wakes me every morning. My writing table is outside.

There are changes I observe with my parents. More geira (sulphur-crested cockatoos) fly over the house, their sharp squawks impossible to ignore. I don't remember many of them when I was last living here, a decade ago. Neither does my dad. But we remember other birds, smaller birds, that we no longer see. We see fewer insects in the backyard.

I have other conversations with my blackfella and People of Colour friends of a similar age, millennial babes through and through. We've been told that people, animals, plants and the rest of the living must 'keep pace with climate change', keep 'evolving', keep adapting to the changing world. We speculate about the frightening changes we will observe in our lifetime. Should we have children? Would it be responsible of us? Could humankind become extinct in our or their lifetime? Should we live in a state of panic or try to enjoy the last days of the world as we know it? Which would be the most respectful to our ancestors? What would a post-human world mean in an Aboriginal way? As a coping strategy, we dissociate from climate crisis through music.

I grieve the colonisation of my people and fear that the efforts we have taken to recover and revive our culture will be 'too late' as human-created environmental change has rapid effects on our land and waterways. As I learn more from my Elders and peers, as Yugambeh rolls its way onto my tongue, I think, is the little I'm doing enough? Maybe that's just shame and guilt talking, two emotions so easily pushed onto a colonised people's psyche.

It takes a while before I activate the real question I want to ask. How can we heal and recover from the past while at the same time preparing for a dangerous future? Can one lead to another?

It does help, talking to my friends, realising that I am having normal emotional responses to the circumstances we live in, that they also feel torn up, anxious, exhausted and unprepared. I feel my energies scattered between those two disciplines of healing and preparing.

The intergenerational conversations I have with my parents are slightly different. In the living room where we have our dinner, the TV flicks over one commercial channel to another – segments on fish dying in the Murray-Darling Basin, 40 per cent of insect species threatened, ocean acidification, habitat loss, floods, droughts, blizzards. I explain dugai terms like 'Anthropocene' all the while knowing that western science has never added value to Indigenous peoples' lives. We are creating our own language around this, my parents and I, embodied through our bush walks. We walk at the back of the house, and sometimes we fill a few water flasks, pack extra strong mints and go for a drive, walk the familiar spots we used to do when my brother and I were young. I am happy to be home. I am happy to be where my ancestors come from, belonging to this place, responsible to this place, in dialogue with this place.

When the settler-invaders came to the east coast they not only committed crimes of rape, murder, torture and brutality to Country and people, they also became narrative terrorists, a branch of terrorism that still goes strong today. The settler-invaders attempted to destroy all evidence of technology, occupation and culture – that mob were here, are here, that they built, lived and loved here. They did their best to rub an eraser over the land and claim it as their own. Remains and cultural objects stolen were taken to museums all over the world or kept in private collections. But Aboriginal people knew they could never destroy everything; traces, connections, sovereignty remained, and all will be returned in time.

Farmers concealed or destroyed items found on their farms. Evidence like tools, huts, fishing nets, compasses and burial sites were destroyed or made their way to the strange storage rooms of museums. After the landmark Mabo decision in 1992, farmers again hunted their properties for evidence of occupation.

In 2017, a Victorian farmer was fined $20 000 for intentionally harming Aboriginal artefacts. In the same year, more than 130 Tasmanian Aboriginal stone tools were seized in Sydney as part of an investigation into the illegal online sales of cultural material. In 2018, the Clarence Valley Council in northern New South Wales was fined $300 000 for destroying a culturally significant Aboriginal scar tree in Grafton. The tree held cultural significance for the local Gumbaynggirr and Bundjalung people and was registered on the Aboriginal Sites Register in 1995, making it an offence to harm or desecrate the tree. The loss of the tree cannot be quantified.

What non-Indigenous people kept and recorded served their narrative purpose. Whitefellas became the 'experts' on our lives, anatomy, land and everything that lived on it. At the time of writing, in 2019, they are not ready to give up that title. During the nineteenth century, archaeology developed out of antiquarianism in Europe, and spread across the world. Archaeology is used by authoritarian bodies to shape certain visions of a past. Tensions between First Nations peoples and archaeologists arise for several reasons. Archaeologists tend to position these objects as belonging to a faraway past, while First Nations peoples believe that disturbing these places has consequences for the present.

It has only been in recent years that museums are opening their doors to community for items to be viewed, being transparent with what they own, and sometimes repatriating remains in collaboration with community, the result of many years of resistance and advocacy. The ceremony of returning of artefacts might be one step towards healing for a community.

Australia's narrative terrorism manifests in legislation that does not recognise contemporary Aboriginal culture, conveniently failing to believe in an ancient/modern continuum and that the diversity of Aboriginal experience is as diverse as the population. Instead, stereotypes prevail. We don't belong in museums.

Eualeyai and Kamillaroi writer and lawyer Larissa Behrendt's book *Finding Eliza* exposes mythmaking in colonial storytelling. Eliza Fraser fraudulently claimed to have been captured by the local Aboriginal people, the Butchulla/Badtjala people. Her narrative terrorism led to the massacre and dispossession of the local people. Today, the island, whose traditional name is K'Gari, is named Fraser Island, after Eliza Fraser, though traditional owners are campaigning for naming rights and still fighting today against the colonial story that has done such damage.

'The Eliza Fraser stories', writes Djugun woman Georgia Mokak in her article about Behrendt's book, 'are the perfect example of how stories have been used by Europeans for their own purposes or for institutional purposes, and how they create the ongoing stereotypes of Indigenous people in Australia and across the world. Any truths surrounding Eliza's relations with the Badtjala peoples were very hastily sacrificed for the traditions of the dramatic tale'.

For mob growing up in suburbs like mine, the erasure – whether at school, or the supermarket – is compounding. Extending beyond the imposed built environment, there's a deeper disregard for Country. It took me a while to figure out that a lot of my neighbours, teachers and classmates live their lives simply 'forgetting' they are on Aboriginal land. I witness this psychosis, the green and gold haze of Southern Cross tattoos and Australian flags.

'Paris Syndrome' is the name used to describe the condition that affects some people when they visit Paris for the first time. In reality, Paris is nothing like the glamorous city that the media shows. Tourists suffering Paris Syndrome can feel shell-shocked by the clash of fantasy and reality, and sometimes they become so sick they need to be hospitalised.

Call it 'Australia Syndrome', the relationship that non-

Indigenous people have with the land. The culture shock of being on Aboriginal land, the clash of fantasy and reality. Where are we?

On one rainy afternoon, I sit at my laptop under the deck, water pouring down. A pair of geira fly in the soft grey sky.

I fill all gaps in my life with music. I obsessively scout artists from Australia, Africa, Europe, Asia and the Americas to build playlists. The general theme is dance to decolonisation through alternative jazz, electronica and hip-hop. I fall in step with Baker Boy from north-east Arnhem Land who raps in Yolngu and English. Laura Mvula, Nakhane, Sudan Archives, and Yaeji. I imagine playing this playlist on the last night of Earth, inviting all my blackfella and POC millennial friends, dancing till the sun comes up.

Arlo Parks (Nigeria/Chad/England) sings 'We're a super sad generation/Killing time/ … And trying to keep our friends from death'. For millennial babes, the internet is a flawless distraction. Being oppressed people without land rights but with high speed internet is a strange thing. One of the first things colonisers do is take language and culture and prohibit the channels for obtaining knowledge. Knowledge is power. But there are question marks about whether the internet really holds knowledge, and therefore power. Whether it really does connect us with each other. We can draw on many examples where it helped us organise our resistance. But we haven't called each other in so long. Remember what our Elders achieved talking on the phone, twirling that cord with one hand – and before the phone.

Responses to the global climate crisis on the internet seem enticing but often leave me feeling hollow. I think about the strangeness of a meditation selfie. Decolonisation is a hashtag.

After watching a documentary with Mum on Netflix about two white men who claim to be saving the world by spreading the word of minimalism, living more with less, I spend hours looking at #Blackminimalism, a movement of mainly British and American women from the African diaspora. I find myself on websites shopping for sports bras made from recycled plastic bottles and scouring for plant-based skin care. 'This minimalism thing is actually encouraging you to buy', Mum points out. So much for these movements being anti-consumerism and anti-capitalism. I get sucked into one Instagram vortex after another, looking at the beautiful black, brown, Asian and white faces that offered solutions to a crisis in consciousness. Are they doing it for the 'Gram or doing it for the planet? It doesn't matter. I go vegan in Feb, plastic-free in March, and my parents roll their eyes, asking what will be next.

After countless hours opening tabs, I finally shut my laptop down. I live each day knowing how precarious life is. I live in the past to comfort our ancestors who have experienced so much pain. I haunt-walk through my existence. It is my radical longing that I'm afraid of, so much that I push it aside. As a young queer Blak person, I want more.

The photo series *Pose, Your Future Descendants Are Watching* (see <everydayfutures.com.au>) grew as the answer to my self-imposed question: how can we recover from the past while at the same preparing for a dangerous future? Can one lead to another?

I replant evidence of our occupation, crafting living objects as evidence of our historic and current occupation. This act resists the colonial narrative. My parents get on board. Together, we craft a soft basket with a clutch handle of tea tree sticks joined together by dyed and natural twine, a digging stick standing to my shoulders, and a coolamon to position on Country. These are items that not only heal a past but also prepare for a future. They are used to source food and water, to dig, to carry, material in balance with Country, without separation.

My parents generously drop what they were doing to help me make these pieces. Mum misses watching the Oscars and Dad misses working around the house. They observe my survival. Their labour is one of love and support. As I watch them flow into work without hesitation or complaint I reflect on the Lebanese poet Khalil Gibran's quote, 'work is love made visible'. Our childhood home came alive with the sounds of carving, weaving and painting. The television was regulated for the moment, the computer sat idle.

When I pick at the scabs on my knees, my blood smells like the bush. Finding the right tools in our present environment and at our disposal: sometimes it was a rock, sometimes it was a knife in the kitchen. Black American author Audre Lorde said, 'The master's tools will never dismantle the master's house'. It is more essential than ever that we move beyond the coloniser's logic and reach outside the toolbox. Micah White, co-founder of Occupy Wall Street, says, 'Let's reclaim our stolen tools'. We can free our minds with the right tools. When I walk through the bush with refreshed eyes (refresh that doesn't involve a scrolling finger), I feel a sense of creative control. While planning and gathering materials for these objects and crafting them with my parents, my eyes change, my mind shifts. I feel calmer, my anxiety levels are lower. No matter what has been done here, no matter what continues to happen, I will never stop thinking of this place as home.

I made my first toothbrush out of macaranga. My teeth and the plant acquaint in my mouth and my gums bleed into the wood. When we are not recognised, we are not well. We are cultural materiality.

When I ask Mum what the living artefacts we have crafted mean to her, she talks about the artificial environment, and machine-made things in our current era. She points to the digging stick, the coolamon and the basket. 'They have no idea what it is and that it is still important, it's still used today', she says, referring to the non-Indigenous gaze.

Mum chooses blue as the central colour of the living objects. We paint the digging stick a bright blue. This represents the past and the future, survival, diversity and visibility. The three of us were wearing that same shade of blue on the day we crafted these objects. The cool-amon carries painted macadamia nuts and gum nuts, in the colours of electric blue and white, as well as gum leaves. The basket is made of electric blue felt. When Mum chose blue, which made the objects stand out, I knew I also had to choose to take these objects with me, instead of leaving them behind to be found as I had planned. They were still being found. We had made them, and we had found them at the same time.

Pose, our future descendants are watching. Only crack out a smile if you want to. Watching us IRL, not through a screen. There is no need to smile if we don't want to, but pose, pose, pose, because pose indicates purpose. We are living for them, we have made these things for them, we have crafted these things for them.

This futurepast evidence all swings back – let our future be our past and our past will be our future. Our ancestors become our dece-dants. Our descendants are our dependents. Those descendants use that stick to pull out them weeds, they take that basket to carry tucker to give to their family. They take that coolamon to carry water from that river that's well cared for now, and they hold it above their head to shelter from the healing rain. Neighbours continue to share mate-rials and feelings.

Readings

Larissa Behrendt, *Finding Eliza: Power and Colonial Storytelling*, University of Queensland Press, Brisbane, 2016.

Georgia Mokak, 'Cannibals and Savages: The Power of Colonial Storytelling', *NITV*, 5 September 2017, <www.sbs.com.au/nitv/article/2017/08/29/cannibals-and-savages-power-colonial-storytelling>.

IWATA

Kate Wright

For the past five years I have been immersed in a postdoctoral research project that has involved collaborating with Aboriginal people to cultivate a community garden on land that used to be part of the East Armidale Aboriginal Reserve, New South Wales.

Following the extremely violent pastoral expansion of the 1830s, Aboriginal people in the newly named 'New England' region had been largely dispossessed from their Anaiwan, Dunghutti, Gamilaroi Gumbaynggirr and Ngarabal homelands, and were forced to travel like fugitives throughout the country. Across Australia, Aboriginal people were relentlessly 'moved on' by authorities from places of settlement and were left with little choice but to camp on the outskirts of town. In the 1950s, Aboriginal people began to settle on the Armidale town dump in an attempt to glean whatever materials they could from the rubbish to create shelter from the bitterly cold winters. In November 1958, with over 100 people living in tents and shacks on top of the contaminated soils of the dump, with one unreliable tap to service everyone, no electricity, and no sewerage, the area was declared the East Armidale Aboriginal Reserve.

From the outset my commitment to the community garden project has been an intensely personal one. The community garden is in my home town (it is about 800 metres from where I went to primary school), and yet, growing up, I never learned anything about the Aboriginal Reserve's history. As Elders shared with me intimate accounts of their childhoods spent on the reserve, filled with profoundly moving experiences of racism and dispossession, it forced me to confront the fact that my places of intimate habitation, the places where I grew to understand myself and the world, are scarred by a genocidal and ecocidal past. As I listened to Elders describe being forbidden from speaking language, scavenging material for tin humpies from the white people's rubbish dump to create shelter from below-freezing winters, and childhood memories of hiding from the Welfare Board so they wouldn't be taken from their families, my physical response, my profoundly affected body, drew me into a new relationship of responsibility. I felt for the first time that I had lived my life on stolen land. I had known that for a long time, but now I *felt* it. It was in the midst of this encounter with the troubling histories of my hometown that Anaiwan Elder Uncle Steve Widders mentioned to me that he would like to cultivate a community garden on the old East Armidale Aboriginal Reserve site, and I asked if I could help. The community garden opened in May 2015, and is now managed by the Anaiwan Language Revival Program.

Aboriginal reserves and missions were established across Australia to confine and control Aboriginal people. Within these segregated sites the speaking of ancestral languages, Aboriginal cultural practices and the hunting of traditional foods were banned. At the East Armidale Aboriginal Reserve, the colonial 'rubbishing' of Aboriginal culture was accompanied by a rubbishing of the environment, with the toxicity of the surrounding garbage dump contributing to the appalling living conditions at the reserve, leading to many preventable deaths in the community.

We are living in the midst of an environmental crisis that is inextricably tied to troubling histories of colonial violence. Questions of environmental recuperation in this era are therefore fundamentally entangled with issues of social justice and decolonisation.

The community garden is a site of Indigenous environmental and cultural rehabilitation, revival and reclamation. The garden brings people, plants and non-human critters together, creating an alternative space where decolonial stories about the past, present and future can be told.

In August 2015, the community garden welcomed a new inhabitant – 'Iwata', a living sculpture of an echidna. Iwata is the Anaiwan name for echidna, and the echidna is one of the Anaiwan's totems. Iwata changed my relationship to the community garden, and she continues to be a generative force in my own, and perhaps in other community garden visitors', thinking.

The sculpture is the result of a community arts project in which local artist Jeremy Rudge worked together with Aboriginal high school and primary school students to create an echidna with spines that are made of lomandra grasses, traditionally used in weaving, and a body that is composed of living soil – a multiplicity of minerals coalescing with organic fragments of the bodies of the living and the dead. Iwata's spines have now grown as tall as me, and it would take four adults holding hands to encircle her round body. Her face is made of sculpted tin, with a long and pointy nose that beckons ants to tempt her. In the summer sun her spines are green, in the winter twilight they are a luminous yellow.

As a manifestation of connectivity and healing, Iwata articulates the more-than-human alliances that are forming in the community garden and brings with her a feeling of warmth and cultural safety.

Iwata is ancient and imminent; she is ancestral but created by the young. She is alive, but she is not singular. She is a heaving multitemporal sea of becomings, and she is a focal point for visitors to the community garden to begin to encounter the incommensurate belonging of Aboriginal people to this land.

I find myself unable to enter the garden without saying hello to Iwata. And I am incredibly proud of my ability to help cultivate and sustain her. As I continue to strive to decolonise my thinking and my life, Iwata is a guiding force – a teacher for how I might learn to live well in the ruins of capitalism and colonialism, and how I can help heal this wounded place. As her spines continue to grow, my labour and the labour of my friends and colleagues weaves our lives into this pocket of land, like a basket made of lomandra grasses. And Iwata is growing alongside us and our garden. In a minoritarian, material language she grounds our experimental hopes in the earth, enunciating our commitments to community and Country.

HIDDEN ECOLOGIES OF A WEATHERBOARD WALL

George Main

The doors are opened wide. Today will be hot. Noises blend inside the old building. Cicadas in creekside trees, the humming fridge, transient blowflies. On the wall outside, bright summer light bounces from overlapping planks of timber, horizontal, painted white. Between the red earth and the galvanised iron roof are nineteen rows of pine weatherboards, each about two hands wide. Sometime in the late 1890s, builders hammered square-headed nails into the boards, the fresh planks exuding the sharp scent of resin, to construct the dining room wall. The great table remains, where shearers gathered on lengthy benches, bodies aching and tired, after hard days in the woolshed, a short walk away, across the paddock.

I examine one timber plank. My eyes and hand follow the flowing grain, streaming like river water around circular knots, each an island, recalling the passage of seasons when this wood stood upright, damp with sap, growing within a tall and vigorous white cypress pine, extending branches of blue-green foliage, shady roosts for white-winged choughs, mudlarks and magpies, bursting pollen clouds into spring winds, a tower of plenitude for a variety of ants. The old timber board, its streaming grain, its rounded knots, its cracks and thick white paint, murmurs of passing time, of the living and the dead.

White cypress pine, *Callitris glaucophylla*, garraa or burradhaa in Wiradjuri, grows across much of inland Australia. Unlike other trees indigenous to this district, on the western slopes of the Great Divide in southern New South Wales, beside the narrow, twisting channel of Pinchgut Creek, white cypress cannot tolerate fire. Unlike kurrajong, yellow box and wattle, flame swiftly kills young pine. Wiradjuri people frequently coaxed fire across these gentle hillsides and creek flats. Fire, strategically applied, kept Country open and grassy. Yams, chocolate lilies and other edible tubers flowered and flourished amid a perennial pasture of kangaroo grass.

A willy-willy dances down the dry slope, a twisting column of dust, as I drive along the fence line, towards the tall and stately pine. I park near the dam and walk across the paddock. My shadow is short, the midday sun above. The shallow creek curves around the tree, standing alone. Butterflies rise as I enter the dense shade, a refuge from the intense sunlight and heat. The billowing north-westerly finds a voice in the feathery foliage. At the base of the wide, furrowed trunk, the compressed surface of grey-red soil is splattered with bird droppings, dispatched from high roosts. Exposed, weathered roots radiate outwards, cradling low tufts of wallaby grass, their fluffy flower heads tossed by the wind. Near the crown, catching the warm breeze, a pair of magpies await the evening cool.

Bark has regrown across a long, deep scar. I peer through the narrow opening, wondering if I might see the weathered remnants of patterns carved into heartwood with a stone or metal hatchet, the artful markings of a grave. Perhaps the tree is not that old. It could have germinated in the 1850s, after squatter John Hurley and his stockmen seized this fertile terrain. Across the region, regular burning ended when Wiradjuri clans lost control of their Country. Within decades, dense forests dominated by the fire-sensitive white cypress pine replaced the open, grassy woodlands stocked with cattle and sheep. Pastoralists urged the colonial government to 'take steps to have this great evil removed'. In a letter to the *Sydney Morning Herald*, one 'old squatter' who had owned 'large squatting properties' described the capacity of fire to solve the problem of the spreading pine:

> There is no kind of scrub so easily destroyed and got rid of as pine scrub, simply because the tree is resiniferous, and the least scorching by fire kills the young scrub, and when once scorched it will never grow again from the roots. A bush fire kills all pine scrub it comes in contact with; but generally the grass is too valuable, and some people would much prefer to have pine scrub on the run than lose even one season's grass in fire.

A pastoral inspector came here in February 1894. He described the country as 'undulating box country, with a few belts of pine, and in parts open', with grasses 'of a fattening nature' growing 'where timber has been long killed'. Pastoralists had discovered a method to destroy the new forests. Gangs of men with sharp axes cleaved belts of sapwood from around the trunks, halting the flow of moisture and nutrients upward into branches. 'A good deal of the country has not been very long ring-barked', the inspector noted, 'and the trees are still throwing out suckers, which require constant attention. This the overseer Mr Dunn seems to be thoroughly alive to. When these suckers have been destroyed thoroughly, the carrying capabilities of the country will be slightly increased'.

Thousands of emptied brown seedpods lie scattered beneath the pine, crunching under my boots. Some appear chewed, perhaps by hungry galahs or superb parrots. Most of the winged seeds, I imagine, had escaped beaks. On the branches in late spring or early summer, pods had opened, scattering their contents across the paddock below. Despite the record heat and dryness, the tree is sprouting fresh foliage, new stems holding tiny green seedpods. The old pine will try again to reproduce. Nowhere in sight does a single white cypress pine sapling grow.

The neighbouring paddock to the west, my father remembers, was called 'The Pines', though it held few pine trees. Across the region, sweeping stands of white cypress pine were felled to supply building timber. Renowned for its termite resistance and durability, as polished floor and ceiling boards the timber glows in honeyed tones. 'Bill's Camp' was a nearby paddock. Bill was a timber getter. In the late 1930s, he felled and milled timber for a new homestead, built on a stony rise for my father's parents.

On my drive back to the shearers' quarters I pass a small plantation of pines, a rectangular formation on the western boundary. Molly, my father's aunt, planted these trees, fifty or more years ago. The steady disappearance from her beloved paddocks of the graceful white cypress pines had saddened her. Purchasing the seedlings, and planting them inside a barbed wire and netting enclosure, she strove to maintain the character of country she cherished.

It is unthinkable that Molly saw the stately pine trees in her paddocks as markers of a brutal transition, of a forced end to millennia-old practices of tending land, of the profound shift from an 'Organic mindset to our society's dominant Mechanical world view', as regenerative farmer Charles Massy describes the cultural revolution imposed across inland Australia by colonisation. Likewise, it is unthinkable that neighbouring farmers using powerful tractors to uproot the few remaining pines in cropping paddocks, to make way for ever-widening farming equipment, could know the monumental history held by these trees. Here, our past is hidden.

Back at the quarters, I try to grasp the poetic meanings skittling through the old, cracked weatherboards that form the dining room wall. Such walls sheltered my family. They sheltered the shearers and other rural workers whom my family engaged, including descendants of Wiradjuri men and women who survived frontier diseases and warfare, survivors of the same tumultuous history that gave rise to the pine scrubs. Now they are sheltering me, from the hot north-westerly, as I write and think about the Anthropocene, informed by the expressive materiality of Country.

Last year I walked up the creek with a friend. She was staying at the shearers' quarters, finishing a thesis about the history of Yuwaalaraay Country in northern New South Wales. As we passed a clump of aged red gums, their sturdy bases stained by resting water, I explained the source of the name given to this property, Retreat. In the early days of pastoral settlement, squatters established their headquarters beside major waterways. Here, where we walked, far removed from the Murrumbidgee River, near hills from which creeks begin long and winding descents to the Lachlan River, herds of feral horses found water and refuge, beside the expansive swamp on Pinchgut Creek. Not only horses, my friend suggested, gathered here to escape threats posed by squatters and their men. Wiradjuri knew well these places where feral horses came. It is likely they called this place Yarramalang, which according to a recently published Wiradjuri dictionary means 'place of wild horses'.

In the 1980s, Tom and Anne lived in a small cottage, walled and floored in white cypress pine, beside Pinchgut Creek, with their three sons. Tom was employed as a farmhand, responsible mostly for the sheep and cattle. Each morning he drove up to Retreat homestead with a white enamel bucket of warm milk, drawn by his hands from the udder of a milking cow, its head bailed to the trunk of an ancient yellow box tree, its roots branching out towards the dark swamp earth. With a smile as broad as his Scottish accent, Tom told stories of digging calves from deep snow, before migrating to Australia. One night inside the cottage, the family watched a television program about Aboriginal heritage sites. Later they told the farm manager about a circular arrangement of stones beside the swamp on Pinchgut Creek, not far from the cottage. The unusual, curving line of single, rounded stones looked very similar, Tom said, to the stone arrangements they had seen on television.

The poet Mary Gilmore, who grew up in the region, remembered Wiradjuri gatherings beside swampland, where hunting restrictions ensured plentiful supplies. She described in *Old Days, Old Ways* a gathering of about 300 men, women and children alongside the swamps of Morangarell, roughly a two-day walk north of Retreat, in 1879:

> It was only half the number expected, as those from the Lachlan could not get across in time, owing to drought. It was held at Morangarell, the home of my father's cousins, the McGregors. There I saw the last Gundagai chief. The blacks had called the meeting of the localized tribes, expecting and knowing it would be the last they would ever hold.

An arrangement of stones beside Pinchgut Creek. Hatchet heads and grinding stones on low rises above the swamp. Stories passed down of trees marked to indicate graves. Flakes of worked stone on creek banks. The hard-baked remains of earth ovens. Fragments of ochre. Here, people gathered to develop strategies of resistance and adaptation. They had witnessed, or heard told, the behaviours of newcomers bound to the burgeoning industrial culture of western Europe, of squatters and their workers driven by the insistent machinations of globalised capital and trade, freed by the tenets of Enlightenment science to harness and transform Wiradjuri Country for commercial production.

LAST NIGHT A THUNDERSTORM DROPPED A FEW MILLIMETRES of heavy rain, clearing the air and settling the dust. After lunch I drive west, through an expanse of sun-bleached stubble, rippling in the heat. About 30 kilometres from Retreat, as the crow flies, extends Mimosa Station Road. On either side of the long ribbon of dirt, large signs assert ownership of vast tracts by a single company: 'BFB. Logistics. Agriculture'. The logo shows an arc of green crop transforming into a sweep of bitumen road. Produce efficiently trucked away to distant markets, the imagery suggests. Owned by a Canadian superannuation fund, BFB owns almost 50 000 hectares (about 120 000 acres) of farmland in the region, a conglomeration of twenty-eight farms once held by individual families. The company is renowned for the scale of its broadacre grain production. When BFB buys another family farm, workers demolish internal fencing and push down paddock trees. No sheep or cattle are grazed. Across the opened country, operators of towering machines use satellite GPS systems to apply tremendous quantities of synthetic fertiliser, herbicide, insecticide and fungicide to grow cereal and oilseed crops.

Clumps of western silver wattle, *Acacia decora*, grow beside Mimosa Station Road. The shrubs carry brown pods of ripened seed, and I stop to collect some. We have successfully planted many of these hardy shrubs on Retreat. Perhaps this variety of wattle gave Mimosa Station its name, in the nineteenth century, when people called *Acacia* species either wattle or mimosa. Further along, where another BFB sign stands before the stretching stubble, the spiked tufts of spreading flax lily stand alongside the wire mesh fence. Known as nidbul in Wiradjuri, its long leaves comprise strong silky fibres, and are valued for weaving.

I turn onto the laneway that leads down to the abandoned settlement of Mimosa, near the large station homestead of brick walls and shaded verandahs. The village grew beside the homestead after the subdivision of the great pastoral run into a patchwork of small farms in 1906. Thickets of white cypress pine, of varied ages and sizes, bustle inward as I drive along the narrow lane. Their abundance is surprising, as if the community of trees rejoice, in a recent end to burning, as if a depth of time has dissolved. I park beside an interpretive sign. 'Mimosa Station', the sign tells, 'was originally held by Messrs Macansh and Windeyer in 1857 and consisted of approximately 246 000 acres.'

In her poem 'The Hunter of the Black', first published in 1930, Mary Gilmore centres a chilling story here, on Mimosa Station. 'I heard it when it happened', claimed Gilmore, recalling the talk of her father and other men, overheard as a child. The poem describes the work and reputation of a killer, hired by 'him who stole the country' to shoot a Wiradjuri man 'who killed a sheep'. Through the scrubs and pastures of Mimosa, 'three days and nights he tracked him, never asking sleep'. Across the region, pastoralists and their workmen considered the skilled mercenary 'something like a king'. When warfare finally ended, silence shrouded his bloodied legacy.

> Tomahawk in belt, as only adult needed shot,
> No man knew how many notches totalled up his lot;
> But old stockman striking tallies, rough and ready made,
> Reckoned on at least a thousand, naming camps decayed.

> Time passed on, and years forgotten whitened with the dust;
> He whose hands were red with slaughter sat among the just,
> Kissed the children of his children, honoured in his place,
> Turned and laid him down in quiet, asking God his grace.

Downhill from the derelict Baptist church, I face Mimosa homestead, and read aloud the entire poem. In a nearby paddock, beyond the old cricket ground, a giant red tractor rumbles past, raising a cloud of dust. I turn towards the church. Along the decrepit wall of white cypress pine weatherboards, a row of gothic windows have lost their delicate framework and glass. The dark shapes point skyward, stare blankly at the ruined village. Inside, the polished floor and wall linings are all pine. Did the soulful singing of those who had known the hired killer engaged by Mimosa Station reverberate within these timbers? Did the singing of the elderly killer himself, of accomplices and perpetrators of atrocity, carry through these windows?

Late in the nineteenth century, the loss of wide stands of valuable building timber, as ringbarking teams converted pine forests into wheat paddocks, raised concerns. Timber reserves, proclaimed and managed by the colonial government, were a solution. A short drive west of the decaying structures of Mimosa village lies Currajong State Forest, a long rectangle of cypress pine trees, peppered with yellow and grey box, amid the uniform spread of industrial farmland. Maps of the Robertson Parish over time show the forest is a tiny remnant of the expansive Currajong Timber Reserve, resumed from Mimosa Station in 1878. As the spreading network of railways bolstered the economic viability of wheat farming across the southern inland slopes of New South Wales, the pressure to unlock the reserved swathe of pines for agriculture was unstoppable.

I drive down Currajong Lane and turn into the state forest. 'Tree Felling in Operation' declares a warning sign fixed to a pine trunk. There are no fresh tracks, so I keep going. Some of the stumps are old and weathered. Others are fresh. Machines have recently disturbed the earth and tousled the forest. Harvesting and thinning is underway, it appears. Stacks of pine logs await trucking to the saw mill. The warm afternoon air is pungent with cypress resin, a sticky substance long used to fix sharpened stones to handles and spears. Golden drops of the sticky substance, hardened by summer heat, decorate the sawn ends of each log.

MY BROTHER ASKS ME TO CHECK THE COWS AND CALVES. THE Weather Bureau forecasts a top temperature of 42. Late morning, the thermometer in the kitchen registers 39. I drive through the paddock gate and follow the fence around to the dam, to make sure that no cattle are stuck. Crows fly between yellow box trees, crying to each other. In the soft, muddy verge, a pattern of deep hoof prints frames the circular pool of brown water. Small wasps, orange with black stripes, land gently on the water's surface, drink momentarily, and depart.

I continue driving, staying close to the fence. Grasshoppers with yellow wings whisk across the bonnet. I recall driving through summer paddocks with my grandfather, a blue plastic fan mounted to the dashboard of his Holden ute, small seedpods of thistles working their way into the cabin through the opened air vents. The cows and their calves are in good condition. Despite the heat they look content, resting in the dappled shade thrown by yellow box. The drinking trough gurgles, slowly refilling with water pumped through an endless maze of pipes from bores on the Murrumbidgee River floodplain, stored in cement tanks on hilltops throughout the region.

Near the trough, fleabane, thistles and pademelons grow across furrows. After my grandfather died, Retreat was managed by a farm consultant, then leased to local farmers. Now my brother, a regenerative grazing enthusiast, runs part of the property. During the industrial farming phase of the past forty years, beneath the soil surface, repeated tillage and the application of synthetic fertilisers, fungicides and other chemicals destroyed a teeming and diverse community of micro-organisms, bacteria and fungi. The long, branching, tube-like forms of different fungal species are especially valuable. Soil fungi protect plants from disease, retain and transfer crucial nutrients, and form passages that allow the flow of air and water. Ten years ago, where we fenced the creek and planted trees and shrubs, fungal networks began to slowly rebuild. The thin feeding tubes of fungi are easily crushed. Now we drive only along fence lines and established tracks. Agricultural chemicals that harm soil biology are no longer applied to Retreat paddocks. Strategic, regenerative grazing methods are reactivating water and mineral cycles, and fostering the return of a diversity of species, above and below ground. Soil carbon levels are restoring. Fungi creep back through the red earth.

Back at the kitchen table, I inspect a grey, heavy stone, a multi-purpose tool. One end is ground smooth on either side into a hatchet blade. As well as the sharpened end, both sides of the hatchet head carry deep pits, perhaps used to steady timber being worked, to make fire, or open hard shells protecting quandong kernels. I found the stone last year, beside stone flakes and pieces of ochre, near the creek, maybe one of the 'camps decayed' tallied by old stockmen in Gilmore's dark poem. Marks on the hatchet head record a century or more of cropping. Plough discs and sowing points have chipped the stone, etched lines across its surfaces. Like the tyres and blades of heavy farm machines that crush and sever delicate networks of fungal pathways, the turbulent passage of steel through earth has chipped and gouged this stone tool, evoking broken, intangible threads of connection, as invisible and real as soil fungi, the stories and living memories that tied Wiradjuri people to these hillsides and creek flats.

North American scholars Heather Davis and Zoe Todd argue that 'the Anthropocene is not a new event, but is rather the continuation of practices of dispossession and genocide, coupled with a literal transformation of the environment, that have been at work for the last five hundred years', since the inception of European colonisation. Underlying the Anthropocene is 'a logic of the universal which is structured to sever the relations between mind, body, and land'. Across the Americas and throughout the world, 'the logic of the Anthropocene' has imposed 'a severing of relations between humans and the soil, between plants and animals, between minerals and our bones'. Davis and Todd issue a powerful call 'to tend to the ruptures and cleavages between land and flesh, story and law, human and more-than-human'.

Over the last decade, regenerative agriculture has become a widely used term. In contrast to industrial modes of production, regenerative methods of grazing and farming restore biological diversity and rebuild ecological connectivity. 'Regenerative' implies a particular stance towards history and place, an acceptance that processes of severance and wounding have unfolded through time. In the Anthropocene, actions may be taken to address the wounds of history, to restore the wellbeing of Country and its people. Unlike the triumphalist narratives of industrial farming, which celebrate the harnessing of land via the application of abstract scientific knowledge and mighty technologies, the cultural framework of regenerative agriculture fosters a more humble disposition. In his landmark book *Call of the Reed Warbler: A New Agriculture, a New Earth*, Charles Massy reports on his visits to regenerative farms across Australia. While undertaking his research, Massy noticed an 'openness to Indigenous people and a different world view' among 'leading regenerative farmers who had rejected industrial agriculture'. The exploration and application of regenerative methods, Massy observes, 'unlocks an entirely new way of thinking, perceiving and feeling, which is connected to a different set of values and ethics'.

A common characteristic of regenerative thinking, Massy learned, is an acknowledgment of 'the inherent self-organising capacity of natural ecosystems and other complex dynamic systems'. As one farmer told him, 'Nature will just drive it for you. Most of the time, all we've got to do is get out of the bloody way and stop interfering and it'll fix itself'. Such a stance, which holds that land and its communities of different species possess an inherent logic, that Country is meaningful, expressive and dynamic, is far from imported Enlightenment understandings that define land as inert and mechanical, as blank terrain available for industrial transformation. In a regenerative farming system, the production of food and fibre is grounded in respectful dialogue with land and other species, in the honouring and building of relationships.

To regenerate, according to the *Oxford English Dictionary*, is to be 're-born', to be 'formed anew'. The process enables 'a nation' to be 'restored or raised again from a sunk or base condition'. The word has spiritual connotations. To regenerate is 'to invest with a new and higher spiritual nature'. A 'person or state of things' may 'reform completely'. Regeneration promises a fresh and improved reality. 'To reconstitute on a higher plane; to place on a new basis.' As I write inside the old kitchen at the Retreat shearers' quarters, the farmland that stretches out – haunted by a dark and hidden history, stifling under another heatwave – holds potential for a profound transformation of land and society. The fertile red soil of Retreat, through which fungal networks are now gently rebuilding, cannot sustain the cultural frameworks that delivered the severances and atrocities of the Anthropocene. Thinking and action that foster farmland regeneration 'begin to address the root of the problem', as described by Davis and Todd, 'which is the severing of relations through the brutality of colonialism coupled with an imperial, universal logic'. By nourishing relationships and responding to the particularities of place,

> we might then begin to address not only the immediate problems associated with massive reliance upon fossil fuel and the nuclear industry, but the deeper questions of the need to acknowledge our embedded and embodied relations with our other-than-human kin and the land itself. This necessarily means re-evaluating not just our energy use, but our modes of governance, ongoing racial injustice, and our understandings of ourselves as human.

In the afternoon I drive south towards Junee, to meet my brother and his family at the town pool. On the hill to the west stands the house of cypress pine weatherboards built for my grandparents, where I spent part of my childhood. I remember spiny thickets of blackthorn, *Bursaria spinosa*, in the home paddock, where we made cubbyhouses under the pines. In summer, blackthorn carries bursts of creamy flowers, sweetly scented. Beside the road I notice a lone blackthorn shrub, knocked about by a herd of hungry cattle that drovers escorted through here a few months ago, and stop to have a look. I stoop to draw in the delicious aroma, but pull back when I see the wasps. Small and orange, with black stripes, darting across the pale flowers, drawing nectar, the same species I saw drinking from the surface of the muddy dam this morning.

John Hurley was the first squatter to secure control over this part of Wiradjuri Country. He lived in Campbelltown, near Sydney, far from the brutality and dangers of the pastoral frontier. Hurley based his stockmen on Houlaghans Creek, just upstream from its swampy confluence with the smaller, intermittent Pinchgut. In 1847 the colonial government gave squatters the right to lease the wide lands occupied by their cattle and sheep. No longer was their occupation of vast inland tracts considered illegal, in the eyes of colonial officials, and rents would soon be due. The following year, surveyor James Larmer set forth from Sydney to map the newly proclaimed Lachlan squatting district, between the Murrumbidgee and Lachlan rivers, where Hurley held several squatting runs. Larmer knew that Sir Thomas Mitchell, the celebrated explorer and surveyor general of New South Wales, required his surveyors to record and use Aboriginal place-names. To one surveyor Mitchell wrote:

> You will be particular in noting the native names of as many places as you can on your map of that part. The natives can furnish you with the names for every flat and almost every hill, and the settlers select their grants by these names.

Larmer eventually reached the sloping terrain drained by Pinch-gut and Houlaghans creeks, grazed by Hurley's livestock; he recorded Warre Warral, the Wiradjuri name for blackthorn, as the placename of the squatting run. Mary Gilmore, whose father learned much from the senior Wiradjuri men he befriended, noted that places holding the names of plants and animals were sanctuaries for that species. Within the boundaries of the sanctuaries, no gathering or hunting of the plant or animal was allowed, ensuring abundance:

> All billabongs, rivers, and marshes were treated as food reserves and supply depots by the natives. The bird whose name was given to a place bred there unmolested. The same with plants and animals. Thus storage never failed.

Across Australia, such sanctuaries are religious sites, anthropol-ogist Deborah Bird Rose explained, part of a holistic system wherein people who do 'the right thing ecologically' know that 'the results will be social and spiritual as well as ecological'. Likewise, those 'doing the right spiritual things' evoke 'social and ecological results'. Relation-ships of care cannot be categorised; they are integrated. Here beside Pinchgut Creek, the old records suggest, 'a unified field of Dreaming ecology' drew blackthorn and red earth, pine and magpie, people and swampland, into mutually nurturing bonds of kinship.

Ecologists recognise the significance of blackthorn in agricul-tural regions. In a guide to revegetating the Southwest Slopes, Fleur Stelling notes that in the summer, wasps energised by blackthorn's sweet nectar parasitise and kill grubs that destroy pasture and scarab beetles that denude paddock trees. On farms managed along ecolog-ical, regenerative principles, blackthorn and the wasps it nourishes are valued.

Within the hidden ecologies of pine, fungi, blackthorn and wasps lie histories of atrocity, severance and loss. In an overheating world, the fertile soils of Wiradjuri Country also hold the promise of regeneration. We can choose to honour and maintain the heritage and function of Retreat, its gentle hills and restoring swampland, as a place to gather, to build strategies for countering the violent machinations of the Anthropocene. Those who adopt 'a holistic world view', wrote Deborah Bird Rose,

> which situates life forms as part of living systems, will conceptualise loss in complex and non-absolute ways, and will place confidence in the earth's capacity to recover from damage. If the regeneration of ecosystems is to involve Aboriginal people, as I believe it must, it will of necessity depend on sharing understandings in complex and non-absolute ways. Everybody will benefit.

I continue driving through the afternoon heat, the blackthorn of childhood memory behind me, towards the cooling relief of Junee pool, towards the company of kin, hopeful that shared understandings may regenerate our wounded land.

Readings

Australian National Botanic Garden, <www.anbg.gov.au/apu/plants/bursspin.html>.

'BFB Seeks Investment Partner for Cropping Portfolio Expansion', *Grain Central*, 29 August 2018, <bit.ly/graincentral-bfb>.

Heather Davis and Zoe Todd, 'On the Importance of a Date, or Decolonizing the Anthropocene', *ACME: An International Journal for Critical Geographies*, vol. 16, no. 4, 2017, pp. 775, 776.

'Eradication of Pine Scrub', *Riverine Grazier*, 25 August 1883, p. 4.

Mary Gilmore, *Old Days, Old Ways: A Book of Recollections*, Angus and Robertson, Sydney, 1934, pp. 198, 207.

Mary Gilmore, 'The Hunter of the Black', *The Passionate Heart and Other Poems*, Angus and Robertson, Sydney, 1979, pp. 66–68.

Beth Gott, *NSWUSE – Database of NSW Plants Utilised by Aborigines*, 1995.

Stan Grant and John Rudder, *A New Wiradjuri Dictionary*, Restoration House, Wagga Wagga, 2010.

'Have Offshore Players Got the Jump on Local Investors?', *Land*, 26 November 2018, <www.theland.com.au/story/5777714/>.

NSW Land Registry Services, Various maps of Robertson Parish, County of Bourke, Historical Land Records Viewer, <hlrv.nswlrs.com.au/>.

Charles Massy, *Call of the Reed Warbler: A New Agriculture, a New Earth*, University of Queensland Press, Brisbane, 2017, pp. 78–79, 168–70, 202.

'Mimosa Subdivision', *Farmer and Settler*, 7 February 1906, p. 14.

CT Onions (ed.), *The Shorter Oxford English Dictionary*, Oxford University Press, Oxford, 1978, vol. 2, p. 1781.

'The Pine Scrub Scare', *Sydney Morning Herald*, 13 August 1887, p. 8.

Retreat station report, 26–27 February 1894. Noel Butlin Archives Centre, 21306/1.

Deborah Bird Rose, *Nourishing Terrains: Australian Aboriginal Views of Landscape and Wilderness*, Australian Heritage Commission, Canberra, 1996, pp. 49, 85.

Fleur Stelling, *Southwest Slopes Revegetation Guide*, Murray Catchment Management Committee and Department of Land and Water Conservation, Albury, 1998, p. 300.

Alice Williams and Tim Sides, *Wiradjuri Plant Use in the Murrumbidgee Catchment*, Murrumbidgee Catchment Management Authority, Wagga Wagga, 2008, pp. 25, 75.

Greg Windsor, 'The Recognition of Aboriginal Placenames in New South Wales', in Luise Hercus and Harold Koch, *Aboriginal Placenames: Naming and Re-naming the Australian Landscape*, ANU E Press and Aboriginal History Incorporated, Canberra, 2009.

MARRA CREEK WATERPONDING

Ray Thompson

Reclaiming scalded landscapes has become my lifelong work in the rangelands of New South Wales. In 1984 I mapped out 100 000 hectares of scalded duplex soils in the Marra Creek district north of Nyngan, New South Wales. Duplex soils are distinctive for their loose, sandy-loam dry topsoil layer that rests on dense subsoil. The loose soil is vulnerable to erosion, and vast tracts of land out here have scalds: land completely devoid of vegetation through the effects of erosion. I believed that these eroded landscapes could be reclaimed by the waterponding rehabilitation technique. Waterponds are shallow U-shaped earth banks that retain water on flat scalds and help vegetation to establish.

The Soil Conservation Service's Marra Creek Waterponding Demonstration Program ran from 1984 to 1988. It was so successful that it continued to grow, and the waterponding technique has now reclaimed 40 000 hectares of scalded landscape, which is a win-win for the environment and land-holders.

I have surveyed 80 000 waterponds since the program started. I've also spread the waterponding technique across the world. Through the Australian Aid program, I have taught seventy-one African trainees from twenty-one African countries. I've spoken on waterponding at international conferences in India, Argentina, China, Canada and Australia.

For some reason now unknown, on the first day of my water-ponding career, I began a logbook covering every day that I went into the field. I recorded the property name, number of waterponds laid out, number of surveyed hectares, laser hours, tine marker hours and average waterpond bank length.

This book has become my living bible of facts and figures over the last thirty-two years, which is why I know how many waterponds have been surveyed, how many hectares have been rehabilitated and how many properties have been waterponded. The logbook has become battered and full of so many entries – a second book has carried on.

From the first, 'Number 1', waterpond that I surveyed in 1984, to the 80 000th waterpond, my passion has not changed; that desire to revegetate the landscape has remained my number one focus.

The Marra Creek district is unique in its landscape and people. It has engulfed my working life with so many highs and given me opportunities to spread the success of waterponding across the world. Marra Creek's duplex soil is very responsive to change: it is like birth – you plant the seed and rehabilitate, and the vegetation growth is mind-blowing. I have a sense of awe when I walk around out here, knowing it is possible to take this claypan – land that has lost 30 centimetres of topsoil, that is barren and denuded of life, and just continuing to blow and wash away – and regenerate it into a landscape of waving native grasses, perennial saltbushes, full of wildlife and birdsong. When I see that the dust storms have stopped, the erosion has stopped, and the landscape is back in production ... you can't beat that feeling. This is a place that has been given a second chance at life.

When I walk onto a claypan with a land-holder and he or she says, 'What can I do with this?' I begin thinking about what this scalded site is going to look like in five years time, covered in saltbushes and grasses; reborn earth to enhance the environment for a far better functional landscape.

You just have to get down and get your hands dirty – it will not happen by sitting behind your desk, you have to get out in the paddock every day. I set a goal to cover 50 hectares of scald every time I go out. I have just chipped away at it and ridden the waves over the past thirty-seven years of rehabilitation work.

The Soil Conservation Service still exists, but seven department name-changes later, I've been able to continue with the waterponding work, all the while using the same faithful equipment that I started with. The Marra Creek Waterponding Demonstration Program owned this laser equipment, which prevented it being sold off each time we changed department names (thank god for that).

I believe the equipment has made this job the success that it is. I know there are a lot of components in the job that have to be brought together – reading and understanding the landscape, survey skills, timing, survey equipment and back-up – but the laser equipment virtually talks to me inside the cab of my ute. I treat it well and it treats me well. The two of us have been together every day for thirty-two years. I hit the switch and the laser springs to life – more numbers today. Without this equipment, I would have never walked the 17,040 kilometres that the tine marker has marked behind my laser truck.

Two days that I will never forget, back in 2005: I was surveying waterponds at Melrose, Frank and Rochelle McKillop's place. At the end of the day I handed Frank the waterponding survey sheet with all the ponds drawn on it so he could build them with his road grader.

I said to Frank, 'I have put an X on a pond on the sheet, which is the 50 000th waterpond that I have surveyed.'

Frank took the sheet and away I went.

A month later, Frank rang up and invited me out to do the final inspection on the new fence and the waterponds he had built. That was fine, so out I went. When I arrived at Melrose homestead only

Frank was there, nobody else, which was a bit strange, but off Frank and I went to do the inspection along the shiny new fence. Then I saw way over in the distance that there were four-wheel drives parked out in the middle of the waterponds.

Frank said, 'Just head over to the vehicles.'

I pulled up beside an object covered in a woolpack. Something was about to go down. (It still makes me choke up today.) I lifted the woolpack off the object and found it was a plaque, engraved and welded to a steel pipe cemented into the middle of my 50 000th water-pond. It read: 'Mr Ray Thompson CMA (Soil Con) marked out this Pond No: 50,000 on 6-12-2005'.

The gratitude of the land-holders for the job I was doing really hit home to me. I appreciated Frank's actions, putting that pond into history, for the recognition of all those days just going out surveying, day-in-day-out, working to regenerate the environment.

MUDSTONE AND MEMORY

Penny Dunstan

Did you know that rock has memory? In its form and shape, rock remembers long-distant times. This is a story about a rock type known as mudstone, which interleaves between coal measures in the open-cut coalmines in the Hunter Valley.

Stone is made from even older stone. Mudstone is made from ancient pasts, weathering, washing and dribbling down Permian mountain sides to lie on ancient forest floors, where it formed soils to grow the giant forests that made the coal seams we now mine. Mud from ancient soils was carried by heavy rain into salty lake bottoms between bands of flattened forest, where, with aeons of resting, drying, squashing and squeezing, it was pushed into layers and transformed by deep time into rock. That rock rested as deep as 500 metres below the surface for around 260 million years, until its slumber was interrupted by humans looking for coal. Great seams of rock from the Permian age were broken up as the coal was retrieved. The layered mudstone was blasted, dug and transported to the non-working side of the open-cut void to form Anthropocene mountains of mine overburden.

But does rock remain rock once the pressure of layers of time is removed, once the stopwatch of creation has been set back to zero?

Free of the weight of history, the stone is now jumbled boulders with air spaces and water voids. Mudstone remembers it was once soil, full of fungi and bacteria, plant roots and humus. It remembers that it was once living and breathing, generating food for countless flora and fauna. The stone again shifts form, disintegrating in a geological blink of an eye (between three months and two years), forming a substrate of small particles, a 260-million-year-old approximation of soil.

But it is not soil.

Decomposed mudstone is both highly saline and highly alkaline and this makes it unable to host the fungi and bacteria required for plant growth; it is also chemically hostile to most plant roots. Even when topsoils rescued from the working side of the pit are spread, carpet-like, over the degraded mudstone, most plants cannot use mudstone-derived 'subsoil' for nutrients or even anchor points.

Yet, mudstone remembers what it was to be a soil and, given time, will become fertile again. The catch is that time for mudstone is measured in Earth time, rather than human time. The Earth will heal itself, but perhaps not at the pace that humans would like.

To record the start of the transition of mudstone into soil, I dug pits 1 metre deep in three locations on one mine site near Singleton, New South Wales, and collected a vertical soil section from each pit (see <everydayfutures.com.au>). Vertical soil sections are known as *soil profiles* and they show the transitions of soil types, soil colours and how plant roots interact with soil changes to depth. Soil profiles are used to determine soil composition and soil health. From these metre-deep holes in the earth, I made three soil profiles: the first was collected from a natural, undisturbed soil; the second and third came from rehabilitated mine land.

The unmined natural soil profile, collected from an open forested area, shows a bright orange sandy clay loam topsoil transitioning into a brown sandy clay subsoil. There are lots of healthy plant roots of many species throughout the soil. The soil has a strong structure that lets water and air into the root zone. The strong and healthy roots throughout the profile show that the soil is functioning well.

The two post-mining profiles show a transported topsoil layer over mudstone overburden. The second soil profile is only two years old and shows a defined layer between the orange topsoil and the grey degrading mudstone that substitutes for the subsoil. Plant roots are common in the topsoil but almost non-existent in the mudstone subsoil, and those roots are twisted, shortened and gnarled from the excessive alkalinity released from the mudstone as it breaks down. The soil structure in the topsoil is weak (it has been dug up, transported and bulldozed, and has not yet recovered). The mudstone 'subsoil' still looks like rock chunks rather than soil peds – small lumps of soil that allow easy penetration of water and air, and enable plant roots, funghi and microbes to colonise the deeper layers of the profile.

The 22-year-old profile shows a less obvious layer between an orange-brown topsoil (more organic matter) and mudstone 'subsoil', and, encouragingly, there are Rhodes grass (*Chloris gayana*) roots in the mudstone-derived part of the soil profile. Rhodes grass is a very tough plant and, along with *Acacia saligna*, seems happy to tolerate extreme root-zone conditions that most other plants cannot. But can the mudstone section of the soil profile be classified as a soil? My soil science colleagues say no, since there is no formation of soil peds.

In the Hunter Valley, there will be tens of thousands of hectares of rehabilitated post-mining land when the coal industry is done. But that is not the end of the story; the land will continue to change over many hundreds, perhaps thousands, of years. Mudstone boulders brought to the surface by mining will be breaking down into component parts not just on the surface, where plant roots can reach, but also in the depths of the hills. Whole landscapes made of mudstone may drop in height. Concrete structures that now direct water flow down the hills will fail as the mountain sides move and settle. Obvious gully erosion that exists in this present day around post-mining overburden hills will become vast if left untreated. Erosion makes land unsafe and unproductive, and runoff often affects surrounding lands. Care and maintenance of post-mining land is a problem that we leave future generations to solve. The human-made mountains are imperceptibly on the move, weathering, washing and dribbling down engineered hillsides to lie on agricultural lands where we used to grow our food, changing the water quality of our aquifers and rivers on their way.

Bringing Permian rock to the surface gives rise to many environmental issues. We are familiar with the relationship between mining coal and climate change, but there will be other penalties associated with mining that we impose on future generations. The loss of functional subsoils restricts soil water storage, making the land more drought-prone; it restricts nutrient availability for plants, making the plants smaller, weaker and more prone to disease; it challenges the stability of large trees; and it changes the flow patterns of water and air.

In the short term, degraded mudstone cannot act as soil no matter how much we might wish it, but, with certain levels of ongoing care, mudstone will do its best to remember how to act as a soil. With geological time on its side, mudstone-derived soils will provide shelter for fungi and bacteria, plant roots and micro-organisms. In Earth time, mudstone will remember that it once knew how to grow forests.

RAISING A GREEN WOOD SHED

Gib Wettenhall

Last winter, I stood on the white sands of a remote tropical beach watching a Macassan man conducting the crafting of seven teak-flanked phinisi boats, in much the same way they had been conceived for over a thousand years. No plans on paper needed. The template, passed down from generation to generation, was inside his head. And his workers bantered amiably, as each of the seven ships of seven different sizes sprang into being from a well-grooved, familial structural form. Ships whose sails on the horizon had for centuries signalled for the Yolngu people of north-east Arnhem Land the arrival of the Wet and trading opportunities for swapping trepang for tobacco. Ships whose ageless grace and function are now coveted globally as the epitome of authenticity.

In spring, I went with fellow farm foresters on a field trip to Victoria's northern plains to see a splendid barn built the old European way, out of green wood. Not a plan, nail nor machine was in sight. Like the phinisi boats built on the beach at Bulukumba in Sulawesi.

Once, building with green wood was the norm, not abnormal. Trees were felled, hewn with axe and adze, and a barn or boat of beauty rose nearby. The process made sense. Wood when green and dripping wet is ten times more workable than when hard and dried.

Unlike metal nails, wooden pegs joining post to beam and truss can cope with shrinkage. Only a few tools are necessary. A broad axe for hewing a log into a post or beam. A handsaw and chisel for fine detailing, such as carving beam ends to fit snugly into a rectangular slot on either side of a post's top. An auger for drilling holes through post and beam for the wooden pegs. A drawknife for shaving pegs to a point so they can be hammered into place, locking post and beam together.

Building with mortise (Old French for 'hole') and tenon (literally 'tongue') must have been based on natural principles, analogous, as it is, with the sockets and joints of animal bodies. Pegs replace muscles, fixing beams to posts firmly. Linked posts and beams appear similar to a row of people standing with their arms on their neighbours' shoulders.

The technique never caught on in Australia. Why? The Industrial Revolution disrupted tried-and-true traditional pathways. Mechanisation sped up processes, exponentially increasing milled timber volumes and profit potential. Axe and adze were vanquished by chainsaws and steam-powered saw benches. Moist and flexible green wood was abandoned in favour of the inanimate uniformity and rigid precision of kiln-dried wood.

What if, I thought, I commissioned the young maker of the splendid barn to try his hand at reinventing the traditional Aussie-style farm shed, out of green wood? We would source the wood from my patch of native forest on the edge of the Wombat Forest at the southern end of the Divide. We would choose for the mortise and tenon frame the common native hardwood, messmate, once described by the explorer William Howitt as 'the most useful' of trees; today, little used, displaced by that inferior Californian exotic, radiata pine. What could act as a more apt example of localism, reconnecting people to place, slowing the creative act down so it swung in tune with the planet's beating heart?

Lachlan Park, the 28-year-old fine wood craftsman, was keen.

He and many of his fellow millennials are sick of spewing out poorly made, toxic stuff to serve the treadmill of economic growth. He wants to work with wood, rather than fight it, let alone lay waste to forests.

In the 1850s, over 570 000 immigrants arrived at the port of Melbourne, en route to the goldfields 'up country'. It was the greatest gold rush the world had ever seen. What also ensued was 'a great slaughter of trees', as the region's first forester, John La Gerche, confided to his journal. Much of the gold lay under the Wombat Forest; it was stripped bare and turned upside down. By 1897, a Royal Commission had declared the Wombat 'a ruined forest'. Although it was to recover, the late twentieth-century innovation of clear-felling stripped the forest bare once more, reducing it to woodchips for papermaking.

Overcut, exhausted, the Wombat Forest was closed to clearfall at the turn of the twenty-first century. As happens when a forest is laid bare, thousands of seedlings germinated and strove for sunlight per hectare, replacing what were originally open woodlands with dense, even-aged thickets of eucalypt saplings.

This was the 'young', dark, impenetrable forest that greeted my family and me when we bought our 15-hectare block over twenty-five years ago. I took a Master TreeGrower course and learned about the key silvicultural tool for breaking sapling gridlock in a regrowth forest – thinning. In the Wombat Forest, this has for many of us taken on the form of felling every second tree for firewood. By halving density, the remaining trees are released from fighting for their place in the sun. They gain space to survive and spread. And to our joy, the light let in has allowed the return of orchids and wildflowers, adding a pointillist palette to the bush at our back door.

Summer came and Lachlan and I began the green wood shed project by diverting some messmate thinnings from an ignoble fate as firewood. We selected 5-metre lengths of straight messmate from a firewood cutter and brought in a mobile bandsaw mill for shaping into post and beam. A friend found an old US Army manual online that showed Lachlan and his brother Joe how to pull the frame into place using a block and tackle.

Where possible, we decided, we would use only low embedded energy, materially renewable resources. So, we have locally sourced stone for the foundations, secondhand bricks for the posts' piers, a wind-blown oak for the pegs, recycled galvanised iron for the roof and local plantation timber for the cladding. Putting theory into practice has required patience, but has proven immensely satisfying.

Once, the land, forests, rivers, seas and sky appeared endless. We know this viewpoint no longer holds true. But what are we doing to change direction from an ideological pathway of planetary plunder that heralds catastrophic global warming and the sixth wave of extinction? Despite what many people imagine, human history is not rationally ascending to some sort of Star Wars domination of the universe. Rather, we have made choices at crossover points in the past, like pursuing capitalism and mass production, which have had unintended consequences that are not necessarily proving benign.

We stand in the middle of another crossover point. Many of the slow, place-based ways of the pre-industrial era are more suited to the rhythms of the Earth. Like walking, wind power and eating the food that you grow, working with green wood connects people to nature, creating cultural artefacts of lasting strength and beauty. In our search for a more authentic and meaningful way of living, Lachlan and I like to think that rediscovering lost arts could contribute to bringing us back into balance.

ANCIENT RED GUM

Billy Griffiths

With a mischievous smile, Damien Wright gives the exhibit an uncere-
monious kick. The enormous, curved slab of river red gum rocks back
and forth on the gallery floor, casting a wavering shadow over the 'Do
Not Touch' sign at its base. A couple of anxious visitors shuffle over
to investigate as Damien tells me how he made this wobbling wooden
bowl, and why he chooses to work with the hardest, most challenging
timbers.

The river red gum (*Eucalyptus camaldulensis*) once grew on the
banks of the Murray River. Damien discovered the thick slab in a
miller's yard in Wodonga, where it had lain exposed to the elements
for years, slowly warping in the heat. What others had dismissed as
damaged wood, Damien saw as creative possibility: he relished the
opportunity to work with wood that had been 'cooked, cured and
crazed by the sun'. In his workshop in Northcote, Melbourne, he
worked to accentuate the warp in the wood by curving the edges of
the slab, creating a long, bowing channel, almost 3 metres in length
and over a metre wide. Like all his work, this object is an argument he
has made with his hands. The rough, red, cracking grain of the wood
runs lengthways across the piece, like gullies and rivulets spreading
across a parched, burnt land. Damien encourages this comparison

with his title, which is a pointed commentary on the mistreatment of the waterways on which the tree grew.

'It's called *Food Bowl*', he tells me. And then, gesturing to a knot in the centre, 'It drains in the middle'.

For Damien, wood is a way of thinking about place and time – even deep time. A river red gum may grow for anywhere between 400 and 1000 years before it falls. And as it decomposes over centuries it becomes a home for new life. Murray cod lay their eggs in drowned red gums. To work with wood is to think beyond a human lifespan. When you look at something like the Murray-Darling system from the perspective of a grand old red gum, you see the fragility and inter-connectedness of the waterway, and how rapidly it has degraded with recent human interventions.

'And if you have that conversation about deep time in this country', says Damien, 'you have to talk about Indigenous people and this continent as an occupied and cultural space, not just a physical place'.

River red gums were a part of Australia's environment long before people arrived here. They grew beside the Murray River when it was a wide, cold, fast-flowing stream; they witnessed its transformation in the late Pleistocene into a narrow, sinuous, seasonal river; and they have remained, over the past 13 000 years, as the water has slowed and warmed, forming swamps, low sand dunes and small lakes along the channel, and seasonal wetlands in the wider riverine plain. These mighty trees have also been absorbed into the social and cultural worlds of Indigenous Australians. Their roots have been dug and hollowed out to create bowls, their bark cut to craft canoes, and their limbs burned to warm camps and cook food. In recent millennia, they presided over the most densely populated areas of the continent.

Damien tells me how he seeks to evoke this deep history through his craft as he shows me two of his other pieces: a striking lantern (*Black Lighthouse*) he made in collaboration with Yolngu craftsman Bonhula Yunupingu, which glows like a fire through thin, black wood; and an elegant reading chair and angular side table called *Ned* – a riff on Sidney Nolan's Ned Kelly helmet, which it closely resembles. Each piece of furniture has been made from red gum in a stage preliminary to fossilisation. The wood is black and almost as hard as stone. It is known as ancient red gum.

While other native timbers enable Damien to explore relationships with the Australian environment, the ancient red gum opens a conversation about deep time on this continent.

Geomorphologist Jim Bowler was the first to identify the material as red gum; he used radiocarbon dating to place its age at about 8000 or perhaps 10 000 years old. Later I call him and, over the phone, he sketches out the wood's journey from the banks of the Murray River to the workshops of inquisitive artisans like Damien.

The tree would have seeded after the end of the last ice age, at a time when sea levels were rising and the climate was warming. The rapid snowmelt in the Victorian Alps caused the mountains to shed huge amounts of gravel, which was then swept into the Murray River. As red gums fell into an ancient channel they were covered by this new gravel, which sealed them in the riverbank. Preserved from decay by the acidity of the water, the entombed wood slowly absorbed enormous amounts of iron and silica. This oxidising and ebonising process is what makes it black through to the centre and hard, much harder than other red gum.

JIM FIRST BECAME AWARE OF THE RED GUM WHEN HE received some samples at the Melbourne Museum in 1990. The damp and fibrous wood had been unearthed in a quarry on Yorta Yorta land in Wodonga, where it was regarded as a nuisance by those more interested in the gravel around it. Jim and his wife Joan Bowler recognised the significance of the timber and were eager to see it preserved and used. They helped arrange for the director of the museum to provide 'authentications' for woodworkers to make it into furniture, and Joan and her friend Annetine Forell travelled the country over the following two decades, drawing the remarkable material to the attention of millers and craftspeople. The late Kelvin Barton, a miller, woodworker and seventh-generation farmer, became a crucial intermediary. He collected the ancient red gum in Wodonga, reducing its water content in his ersatz kiln to turn it into workable timber. This was how Damien, a long-term friend and collaborator, came to encounter the ancient red gum – indeed it was in Kelvin's yard that he found the much younger slab that became *Food Bowl*.

Damien uses the ancient red gum to articulate his vision for Australia. He sees craftsmanship as a language: a practice that is refined over time to communicate knowledge, beauty and ideas. He considers his furniture – in its functionality as well as its elegance – as an embodiment of this philosophy. Objects tell stories. They become part of our everyday lives and express everyday futures:

> My argument is that to take a material that is ten thousand years old and to articulate that in a beautiful and passionate way and to make that a relevant thing to our lives or to peoples' lives is a way of articulating a future for this continent. It's a way of understanding our place in time. It's a way of dealing with people. It's a way of projecting forward.

Joan Bowler shares this vision for the ancient timber. In 2008, her company Australian Ancient Redgum donated a 6-metre 'Fossil Tree' to the Children's Garden at the Royal Botanic Gardens Victoria, so that 'children can sit under this ancient tree and look up through the hollowed-out centre and dream of what was and what might be'.

Trees that were seeded after the end of the last ice age, that survived the ruptures of invasion and industry, have re-emerged to offer a deep-time perspective of the continent. It is a scale that reveals the long-term costs of short-term exploitation, and renders processes like the degradation of the Murray-Darling river system into sudden events. Ancient red gum also invites a longer view of Australian history. And in the hands of Joan and Damien, it calls for the acknowledgment of cultures and histories that for so long have gone unrecognised.

BIG HUNKS OF STONE ALWAYS MAKE ME SMILE

Ian Lunt

When I despair that the world is changing too fast – or not changing fast enough – I often visit a favourite place: an outcrop of rocks in north-east Victoria.

I drive down the Hume Freeway, turn off to Beechworth, and bump along a track, winding through pine plantations, until I arrive at a gully in Chiltern – Mt Pilot National Park. I lock the car and walk past the motorbike trails, up a stone path dug by goldminers, to the ridge, where there are no tracks. I keep going till I get to the rocks.

My favourite rocks don't have a name. They have a presence. There's this thing about a granite boulder. If you sit on a log in a quiet patch of bush, you can imagine you're the only person ever to sit there. But when you stand by an enormous, round rock, you know you stand where others have stood and sat and laughed and slept since people first walked in that corner of the Earth. Not far from here, a rock shelter bears a fading image, painted in ochre, of an extinct animal, a thylacine.

Sometimes when I visit, I climb onto a low, flat shelf and lie down until the wrens hop close and the moss wets through my clothes. As I gaze back down the hill, I see smoke rising from a stubble fire, a truck rusting in a paddock, shiny mobile phone towers. I hear the drone of trucks on the freeway, carting more stuff for us to buy in Sydney, Canberra and Melbourne. Like Thoreau at his pond, it's never lonely at my refuge from the crowd.

Between the boulders stand native trees that were named after trees from Europe: cypress pines, slender trunks in stockings of orange lichen, and long-leaved box, weighed down by sagging, heavy boughs. Beneath the trees are grasses and lichens: soft in spring and crunchy dry in summer. And, of course, the rocks.

The things we are doing to the planet will change this forest forever. I understand that. The pools may dry, down in the creek where the honeyeaters drink. The trees will burn and burn again. But the rocks will stay: quiet, accepting, just hangin'.

Every time I visit, these great big hunks of stone make me smile. Every single time. Before I leave, I nod in thanks; then I breathe in, bounce down the hill, and make my place among the trucks on the freeway below – with peace, hope and the courage to try again.

SHARING THE STORY

THE STORIES WE TELL

Sophie Cunningham

1.

True, the word 'plague' had been uttered; true, at this very moment one or two victims were being seized and laid low by the disease. Still, that could stop, or be stopped. It was only a matter of lucidly recognising what had to be recognised; of dispelling extraneous shadows and doing what needed to be done. Then the plague would come to an end, because it was unthinkable, or, rather, because one thought of it on misleading lines. If, as was most likely, it died out, all would be well. If not, one would know it anyhow for what it was and what steps should be taken for coping with and finally overcoming it.

The Plague, by Albert Camus, was written in 1947 and taught to me as a part of Year 12 English, in 1978. Other novels on the syllabus were *I Heard the Owl Call My Name* and *Zorba the Greek*. The theme we were studying was: DEATH.

The Plague was, I learned, an 'existentialist' novel, though I was pretty foggy on what existentialism was. I do remember being struck by the fact that there was a character called Grand, who was an author, and that Grand spent *The Plague* writing and rewriting the opening lines of his own novel, a work that he failed to finish before he caught (but recovered from) the actual plague.

2.

The Day After Tomorrow came out in 2004. I watched it on release, and have watched it a dozen times since. This much-maligned disaster film riffs on a scenario known as Abrupt Climate Change in which a melting Antarctic forces too much fresh water into the Atlantic and triggers a flip of the Atlantic Meridional Overturning Circulation Currents (or something). I've since learned that it's not impossible this might happen – the currents are weakening – but I'm not arguing that science is the film's strong point.

As the film opens our hero-scientists frantically drill for ice cores in the Antarctic. Their work is interrupted when an 'ice sheet the size of Rhode Island' breaks away, almost killing the entire team. Soon enough there are speeches being made about global warming and 'the cost of doing nothing' versus the cost of doing something. Dennis Quaid, who plays a paleoclimatologist, makes eloquent pleas to the Vice President – I'll call him Fake Dick Cheney – regarding the fate of our children and grandchildren. He chases Fake Dick Cheney down a hallway yelling, 'Mr Vice President, if we don't act now, it's going to be too late'.

There is snow in New Delhi. There are massive hailstorms in Tokyo. Birds begin to fly south, 'typhoons' hit Australia and tornadoes destroy LA. One day, Dennis Quaid's pretend son, Jake Gyllenhaal, is looking moody and flying to some giant quiz meet-up in New

York; the next day he and his friends are visiting the Natural History Museum and looking at a mammoth that was snap-frozen 10 000 years ago; the day after that they are trapped in the New York Public Library as a storm surge engulfs lower Manhattan. Ships float down Fifth Avenue. The temperature begins to drop rapidly and within a couple of days Jake and his friends are burning books so they don't become snap-frozen, *like mammoths.*

Millions die but there is little talk about the loss of life and it seems the only animal affected is a homeless man's dog and the wolves from the zoo. Books, however, are a subject of much discussion. 'As far as I'm concerned the written word is mankind's greatest achievement', says the librarian, as he clutches the Gutenberg Bible to make sure it isn't cast into the flames. This was the first printed book, he argues, it is a relic of the age of reason. It must be saved even if western civilisation is lost.

Laura, the girl Jake is in love with, is sad, and he mansplains to her that she's having trouble adapting. The girl asks, not unreasonably, 'How am I supposed to adjust? Everything I've ever cared about, everything I've worked for has all been preparation for a future that no longer exists.' Then she gets blood poisoning and receives what might be one of the last penicillin shots in the world.

Further south we see hundreds of thousands of Americans wade across the Rio Grande trying to break into Mexico. *Ironic.* Dennis Quaid shuffles past the Statue of Liberty in his snowshoes, musing that humankind survived the last ice age and is therefore able to survive this one. 'It all depends if we're capable of learning from our mistakes', he tells his friend, a friend who, inexplicably, has walked from Philadelphia to New York, through the biggest storm in 10 000 years, just to be with Dennis Quaid.

Can we learn from our mistakes? That's the kicker really. This film seemed like a joke fifteen years ago, but I'm not laughing now. If only we did learn from our mistakes, as Fake Dick Cheney learns from his. He makes another speech. 'For years we lived under the belief that we could continue to consume our planet's natural resources without consequence. We were wrong. I was wrong.'

3.

Ten years ago now, I bought a book called *The Place You Love Is Gone* by Melissa Holbrook Pierson. The title was so dispiriting that I never read the book, though I thought quite a lot about it when I visited one of my favourite places in the world not so long ago: Wilsons Promontory, the southernmost tip of mainland Australia. Boon Wurrung, Bunurong and Gunaikurnai land. My wife and I walked to Sealers Cove and back in a day. George Bass and his crew sailed into Sealers Cove when they were seeking shelter from a storm in 1798. They found abundance: crescent of white sand, cavorting seals, soaring eucalypts. Soon enough there was industrial-scale slaughter of seals, and of whales. By the 1850s so many of the animals were dead the Europeans moved on to felling timber. Colonialism really does hit the ground running. I was oblivious to all this when I did the walk as a child back in the 1970s. My father carried me on his shoulders through the forest, down into the fern glades, to the wetlands that sit back from the beach. The scars left by the place's violent past were not visible. New wounds have opened though, and doing the walk in 2019 is testimony to the feats of engineering required to salvage the track after a series of bushfires, and then floods in 2011, gouged trenches down the sides of Mount Oberon, taking a lot of forest, and slabs of the walking track.

If you go there in winter you can fool yourself that the Prom is a remote place. Massive granite boulders loom above and – when reflected in the golden tannin-stained rivers – beneath you. If it has rained, water streams from these boulders and the sheen of water acts as a mirror, reflecting a savage sky. The Prom was once full of coastal banksia but they are in retreat now and tea trees are moving in. The *Xanthorrhoea* (grasstrees) are infected by *Phytophthora cinnamomi*, which is more colloquially known as root rot. I see them as I walk: trunks collapsed in on themselves, the drying grass of the fronds splayed in a circle around the dead centre. I walk along the beach at Tidal River and, like a bower bird, pick up dozens of tiny blue pieces of plastic. I walk to Little Oberon Bay and a magpie struts around me as I sit on a rock, then marches or flies ahead of me for an entire kilometre as I walk home. It's clear to me I'm being escorted out of his territory. I see a wombat and her baby grazing by the river under a full moon. Swamp wallaby hang their heads low as they browse. Casuarina that have grown horizontally for decades form lattice work on dunes. The setting sun hits the western side of the promontory until sand, rocks, casuarina, sea, begin to glow.

4.

When I first became seriously concerned about climate change, I decided to write a book documenting the power of a single weather event: Cyclone Tracy, which almost wiped out Darwin in 1974.

A pilot called Len Garton, who saw the cyclone hanging from the sky, later commented:

> I don't know whether it's the greenhouse effect or these
> alleged currents that are floating around creating problems. I
> know, in flying, the weather patterns are completely different.
> One time, going back five, six, perhaps seven years, I never
> used to mind flying in the wet season. You did see a weather
> front in front of you, a rainstorm, and it would be ten [or]
> fifteen miles wide and not very severe. And you could

invariably see the tops at about twelve or fourteen thousand feet or something. But now, when you see them they're a hundred and fifty, two hundred miles wide and they seem to go up out of sight in twenty, thirty thousand feet. And very dense. I have flown in them a couple of times and frightened myself. The old ones you'd get a bit of buffeting, but nowadays there seems to [be] a lot of turmoil in them. I've never seen any records that substantiate this or otherwise but talking to private pilots like myself they all say: 'Oh yes, it's different we won't fly through a storm any more'.

When I was working on the book, I was shown around Darwin by Robert Mills, a Larrakia community leader, who I'd ask to talk to me about what this place was like before white settlement. We'd never met before, so I figured the weather was as good a conversation starter as any. As we drove along I asked him, 'Is it true that the Wet is coming later? And that when it hits the rain is heavier?'

Mills sat in silence beside me. I barrelled on. 'Do you think the climate is changing?'

After a few more moments of silence, Mills turned and looked at me. 'My people don't really like to talk about the weather', he said.

I think about that exchange often. Why did I think the weather was a topic for casual conversation? Weather is knowledge, weather is *everything*. If I didn't get that, did I really think I could fix anything? With my limited understanding? Did I think I could fix anything by *writing a book*?

5.

I recently had a public conversation with the author James Bradley about an essay he'd written for *Meanjin* called 'Unearthed: Last Days of the Anthropocene'. During our conversation Bradley discussed the difficulty of alerting readers to the dangers ahead, while arguing for constructive action. He mentioned that some days he feels as if he's walking around wearing a sandwich board that reads 'The end of the world is nigh'. I nodded wildly in agreement. Me, I feel like Dennis Quaid chasing Fake Dick Cheney down infinite hallways yelling, 'If we don't act now, it's going to be too late'. But this is hard to talk about because how we feel is not the main game. The main game is doing all we can to mitigate the more extreme effects of climate change. The main game is to save what we can. The problem with feeling crazy is that it can make it harder to do anything useful.

I emailed someone I love and trust recently, and asked them a question: What can I do?

They wrote back, 'Do SOMETHING. Have realistic goals. Then make the best of it.'

6.

In the spirit of doing SOMETHING I sit and meditate on the steps of Parliament House with a dozen others during Extinction Rebellion's Spring Rebellion in October 2019. I felt very self-conscious at first because I remember what I once thought of middle-aged ladies wearing beanies and sitting cross-legged in public places. But the idea that people like me – people who are terrified of living on a planet that has warmed 2 degrees, or more – might be overreacting is a comforting thought. I *hope* that those of us who are dancing, meditating, gluing ourselves to roads, taking our clothes off, being arrested, are *wrong*. I relish this thought a moment: that we don't have to worry; then I open my eyes because a tram has dinged loudly, and find myself looking straight down Bourke Street, all the way to the wet heart of the CBD, Elizabeth Street.

I know a lot of stories about Melbourne and a few about this land pre-white settlement. I imagine that time as I sit here, at the high end of the city. Creeks worked their way down what we now call Treasury Gardens, towards the Yarra River, for this was a watery place. Expanses of swampland sat alongside grasslands and open forest. There were platypus in the creeks and swamps full of frogs; dingoes were common. Swamp wallabies abounded, wombats ambled, emus strolled. Eels wound their way through the waterways. When the settlers arrived aggressive clearing began and the Wurundjeri, the Boon Wurrung, noted a drop in rainfall caused by the loss of trees.

I know this, I realise, because I have written a book about Melbourne. I love Melbourne because I went to the effort of getting to know it. It is nice to realise that while books can't change the weather, the writing of them has changed me and the reading of them has changed many of us.

Meditation over, I get up to take a photo of the signs on the steps. They read: Grief, Loss, Courage, Action.

7.

'You have stolen my dreams and my childhood with your empty words,' says Greta Thunberg. Her words aren't empty: they are fierce. Powerful. 'We are in the beginning of a mass extinction. And all you can talk about is money and fairytales of eternal economic growth.'

We're all hooked on fairytales. I've always dreamed, or hovered in that place between wake and sleep where one can weave fairytales to order. When I was young these were often romantic fantasies. Or sexual. But as I got older these fantasies morphed to ones of travel, and adventure: I walked across the Himalaya with only a snow leopard for company; I escaped an avalanche, a tidal wave; I saved a mob of kangaroos, some wombats, an echidna from a fire storm. For a while the fairytales turned to an imagination of the speech I would give when I won the Booker Prize for the novel I've been writing since *The Day After Tomorrow* came out.

Lately, though, my daydreams have been more pragmatic. I want to buy a block of land. I want to plant as many trees as I can. I want to keep those trees alive.

8.

'What can writers do', Delia Falconer asks, 'faced with a world whose abundance, in the fuller sense of frail complexity, is vanishing before our eyes? Apart from the question of whether art can have much real effect against the overwhelming threats we (humans and other living beings) face, it's possible that the underpinnings of storytelling itself may be endangered.'

My characters, my novels, keep unwriting themselves, or perhaps what I mean is they write themselves so far off-topic that the work unravels. Scene after scene of a novel I've been writing for years end up deleted, in a file marked 'offcuts'.

Here's how it goes: I write a character I call 'author' and I encourage her to write a scene in which a group of Bloomsbury types sit around on a long summer evening in Sussex. I ask her to imagine the sounds they might hear on such an evening. The 'author' ignores me and googles *Cicadas, Britain*. She learns that the New Forest cicada is endangered in Britain, possibly extinct. She googles *Crickets* and learns they are precipitously declining. So too the turtle dove, the hedgehog, some toads and moths, beetles and squirrels. Next she tries *Rapeseed* and then she falls down a rabbit hole of reading about monocultures, the destruction of traditional agriculture and genetic modification. The 'author' stops writing, closes her computer, and goes for a walk.

It's not just my characters who misbehave. I too am losing focus. When I'm at the Lilly Library in Bloomington, Indiana, to research the Bloomsbury set, I walk out of the library and drive several hours to the Cincinnati Zoo to see where the world's last passenger pigeon, Martha, died. Then I go to downtown Cincinnati to see the mural dedicated to Martha, a mural that brings passenger pigeons to vibrant life swooping and swirling above a carpark, above the cages that imprisoned them, over the humans that destroyed them, flying into the cavernous heavens, the blue hot sky that sat over the mid-west.

When I return to my computer I hope that finally I might start to work on the novel I'm here to write, but instead I find a website on de-extinction and read about plans to bring passenger pigeons back to life. It can be done in five steps, apparently:

1   Compare the genomes of the passenger pigeon and band-tailed pigeon.
2   Identify regions of the living band-tailed pigeon's genome to edit.
3   Edit the germ-line of living band-tailed pigeons.
4   Breed a new generation of passenger pigeons in captivity.
5   Reintroduce passenger pigeons to the wild through proper conditioning and monitoring.

I learn that once passenger pigeons were numerous. How had Audubon put it? 'The light of noon-day was obscured as by an eclipse, the dung fell in spots, not unlike melting flakes of snow; and the continued buzz of wings had a tendency to lull my senses to repose.'

By the time Audubon reached Louisville the pigeons were still flying and the banks of the Ohio River were crowded with men and boys shooting at the flock. Dead pigeons piled high as snow drifts. Still they endured, flew, as if undiminished, for the next two days. Maybe there were three billion, maybe six. Give or take. They stripped entire forests of white oak, encouraging a plethora of red oak, bitter, less pleasing, in their stead. Their droppings destroyed entire understoreys. Alder and willow bowed to the ground under the weight of them. These pigeons had no sense of proportion but then, nor do humans, and it was humans who failed to account for systems collapse, failed to understand that the sheer size of the pigeon's populations was no guarantee of resilience. It was humans who shot and netted them, baited them with alcohol to make them drunk and easy to catch, sewed the eyes of pigeons shut – why? I don't understand why they *sewed their eyes shut* – posed them as decoys, used nets to drag them down out of the sky, ate them, tossed the excessive numbers of the dead (who could eat that much pigeon pie?), smashed their eggs, set fire to their nests, cut down the forests so they had no roost.

And so it was that a century after their murmurations swept and curved through the sky, a force of nature akin to the weather, the skies cleared. By 1900 there were only three flocks left. One flock survived at the Cincinnati Zoo but the captured birds wouldn't reproduce. These creatures did not operate as individuals but as swarms. Insect-like, their survival depended on the sheer extravagance of their numbers. By 1902 Martha and George were the last pair left. They'd been hatched in either the Milwaukee or Chicago flocks. George died on 10 July 1910. Martha was getting old. She became less likely to flutter, or to walk, just sat, in the semi-darkness and cold of her pagoda in the China House, sporadically pelted with sand by the crowds that surrounded her who wanted to see her move. The zoo finally took measures to protect her but she died on 1 September 1914. Martha's carers, poised for this significant moment, took her out of her enclosure and packed her into a 300-pound block of ice before putting her on a train headed to Washington.

Once at the Smithsonian she was tended to by a taxidermist and white supremacist named RW Shufeldt, who felt Martha's loss keenly.

Her thin and delicate skin, fine as cigarette paper, cleaved closely to her flesh; the greatest skill was needed if one didn't want to lose the feathers, particularly those on the rump. Her organs were stored in jars of methyl alcohol and then she was formed into the pose that would take her into eternity, head modestly tilted to suggest a certain curiosity, grey and copper feathers dancing with avian gleam. There, for the next hundred years, she sat alongside her massacred kin: the dodo, the great auk, the last Carolina parakeet, a heath hen. Over the decades the ranks of her colleagues grew, the cases at the Smithsonian, at museums around the world, became more crowded, exploded with: the King and Kangaroo Island emus, the Tasmanian emu, the New Zealand quail, the double-banded argus, the Mauritius and Reunion shelducks, the Amsterdam, Labrador and Mauritius ducks, the Auckland Islands merganser, the large and small St Helena petrel, the long-tailed triller, Colombian grebes, the Reunion ibis, the black-backed bittern, the Reunion, Mauritius and Rodrigues night-heron, the Pallas's cormorant, the Guadalupe caracara, the Reunion kestrel, many rails, many crakes, many types of gallinule, Mascarene coots, the Canary Islands oystercatcher, the paradise parrot, the robust white eye, the grey fantail, the grey-headed blackbird, white-winged and Tahitian sandpipers, the Rodrigues solitaire, the St Helena dove, Martha's cousins the Reunion, Bonin Wood, blue, Ryukyu and Liverpool pigeons, both thick-billed and Norfolk Island ground-doves, the western rufous bristlebird, the red-moustached fruit-dove, two types of red-crowned parakeets, parrots, macaws, and cuckoo, so many types of owls – and are owls not perfect creatures, how diminished is the world by their dying? – wrens, bellbirds, warblers, some starlings, many types of thrush, the Lanai hookbill joined Martha as did the lesser and greater koa-finch, the lesser and greater akialoa, two types of mamo, the slender-billed grackle. Others will join her soon: the night parrot perhaps, the orange-bellied parrot certainly, the Regent honeyeater.

9.

There is a game – I'm sure many of you have played it – in which you sit around a table with a group of friends and describe the skills you could utilise when the apocalypse comes. I can garden, I offer, when my turn comes.

And this is true. I have gardened in heritage gardens at home and overseas. I have a range of pot plants on my Fitzroy terrace. My speciality is tending unloved garden beds that don't get enough water but can sustain spiky unlovable plants. Aloe vera, artichokes, cactus, succulents. I don't have much experience keeping vegetables alive but feel confident that, if pressed, I'd figure it out.

I can look after animals. I can look after children. At this point I might quote research that suggests that, evolutionarily speaking, human women live a long time once they are no longer fertile because they can help with the tasks that young families need done if they are to survive. They are *useful*.

In a romantic version of this essay I'd also say: I can tell our stories. I can bear witness. But I have to be honest. Some days bearing witness doesn't seem like enough.

> Rieux was listening to the curious buzzing sound that was rising
> from the streets as if in answer to the soughings of the plague.
> At that moment he had a preternaturally vivid awareness of the
> town stretched out below, a victim world secluded and apart,
> and of the groans of agony stifled in its darkness. Then, pitched
> low but clear, Grand's voice came to his ears.
> 'One fine morning in the month of May an elegant young
> horsewoman might have been seen riding a handsome sorrel
> mare along the flowery avenues of the Bois de Boulogne.'
> Silence returned, and with it the vague murmur of the prostrate

town. Grand had put down the sheet and was still staring at it. After a while he looked up.

'What do you think of it?'

Readings

John James Audubon, *The Birds of America: From Original Drawings*, John J Audubon, London, 1827–1838.

James Bradley, 'Unearthed: Last Days of the Anthropocene', *Meanjin*, Spring, 2019.

Albert Camus, *The Plague*, trans. from the French by S Gilbert, Hamilton, London, 1958.

Sophie Cunningham, *Warning: The Story of Cyclone Tracy*, Text Publishing, Melbourne, 2014.

Delia Falconer, 'The Opposite of Glamour', *Sydney Review of Books*, 28 July 2017.

Ross Garnaut, *Garnaut Climate Change Review, Update 2011*, <www.garnautreview.org. au/>.

Greta Thunberg, Transcript of speech at the UN Climate Action Summit, 2019, <bit.ly/ Greta-UN-2019>.

Lucy Treloar, *Wolfe Island*, Pan MacMillan, Sydney, 2019.

KANDOS DIARY EXTRACTS

Laura Fisher and Lucas Ihlein

The drive to Kandos from Sydney takes about three-and-a-half hours. The first hour is spent moving haltingly through Sydney's congested inner west, and then you're on the freeway that cuts across the western suburbs. At Emu Plains you take a winding road up through lower Blue Mountains suburbia, catching glimpses of dense forest and sandstone cliffs. Once you reach the iconic towns of Leura, Katoomba and Blackheath you encounter an idiosyncratic landscape where eucalypts and banksias mingle with pruned cherry trees and monumental evergreens in neat rows. Cockatoos and king parrots dismember pine cones and drop their remnants over groomed European gardens. Around Hartley the tame domesticity of that environment is suddenly gone. The air becomes clear and dry, and as you descend the escarpment, forest gives way to paddocks, sporadic shacks of corrugated iron and timber, abandoned cars and signs pointing to businesses that no longer exist (a herb farm, a motel, an arts and crafts shop). In Lithgow, you revisit suburbia and traffic lights, slowing down momentarily. Past the town enormous smokestacks announce the presence of industry: the Mount Piper coal-fired power station, which produces 15 per cent of the energy generated in New South Wales. Now and then a sparse and too-even tree line appears on a ridge and a blast notification sign pops into view. The highway between Lithgow and Kandos winds between gargantuan land-holdings licensed to Energy Australia, Centennial Coal, Glencore and Castlereagh Coal. You can't see the mines themselves as you drive, but from Google Earth you can scroll around and scrutinise their puzzling shapes, edging the forest with artificial curves and sharp sandy elbows. You need to zoom in far closer to view the streets of the tiny villages of Cullen Bullen, Capertee, Ilford and Clandulla that you drive past and through before arriving, finally, at Kandos. The mines are nevertheless dwarfed by the otherworldly Capertee Valley, which emerges to the right of the ascending road just past Cullen Bullen, its vast perimeter hitting you with a sense of vertigo.

This story follows the fortunes of Kandos, from its establishment as an industrial town on Wiradjuri Country in mid-western New South Wales in the early twentieth century, to its decline and possible reinvention in the early twenty-first. We are artists, and our interest in Kandos was sparked by its 'post-industrial problem', when the town began to empty out after the closure of its cement plant. Kandos is a microcosm of environmental politics in twenty-first-century Australia. Native wilderness, coalmining, farming, Aboriginal sacred Country. Treeless pasture, eroded gullies, empty shops on the main street. Boom and bust, and the possibility of imagining a future beyond the extraction economy. Our story takes the form of 'diary extracts' from the town. Some of these extracts are drawn from archives and historical records; some from our own experience; others may be imagined or fictionalised. All these fragments suggest how the art collective we are part of, the Kandos School of Cultural Adaptation (KSCA), sits thoughtfully and precariously in relation to its namesake.

1913

The NSW Cement Lime and Coal Company is establishing a new cement plant to meet the demand for roads, buildings and railway infrastructure in the growing metropolis of Sydney. The town of Kandos is founded to house its workforce. Before this, Australia was importing cement from Germany. Kandos is located 5 kilometres from a large limestone deposit, close to abundant coal seams, and only 7 kilometres from Rylstone, a settler town formerly known as Dabee (the name of the Wiradjuri Clan upon whose land it was established in the 1840s). Kandos Cement becomes a household name. Its most famous projects are the Sydney Harbour Bridge and the Opera House.

1926

From the quarrying of its stone to the final bagging and trucking of the cement, Kandos is a model of efficiency ... Fifty thousand men in allied Australian industries are now engaged in handling the products of Kandos ... From the mammoth turbo-alternators of the beautifully laid out power-house through all the operations to the weird little machines of the testing department, which ensures the even standard of the product, there is an almost automatic process of production. The Cudgegong River supplies the company with unlimited quantities of water. Its coal is hewn from a hill at the back of the works. The mill itself is fed with limestone by 200 skips travelling over an aerial ropeway at the rate of five miles an hour, each carrying up to a ton of stone from the quarry three miles from the main works. Consideration for employees is a feature at Kandos, and every precaution is taken to obviate the possibility of injury. Baths are provided, and the employees can emerge fresh and clean to the free tennis courts or other recreations. Kandos also boasts a golf links, a racecourse, and a well patronised rifle club. With long continuity of employment, Kandos has developed into a prosperous town of 8,000 people, with comfortable homes, well-stocked shops – and a picture show.

JF Higgins, MLC, *Sydney Morning Herald*, 17 August 1926

1962

Harry Oxley, anthropology graduate from the University of Sydney, embarks on a study of Kandos and Rylstone. Oxley rents a house in Kandos for his family, and for the next three years juggles his job in Sydney with his Kandos research. He continues visiting the town regularly until 1971. 'In all this time', he writes:

> I attended as many meetings as possible, joined in working bees, went to fundraising entertainments, visited and received visits, and joined the gossip circles at the bars. I even became one of the founders of a project. In short, I participated.

Oxley's study delves into the complicated relationship between the 'Two Towns'. Rylstone is a 'quiet country town serving a moderately prosperous district', with a local population of 800 people and charming sandstone buildings reflecting its deeper colonial history. Kandos is a lively, 'fairly affluent' working-class society of around 2500 people. While Rylstone had emerged organically as a result of colonial expansion and the establishment of pastoral land-holdings by squatters, Kandos was planned around a single industry. Oxley writes:

Kandos is one thing alone – an industrial town. It owes its birth and continued existence to the cement industry and primarily to the Kandos Cement Company. It will thrive no longer than local coal and lime supplies last. It proclaims its nature by a bucket ropeway across the access road, a factory belching white smoke, men in the streets wearing hard helmets, and caked cement dust everywhere.

As an anthropologist, Oxley's interest is in how egalitarian values interact with economic structures and social bonds. He painstakingly tallies up the membership of various clubs, committees, volunteer organisations and church groups in Kandos and Rylstone, the lists and tables occupying several pages in his book. The local workforce in Kandos ensures that money is invested in schools, the library, the museum, the olympic-size swimming pool, and other projects. He calls his book *Mateship in Local Organization: A Study of Egalitarianism, Stratification, Leadership and Amenities Projects in a Semi-industrial Community in Inland New South Wales*. In his conclusion he suggests that the social system of the Two Towns, with its contending forces of egalitarianism and social hierarchy, is a system 'analogous to the ecological system of a wilderness in which entities jostle one another for living space'. One value or the other will gain leverage depending on the social and economic events that occur. His parting words, after dutifully qualifying the analogy, are: 'ours would be a sorry discipline if we could not leave each research job with a bagful of hunches to take to the next one. And it would be sorrier if we could not think that in studying the minutiae of a single community we were getting a hold on the whole social world'.

July 1977

The *Sun* newspaper features a two-page article titled 'The Ghost over Kandos' Shoulder'. Kandos Works has reduced its workforce considerably. The cement works in nearby Charbon (which fifty years ago had employed 300 people) has now closed. In the preface of the second edition of his book, published in 1978, Harry Oxley writes of Kandos that 'the boom-town of the original study is a boom-town no longer … The Two Towns of the foreseeable future promise to be a continuing charge on the social security bill'. He speculates on the future of Kandos and Rylstone:

> I am convinced that small rural communities like these are eminently worth not only saving but leading to prosperity. Few of the Australian population live in them, but their decline to mere rural slumhood would leave the fabric of national life the worse. Profit-driven private enterprise cannot save them. I see their main future hopes to lie in some government initiative for setting up and subsidising small local industries … [But] rural workers, unlike rural graziers or urban workers, represent Australia's most politically forgotten category. I thus suspect that nothing much will be done for these people or for their communities until it becomes too scandalous and/or too costly to continue doing nothing.

July 2011

Cement Australia announces it will close the cement plant in Kandos. The company claims that it is no longer a competitive enterprise, due to outdated technology, the strong Australian dollar, a shortage of skilled labour and high energy prices. Some commentators report that it is a casualty of the Gillard Labor government's carbon tax. In subsequent years, jobs in mining and industry in the region become scarce as multiple coalmines are closed or placed under 'care and maintenance' contracts with skeleton crews. The economic fortunes of the district are again hit in 2014, when Energy Australia closes the Wallerawang power station located one hour south of Kandos. One of the largest coal-fired stations in Australia, Wallerawang has operated since 1957, sourcing its coal from local mines, powering the electrification of the railways in the region and supplying electricity to Sydney. These are significant socioeconomic impacts for the non-farming population of Kandos. As Oxley predicted, Kandos, being 'one thing alone' and 'belong[ing] to the industrial world' is vulnerable to forces outside its control. By 2016, the population of post-cement Kandos has dwindled to 1300 people. The main street is dotted with empty shops, and local employment is hard to find. If you talk to the locals, it's jobs in the mines they want.

August 2011

Brett and Jennifer Nutting move to Kandos from Rylstone. They begin to observe a trickle of artists and other Sydney escapees making Kandos their new home. Brett wryly describes it as 'far, far, far, west Marrickville'. Real estate is ridiculously cheap now that the cement works has shut down. Brett:

> When the grinding, the lights, the whistles, the bells and the
> fucking dust stopped ... 24 hours a day, lights on at night,
> hump, chunk chunk, hump, wholalalump, gear changes, shift
> changes ... When the factory shut, being in the cement business
> and not in the real estate business, the company put about 20 or
> 30 properties on the market all at once ...

Sydney art theorist and curator Ann Finegan buys a small shop on the main street, as a place to look after her elderly mother. After a while she begins to host artist residencies there, calling the venture Kandos Projects. Early visitors include activist artists supporting communities in the region who are protesting against various mining projects, such as the mine that the South Korean company KEPCO hopes to establish in the Bylong Valley just north of Kandos. If it proceeds, this mine will abut Tarwyn Park, a famous agricultural property and horse stud where Peter Andrews developed his model of land restoration known as Natural Sequence Farming. Among the Sydney artists who visit Kandos Projects in 2012 are Georgie Pollard and Alex Wisser. Late one night, Ann, Georgie and Alex cook up the idea of an arts festival for Kandos. The first Cementa Contemporary Arts Festival is planned for early 2013.

February 2013

A series of *Welcome to Kandos* posters appears in shop windows in the town during the Cementa Festival. The posters feature cheerfully captioned colour pictures of several well-appointed local assets. The southern hemisphere's largest solar thermal power station. A botanic gardens focused on climate change adaptation, housed in the defunct cement works. The Kandos University with its School of Cultural Adaptation. A local plywood-bicycle sharing scheme. Festival visitors are impressed, but the posters cause confusion among locals, who know for certain their town possesses no such things. Have these expensive-looking new infrastructure schemes been installed overnight without their knowledge? And if so, by whom?

The posters are a work of fiction – the creation of artist Ian Milliss, who grew up in the region and knows Kandos, its labour history and social context intimately. The posters are an outlet for his frustration with Lithgow Council, where he has worked for several years. Ian has been arguing that the council has a duty to prepare towns in the region for an economic transition away from coal-related industries, but his arguments have had no traction. The posters' garish fonts, clumsy layout and use of generic images pulled down from a Google image search speak more to amateur 1990s desktop publishing than to the futuristic scenarios they depict. This, perhaps, is what makes them so convincing: it's precisely the sort of thing that a local tourist bureau sponsored by the council might print and distribute to promote the town – except that the content has been tweaked.

With the *Welcome to Kandos* posters, Milliss imagines the town *as it could be*: 'resilient and forward looking', a leader in climate change adaptation, which has turned its main problem (the closure of the cement works) into a golden opportunity. Why couldn't Kandos have all these things?

April 2015

Sydney artist Gilbert Grace looks to Milliss's poster series as a blueprint for action, and declares his intention to make each of its utopian schemes a reality – starting with the plywood bikes and the Kandos School of Cultural Adaptation. While the concept of the School, alongside all the other aspects of the utopian Kandos, is a hastily cobbled together figment of the artists' imaginations, it begins to spark ideas. Half-a-dozen artists from Kandos, Sydney, Wollongong and the Blue Mountains gather together and KSCA is formed.

October 2015

The Cementa Contemporary Arts Festival in Kandos expands its program to include a 'land-based artist residency'. Gilbert Grace is selected as the first artist. Local farmer Stuart Andrews (the son of Peter, Natural Sequence Farming inventor) agrees to host the project on his property near Rylstone. Grace has been looking into materials to create the fleet of bicycles from Ian's poster. Rather than using imported plywood, he wonders whether he can fabricate the frames locally from scratch, using bamboo bound with hemp twine. Grace also proposes that he and Stuart grow a trial crop of hemp as a collaborative work of land art. In time a new idea emerges: the hemp crop could be processed to make masonry. As an idea for Kandos, this is a neat switch from cement (a highly carbon-intensive industry) to 'hempcrete' (which continually absorbs carbon dioxide over its lifespan). Grace begins planning a 'commemorative gate' constructed from hempcrete for the main street, symbolic of the potential for Kandos to reinvent itself as a hub for regenerative industries. It is a provocative idea, one that would have been right at home on Milliss's posters. Why couldn't Kandos' idle cement infrastructure be adapted to the large-scale manufacture of hempcrete and other hemp-based industries? Farmer Stuart likes the idea of trying out a hemp crop. Stuart has recently sold Tarwyn Park to the KEPCO mining company, having decided that the battle was causing too much stress for his family and that he was better off using the money to develop Natural Sequence Farming education. He has acquired a degraded piece of farmland on the Bylong Valley Way. Stuart imagines growing and harvesting hemp as part of his land-management cycle, as a mulch and weed mat, to add fertility to the depleted soils and prevent further erosion. An unusual collaboration between artist and farmer has begun.

September 2016

The proprietor of the Kandos Newsagency on the main street pins up a poster in the window signalling his support of an open-cut coal-mine that KEPCO is hoping to develop in the Bylong Valley. Many Kandos residents expect it to create hundreds of jobs in the area and boost the town's population. In response to the newsagency poster, the windows of Kandos Projects next door have been taken over by local artist Terry Burrows. Burrows installs an exhibition called *@thecoalface*, a display of documents outlining the negative environmental impact of the mine to groundwater and surface waters, and emailed conversations between activists who oppose the mine.

October 2016

It's a crisp spring weekend and Gilbert Grace, Eloise Lindeback, Laura Fisher and her son Max camp out to build Gilbert's hempcrete 'commemorative gate'. Terry Burrows, resident of Angus Avenue (the main street of Kandos), has made his front driveway available and there is space to build a modest, low-lying feature wall. A small, round auger turns over the mix of lime, water and hemp hurds, which are fragments of the woody inner section of the hemp plant's stalk. The artists take turns filling and tamping down the hempcrete in the formwork Gilbert has constructed. Gilbert adds earth-coloured oxides to the mix to echo the tones of the sandstone cliffs that surround Kandos. He embeds the lettering CEMENTA on the face of the wall so that it will remain in relief once the formwork is removed.

The hempcrete materials have been sourced from a commercial supplier. Stuart and Gilbert have been unsuccessful in getting a licence to grow their trial hemp crop. The NSW Department of Primary Industries is concerned about the experimental nature of the project, led by an artist. Industrial hemp and marijuana are different species: the former contains only trace amounts of THC (the psycho-active compound in marijuana), yet the industry is tightly controlled because of the fear that growers will use one as a cover for cultivating the other. The licensing application process has been long and demanding, and Stuart has a terse conversation with a staff member at the department. A few weeks later, the police visit Stuart's farm to check whether he has gone ahead and planted the crop without permission.

November 2016

It is the first day of *Futurelands2*, a public forum hosted by KSCA. Kandos Aboriginal Elders Lyn Symes and Kevin Williams speak to the audience in the Kandos Community Hall about the violent confrontations and arrests taking place in the United States at the site of the Dakota Access (oil) Pipeline in North Dakota. Members and supporters of the Standing Rock Sioux tribe have been occupying a protest camp at the construction site for several months. The construction work has damaged ancestral burial grounds and sacred sites and the pipeline will cross the Missouri River within the Standing Rock Sioux Reservation. Article II of the Fort Laramie Treaty, signed in 1868, had guaranteed the tribe's 'undisturbed use and occupation' of these lands. Lyn and Kevin ask the audience to express their solidarity with the Standing Rock protesters in some way.

March 2017

It is a few weeks before the 2017 Cementa Contemporary Arts Festival opens. Someone has spray-painted the word 'NO' in front of 'CEMENTA' on the hempcrete commemorative gate. The lettering also has a large cross scrawled through it. As the masonry surface is too friable for the paint to be cleaned off, Gilbert decides to apply a layer of white render to the wall, concealing the graffiti, the oxide colours and the texture of the raw hempcrete.

April 2017

During the Cementa Festival Gilbert delivers artist talks at the hempcrete wall, serves hemp cookies, displays hemp-based fabrics woven by local artist Kelly Leonard, and demonstrates how to make hemp paper. He also exhibits a prototype bicycle made of bamboo and hemp twine. Busloads of festival-goers visit Stuart's farm to learn about Natural Sequence Farming and witness how he is addressing deep gully erosion.

As part of the festival, Lyn Symes and Kevin Williams, working with Future Method architect Genevieve Murray, host a breakfast gathering a short drive from Kandos town on a piece of crown land designated as a remnant Travelling Stock Route (TSR). Prior to colonisation, TSRs were sacred walking tracks punctuated by waterholes, used by the traditional owners. As Australia began its pastoral expansion, these pathways were taken over as convenient paths for droving and watering cattle. Kevin and Lyn have been trying for several years to secure Native Title on the land, but they are frustrated by the drawn-out bureaucratic processes and the revolving door of officials in the government department.

May 2017

A group of artists representing KSCA travel to the New England area of northern New South Wales. An alliance has been forged with The

Living Classroom, a community-run land-education facility on the outskirts of Bingara. This trip brings together artists, farmers and people concerned with rural sustainability. It marks the beginning of KSCA's new project entitled *An Artist, a Farmer and a Scientist Walk into a Bar* … The project draws together eight cross-disciplinary collaborations putting forward regional New South Wales as a hub for creative ideas for cultural, environmental and economic regeneration. One of the artists, Diego Bonetto, takes seriously the desire to create new post-industrial economies around Kandos. With his *wildfood. store* project, he collaborates with landowners in mid-western New South Wales, training them to recognise and harvest weeds from their properties, and linking them with high-end chefs in Sydney, who are prepared to pay premium prices for good-quality foraged wild plants. A major challenge for Bonetto's supply chain is how to deliver the weeds from paddock to plate in a timely fashion, given the distance to be travelled between Kandos and Sydney.

January 2019

The Boring Company, founded by tech entrepreneur Elon Musk, is creating a test tunnel in Los Angeles. Musk envisages a future network of tunnels that would see cars dropped in and transported at high speed on an electric platform. Australian politician Jeremy Buckingham tweets @*elonmusk*: 'I'm a lawmaker in Sydney, which is choking with traffic. How much to build a 50km tunnel through the Blue Mountains and open up the west of our State?' Musk replies: 'About \$15M/km for a two way high speed transit, so probably around \$750M plus maybe \$50M/station'. Buckingham: 'Thanks, mate. Sounds like a bargain …'

The exchange sets off the Australian press, primed by Musk's earlier delivery on his promise to solve South Australia's energy problems with a Tesla lithium battery system in fewer than 100 days. Such a tunnel might enable the kind of mobility that townsfolk in the region enjoyed at the turn of the twentieth century, when the Gwabegar Railway Line pushed out far into the west, stopping at multiple towns all the way to Bourke.

April 2019

We wonder: what kind of transformation in urban/rural relations could result from Kandos being connected to Sydney by a giant Tesla tunnel? Is another mega-infrastructure project what Kandos really needs? How will the fortunes of farming families in the district be further affected by the extraction industry, and by the frictions between high-yield industrial agriculture and regenerative models like Natural Sequence Farming? How might we map the emergent gentrification of the town, as artists and others flee the unaffordable metropolis and fall in love with the open sky and the immense Wollemi forest that neighbours the town? At the time of writing, Kandos appears to have weathered the collapse of its cement industry, but how will it withstand the inevitable phasing-out of the coal industry over the next thirty years? Having been the town that built Sydney, what might escapees from Sydney be able to offer Kandos now? What kind of ecological social system, to use Oxley's analogy, might arise through the mingling of miners, farmers, artists and others from far, far, far west Marrickville?

Postscript: September 2019

The NSW Independent Planning Commission refuses development consent for the KEPCO mine. The commission acknowledges that while the mine would bring economic benefits to current generations, unacceptable costs would be borne by future generations as the 'environmental impacts, particularly on groundwater and productive agricultural land, would last long after the mine is decommissioned'. The decision is widely publicised and celebrated by many. However, it prompts a backlash from the NSW Minerals Council, which runs an advertising campaign arguing the decision creates a crisis for jobs, business and investment in the state and that the NSW planning system is flawed. It also triggers heated conversations on social media among members of the communities of Kandos and Rylstone, some of whom argue that the decision was hijacked by the demands of 'greenies' from the city. In a surprise move, local councillor Peter Shelley proposes a charity 'boxing match' between miners and greenies, to raise money for animal feed for farmers affected by the drought.

Note: Laura Fisher and Lucas Ihlein are students of the Kandos School of Cultural Adaptation (KSCA), a collective of artists and others who are experimenting with adaptive cultural change. KSCA aims to support creative work that reaches beyond the familiar contexts of art to investigate new ways of acting in the world. At the time of writing, the other student members are Gilbert Grace, Ian Milliss, Kelly Reiffer, Imogen Semmler, Kim Williams, Diego Bonetto, Eloise Lindeback, Sarah Breen Lovett, Christine McMillan, Leanne Thompson, Belinda Innes, Georgie Pollard and Alex Wisser. You can find out about KSCA's current project *An Artist, a Farmer and a Scientist Walk into a Bar* ... and other activities at their website <www.ksca.land>.

Readings

New South Wales Government Independent Planning Commission, 'Bylong Coal Project Refused Development Consent', Media release, 18 September 2019, <bit.ly/ NSWIPC>.

Harry G Oxley, *Mateship in Local Organization: A Study of Egalitarianism, Stratification, Leadership and Amenities Projects in a Semi-industrial Community in Inland New South Wales*, University of Queensland Press, Brisbane, 1978, pp. xxvii–xxix, 4, 61, 62, 213.

Benjamin Palmer, '"Miners v Environmentalists": Charity Boxing Match Proposed by Councillor and Rylstone Businessman', *Mudgee Guardian*, 16 October 2019, <bit.ly/Mudgee-G>.

440 BRIQUETTE

Libby Robin

In my hands I hold a smooth black block with rounded corners, painted with a fluorescent orange number on one side, on the other the text 'thanks for the warming' in Mandy Martin's distinctive flowing writing. The black block is compressed brown coal from the Latrobe Valley mines. Briquettes like this heated thousands of hot-water systems in Victoria. From early childhood, I can remember the particular smell of briquettes burning and helping my uncle stoke up the sooty water heater outside the back door at my grandmother's suburban Melbourne home. By the 1960s when I was visiting, the dilapidated 'dunny' far away by the back lane had been replaced by an 'almost-inside' toilet next to the briquette heater. The hot-water service also served to (slightly) warm the loo on frosty mornings. Both the hardy briquette heater and the almost-inside toilet survived into the twenty-first century, when the house was sold in 2010 after seventy years in the family.

I was touched to be presented with such an evocative personal object by artist Mandy Martin at the Anthropocene Slam event she curated in Melbourne in May 2015. The #AnthropSlam was part of her exhibition 'The Warming' at the first biennial CLIMARTE festival, which promotes arts for a safe climate. The gallery was filled with wonderful works of art in all sorts of media, including plastic and dripping ice. At its centre was a display of objects created specifically for performing – or 'slamming' – the Anthropocene. The Slam was moderated by William L Fox, director of the Center for Art+Environment, Nevada Museum of Art in Reno, together with Peter Christoff, a former Victorian Commissioner for the Future, and me. For the conclusion, Mandy Martin presented us each with a personally inscribed briquette.

The briquette's 440 inscription referenced the sculpture of Canberra artist David Jensz, one of the artworks in 'The Warming'. Jensz used a briquette to mount a bronze statue of the numbers '440' – 440 parts per million (ppm) being a predicted 'tipping point' for dangerous climate warming. In 2016 we crossed the 400 ppm barrier, and we are now inexorably moving towards 440 and more – with predictions that such concentrations and consequent warming will cause chaotic responses in Earth systems. Jensz's *Coal+440* was a powerful artwork in this context.

The planetary scale is so large – and the briquette is so small. This object personalised planetary responsibilities for me. It enabled me to cradle the Anthropocene in my hand. It was both an everyday object of historical significance and a sculpture. In object terms it explored the fiction/nonfiction border between 'found object' and creative artwork. Mandy's inscription added a historical moment, the #AnthropSlam at the first CLIMARTE festival.

Now I look more closely at the fluoro orange paint Mandy chose for the inscription. This paint was part of a kit she developed and took up to the Djelk Indigenous Protected Area, for *Arnhembrand*, a philanthropically funded 'new wave' Aboriginal art project that raised money to support conservation initiatives in western Arnhem Land. Thus, in this small object, the despair of the 440 number is counterpointed with hope, the hope of new initiatives that might help with adapting to changing climates in Australia's far north, thousands of kilometres away from suburban Melbourne.

ON MIC.

Gretchen Miller

I'm taking a train trip today, to a distant shop on the opposite side of Sydney Harbour to where I live. There are bird calls and rustling trees there, I imagine, and the quiet shifting of large, old houses on their foundations on a hot summer day. I like to write in different places, and this is an hour's journey from the concrete-bound inner west – it's a perfect time for writing and remembering.

The shop sells an expensive, hand-sized digital sound recorder by a brand renowned for its clarity, which I need for my work. I could mail-order this machine, but some things must be done the old-fashioned way. With luck this machine will be a work tool for a long time, so I want to hold it in my hands before committing. More practically I need to hear it – and another microphone I might buy with it – to check that the sound is right.

From my earliest memory, the sparsely populated Australian inland has had a powerful psychological effect on me. In the tiny London townhouse I was raised in, we had Sidney Nolan landscapes on the walls that took me 'somewhere else', and storybooks illustrated with red kangaroos bounding across the desert and a platypus diving into mysterious green river depths. When my parents returned to

Australia, bringing their UK-born children 'home', the inland was where I wanted to be.

Fast forward to my mid-twenties and a time of firsts: first public radio feature and first journey over the Great Dividing Range to the inland. My mentor, graceful poet and elegant radio-maker Robyn Ravlich had carefully set me up with a Sony MS5 microphone, handling it with both respect and affection. It is a rugged creature. Put a good windjammer on it (the ones we call 'dead cats' for their fluffy grey 'fur' and long fat bodies) and the fiercest desert wind cannot faze it. On that first journey it was my reliable companion, a conversation starter with strangers and a genuine workhorse.

I had finished studying music composition. I heard the sounds I recorded as a kind of music and they became an integral part of my radio programs, composed, in a sense, like operas. The stories of the people I met were the singers, their orchestra the sounds of places I recorded around them, often taking turns to solo and punctuate the spoken word. I wrote music with earthy, grounded instruments – double bass, oboe, percussion – and they were woven with the gathered sounds of place. With ABC sound engineers Russell Stapleton and Judy Rapley, I worked to find the depths in these floating sounds and built sonic relationships among them.

Some years ago, I found myself sitting on the edge of Paruku (Lake Gregory) in the northern Tanami Desert. Flat desert sand merged into flat shimmering water. Bessie Doonday, a Napangarti woman from Mulan, was speaking the stories of the place, and as she spoke the microphone picked up the faint voices of black swans far away on the lake. I asked Bessie to pause, so I could record the swans on their own to build into the soundscape. She paused, the swans stopped. She spoke once more, the swans started calling. It happened over and again until, laughing, we gave up. Country was speaking to Bessie – not just the swans, but the lake, the sand, the scrub and the sky as well. Bessie heard it the same way she always heard that place.

But for my unversed ears, it was the microphone, like a talisman of philosopher Jean Gebser's magic consciousness, that revealed that relationship: her voice and Country entwined.

I bought a second hand MS5 of my own. My battered old black microphone with its rich and deep sound capture continues to amplify the otherwise unheard. In the human subject, the lived experience, the texture of the body which powers the voice with its breath, the shape of the vocal cords, throat, soft and hard palate and the shape of the skull are caught and amplified by the microphone's diaphragm. Barthes alluded to this in his 1962 essay, 'The Grain of the Voice': 'The "grain" is the body in the voice as it sings, the hand as it writes, the limb as it performs …'

THIS IS AN INTIMATE SPACE. A RECORDED VOICE, WRITE Australian radio makers and academics Virginia Madsen and John Potts, 'fills the psychic space of the listener'. American cultural critic Susan Douglas wrote that it 'envelops us, pouring into us … including us, involving us', and that it 'oscillates' in a most intimate way with our inner selves, our inner voice. The breath driving the voice emanates directly from the body which physically cradles the heart's emotions. This microphone picks up the physical body's expression of emotions to which we have evolved to be alert. Uncertainty. Hope. Love. Pain. Resignation. Joy. We attune viscerally and respond accordingly. In the Anthropocene we orientate to human presence. But there are other voices to be heard, and these sounds exist in the world outside the human too: the metallic sigh as the outback gate settles back on its hinges, the resonance and tenderness in the soft coo of the corella to its mate, the scratching snuffle of an echidna. Listen from various perspectives: an outback bore-water pump, structurally raw and visually stark with its windmill, can be heard close and urgent, layered with the quick gush of water, or from a distance as it merges with the wind. How vulnerable are those beings that depend on the continuation of that sound. You can put the microphone against the metal like a bionic ear and listen to the steel stress and flex.

Recording technology is a mediator here. It's not ideal for the potential of rupture. But unlike the stealing of an ancient artefact, the sound remains behind when I have gone. The dissemination, the gifting of its facsimile to others, is, I think, worth the mediation.

If we want to pay attention to the world, we have to learn to listen, literally as well as figuratively. As much as we can, we must listen to the cry of the disappearing curlew across the water, to the drip and crash of melting ice.

The microphone is always with me to hear and record. This is my offering back to the planet. It's quiet, it's modest, and I think, sometimes, it captures a momentary beauty, even in the shadow of destruction, absence, loss and mourning.

I wrote this on that train trip, and I came home with that new recorder. It will marry so well with my microphone – the glassy clarity of the recordings like a partly opened window to the innermost worlds.

Readings

Roland Barthes, *Image, Music, Text: Roland Barthes*, Fontana, London, 1977, p. 188.

Susan J Douglas, *Listening In: Radio and the American Imagination*, University of Minnesota Press, Minneapolis, 2004, p. 30.

Virginia Madsen and John Potts, 'Voice-Cast: The Distribution of the Voice Via Podcasting', in Norie Neumark, Ross Gibson and Theo van Leeuwen (eds), *Voice: Vocal Aesthetics in Digital Arts and Media*, Massachusetts Institute of Technology Press, Cambridge, MA, and London, 2010, pp. 33–60, at p. 44.

Kim Mahood and Gretchen Miller, *Paruku: In the Tracks of the Two Dogs*, ABC Radio National, 9 March 2008.

TO STAND TOGETHER

Angela Tiatia

My childhood home in Sāmoa was and still is a magical place. The pungent smell of the tropics, the weight of heat, the silk of salt water on skin, and the strict rhythm of life in accordance with the environment provided fertile grounds for imagination, play, discipline and growth.

As an adolescent and adult I lived between Sāmoa, New Zealand and Australia. With each return to Sāmoa, I witnessed a gradual change in the land and sea. Then, eight years went by. This was the longest gap in my return home. When I went back to my village I was shocked. On my family land, where our home resides, the lush green grass, abundant breadfruit trees, mango trees, guava, taro, hibiscus shrubs and frangipani trees had all disappeared. They had given way to a thick brown sludge that came above my ankles. In our backyard there was nothing green, not even a single bush or tree. Just water and mud. My uncle explained, 'There is nothing – nothing can grow here because of the water.' Turning to the sea, I noticed that the rich coral life was now skeletal. This experience affected me deeply and led to my research into climate change and, ultimately, into the making of *Tuvalu*.

The word Tuvalu comes from 'Tu', meaning 'stand', and 'valu', the number eight, so Tuvalu means 'to stand together' as eight (atolls). Tuvalu is a small nation that lies halfway between Sydney and Hawaii. It is remote. To get there you need to take three aeroplanes, and then a boat for inter-island travel. It is a place of surreal beauty, not only of its land but also of its people.

So why did I choose Tuvalu rather than Sāmoa? I chose Tuvalu because right now it is critically fragile. Standing at an average of only 4.5 metres above sea level, Tuvalu is extremely vulnerable to the impacts of climate change, such as extreme weather patterns, rising waters and constant flooding, warming seas, erosion and dying coral.

I also chose Tuvalu because its language and culture are very close to the Sāmoan language and culture. Social, political and economic connections between the Tuvaluans and the Sāmoans date back thousands of years, which is evident in our language and cultural ties.

When I arrived, rumour quickly spread across Funafuti – the main atoll of Tuvalu – that a Sāmoan woman with a camera had arrived. The Tuvaluans are accustomed to film crews, who have made numerous documentaries about the Tuvaluan environment. As a quick sidetrack – when watching these documentaries I often wondered: is this real? I had to see for myself.

In the making of this work, it was really important for me to make connections with the local community before I began filming anything. I was prepared to abandon this work and take a research break if I couldn't make authentic connections. As the days passed I gradually gained the confidence to join in on conversations with new female friends, teasing them about being 'faikakala's!' – 'cheeky gossips!' – and we would all laugh. Then, a few more days passed and another rumour spread around Funafuti – saying that a Sāmoan sister had returned home. These connections gave me the insights, permission and confidence to commence work. I filmed for two-and-half weeks, from the darkness of dawn rising, to daylight falling in the night.

I shot one terabyte of footage on Tuvalu – which is now edited into a twenty-minute video in three channels. It's one per cent of the captured footage. In this work it was important for me to document the island and its people as they moved throughout the rhythm of their day in time to the rhythm of their environment. This work takes the viewer from dusk to dawn. You see the slow waking of the island, the roads being cleared of debris thrown across them by the overnight waves; we see the erosion and the relentless beating of the shoreline by the waves; we also see the bubbling of salt water up through the ground from beneath the island.

Working with the Australian Museum, Blacktown Arts Centre and Casula Powerhouse Arts Centre, it was clear that they are dedicated to making cultural connections between the public and the objects that they house and protect. They are prompting us to put our minds and efforts into the preservation of our lands and our living cultures.

The global scale of climate change can by its very nature make it seem too big to deal with and instil a sense of inertia. This inaction is further compounded by the fact that many of the most immediate impacts are being felt in faraway places. It is easy for it to become out of sight and out of mind.

My intention when making *Tuvalu* was to face into both of these challenges. To show climate change not on a global scale but on an intimate one. To glimpse how life is lived in an environment where the impacts of a changing environment are part of every day, rather than dramatic one-off events.

Tuvalu is the canary in the global minefield. It is a warning for us to take action now. When I first started my research into climate change in 2014 it was predicted that Tuvalu would be uninhabitable within 100 years. Most recently I heard it is now twenty-five years. What does this mean for us as global citizens? Where are our responsibilities in leaving a habitable world for generations to come?

MUSEUM OCCUPATIONS

Jenny Newell

Douglas looks at me hopefully. The waves wash up against the stone wall beside us, chickens peck around the huts, kids in shorts hop about, watching us with grins. I pause from taking photos of the canoe builder chipping away at the tree trunk under a tarp tied between coconut palms. I say hello to Douglas, trying for the lilting Solomons Pijin intonation, and introduce myself. Douglas says he heard there was someone coming on the ship today who wanted to talk to them about climate change. 'We need someone who knows about climate change', he says. 'We got concrete to help with our sea-walls from the Rural Development Fund. But we're not good with concrete here. We don't know how to make it strong – the wall is already washing away.' My stomach sinks. I tell him I'm sorry. I work for the Australian Museum. A museum worker must always be versatile, but concreting is one skillset I really don't have.

Douglas agrees to record a video interview about climate change impacts on Taumako. He talks of the shoreline being worn away, and is concerned that they will soon be living on a tiny, thin strip of land against the cliffs. He laughs at the idea; I can see it doesn't seem credible to him as an *actual* future. He says the days are hotter now; this is what anyone I talk to in the Pacific says about how things are feeling now. It is getting hotter, in this place that already brings a constant sweat. The weather is so unpredictable – the Elders can't predict storms as well as they used to.

There are small solar panels with batteries on most of the houses here on the island. The Solomon Islands government supplied them. We could have solar power being generated all over Australia. I still can't fathom why we don't. Snapping a photo, the dark looming presence of shame and regret that follows me so much of the time bites at the back of my neck.

The canoe maker continues chipping with his adze, bringing the tree trunk to a shape that calls to the ocean. I talk to some young men nearby; they have been away for a few years to study in Honiara, returned home now. They are concerned about the future of this place. They want to talk to me about climate change on camera; there is an edge of anger, but it is, mostly, gracefully sublimated – kindly not connecting the dots between this and all the preceding devastations and exploitations visited upon their people by mine. I'm planning to include their interviews in our permanent climate change exhibition in Sydney, to give visitors a glimpse of what Pacific Islanders are up against. It is part of the effect that museums can have in the world, that they can help audiences to slow down and take notice of the things the wider world needs them to recognise. Because Pacific Island communities are losing their precious places and living things because of climate change; because of the appalling rate at which Australians and other wealthy, entitled people are still consuming fossil fuels despite everything we know. As if no one is going under because of it. As if there is no tomorrow.

Until recently I worked with Pacific histories and cultural objects in museums. Over several decades I learned from colleagues, Elders and others in Tahiti, Hawaii, Sāmoa, Aotearoa, the Marshall Islands, Guam, Fiji and in the diaspora. They showed me the impacts of rising temperatures, sea levels and storms on their places, their ancestors, all the intimately interlinked people, plants and animals. The more I learned the more I was able to share Pacific perspectives and ways of caring with the audiences we can reach through museums. When I could, around the usual work of administering and supporting public access to a collection, I worked on listening, documenting, sharing and providing platforms for Pacific voices on climate change. I had a growing sense, though, of needing to devote more time in my daily remit to this, to raising understanding and engagement in the rising climate crisis and inspiring the museum sector to step up more fully to that responsibility. In parallel, I was increasingly recognising the extent to which I am an intruder into a potent and sacred cultural space. I knew that it was time for me to leave that space to those ancestrally connected to it.

Several colleagues around the world were taking a climate leap, leaving jobs that had started to feel too distant from the main urgency around them. I've now joined them. Leaving the security of foundations of expertise is not easy, but I have been gradually building up my knowledge of the cultural dimensions of climate change and keeping up with research on effective climate change communication, so I do have growing resources to call on. In these times we are increasingly being called on to rethink ourselves. We need new types of knowledge.

I am now the manager of Climate Change Projects at the Australian Museum. This involves upscaling public understanding and engagement in the climate crisis. It involves continuing research into the impacts of climate change on human and non-human communities, and helping people in Australia recognise all the solutions waiting to be rolled out. We ran a program supporting art and activism, *Oceania Rising: Climate Change in Our Region*, a collaboration with art centres, Angela Tiatia and other Sydney–Pacific artists and communicators. The program of exhibitors, talks and workshops responded to crowd-sourced questions: 'What can I do?', 'How can I motivate my community?'; 'How can I get the government to act?'). We are developing more ways of connecting to people, especially around climate solutions. We can draw on the powerful ways of knowing and caring for the land, water and living things of Country that First Nations colleagues open up for us. We can help non-Indigenous audiences to step beyond ingrained dualisms that continue, bizarrely, to split humans from 'nature', into thinking and feeling instead the deep interconnectedness of life.

It's a roller coaster. It's exhilarating seeing a project of climate outreach start to connect, or meeting with like-minded museum people here and overseas. It is empowering to be soaring up with them, with ideas and collaborations, and start to see other cultural institutions picking up the UN Sustainable Development Goals. There's the excitement of interviewing a wind and sheep farmer in Crookwell, standing with his magnificent turbines behind him, the pride in his smile having fought for them for over fifteen years, now sustaining his own and two neighbouring families, despite the drought, with a river of reliable income. But then there's the sickening dive, daily; the latest research report, today's *Guardian* article, the latest missive about koalas from wildlife groups, the nine-year-old saying he has no real hope for the future. It's a new occupational hazard.

Caught up in the bushfires where my family live in Cobargo, New South Wales, as 2019 turned to 2020, I learned quickly what knowledge I lacked, as my imaginings of climate-changed futures rose into reality around us. Escaping from the fire with a random collection of things thrown into the car, and then trying to secure the basics for our gaggle of children and grandparents for days in a town with no power, communications or petrol, not sure how my brother and husband were managing back at the fire front, made it clear that disaster preparedness was the skillset I needed. We each have our particular strengths and our specific needs for skill-building, to help us cope in this changing landscape.

The museum can surely help provide tools for people's 'back-packs'. Supported by the important work of listening, recording and sharing stories, the museum can ensure visibility for the solutions we need to pursue as individuals, communities and nations: clean energy, natural solutions for regenerating soils, forests and seas, supporting biodiversity, living sustainably and healing Country.

Part of conveying powerful stories and creating connections will include Taumako and other Pacific neighbours. The museum is partnering with local communities in the Solomon Islands on forest and cultural conservation projects, and we can all see that locally-nuanced resilience measures can help people to keep rising to the challenges that we of capitalist economies continue to intensify. At the museum in Australia we will go on addressing the causes of these challenges, where we need rapid paradigm-shifts to end the country's addiction to coal and to support practices of care for living things. More and more of us in cultural institutions here and internationally are collaborating on projects and outreach to support these efforts. The ways we might be able to help threatened communities are always going to need to be carefully crafted, but museums are good at listening and engaging hearts, minds and even hands. We are good at bold, collective and creative action. We won't turn away.

Note: I acknowledge and am grateful for the land on which the Australian Museum sits where this piece was written – the unceded Country of the Gadigal, part of the Eora Nation.

GOOLARABOOLOO FOREIGN POLICY

Stephen Muecke

I was one of the foreigners who came from down south to visit Paddy Roe, celebrated Nyigina Elder, holding office under his old tamarind tree in his Country, in Broome. He would sit cross-legged, crafting an artefact like a boomerang, and all sorts of people would come to consult with him – anthropologists, priests, writers, developers. Paddy's job was to mediate between the desires of the settler colonial society to modernise the country and his own Elders' dedication to maintaining Country as it is – or was – 'living Country' he would call it.

He had a skill, the ability to tell a good story, and you can read some of them transcribed in his own voice in the two books I wrote with him, *Gularabulu* and *Reading the Country*.

When someone visited, like a developer with the idea that building a Surfers Paradise-type resort on the beach north of Broome might be a great idea, Paddy would laugh and say, 'might be … might be …', and then begin a story.

An hour later, the developer would take his leave, feeling better informed and feeling better about Country the way it was. He might have forgotten all about his modernisation idea, the story Paddy told still turning in his head.

From the 1960s until he became too old, Paddy Roe was a passionate protector of Country and law boss, promoting what they call Goolarabooloo Culture as a way of designating a confederacy of 'saltwater' cultures extending from south of Broome up the Dampier Peninsula. Peoples speaking the Karajarri, Yawuru, Jugun, Ngumbal, Nyul-Nyul, Jabirr-Jabirr and Bardi languages were unified in their observance of a ceremonial Dreaming track that had been laid out by ancestral heroes in *bugarrigarra* law and culture. 'We are all one', Paddy would say.

Since his day, things have changed a lot. His grandsons were involved in continuing his protective role when Woodside Energy, in conjunction with the Western Australian government under Colin Barnett, wanted to build a huge natural-gas liquefying factory on the coast at Walmadany, smack in the middle of the Dreaming track. A long and bitter campaign ensued, and the Goolarabooloo, now identified with the Roe family and a consortium of environmentalist groups, won a temporary reprieve when Woodside pulled out in 2013.

During the campaign to stop the gas plant, someone found an old photograph of Paddy Roe screwed up in a wastepaper bin – the Roe family now had enemies, people who wanted the gas plant to go ahead. It may have been the only copy in existence. It was retrieved and the image found its way onto T-shirts worn during the anti-gas protests.

In the image Paddy Roe puts two objects into dialogue, on the occasion when he was photographed after receiving his Order of Australia medal in 1990. He is shown holding the medal, itself like a little round shield, side by side with his own *garbina* – which is carved with the traditional parallel grooves, *ramu*, in the lightning-strike design for Goolarabooloo Country, where the storms come in from the sea late in the season called *laja*, the build-up to the Wet. Perhaps he was wondering what the medal was really for, so he gets the *garbina* to ask it, as recorded by an unknown person at the time:

This is my gulbinna [sic] (shield). The government gave me this medal. This gulbinna is asking the medal, you going to break up the country or keep it the same as in bugarre garre [sic] (dreamtime).

My interpretation is that he is challenging the two objects to perform their protective roles. Why protection? You can gaze at this composition for a moment and think back beyond when it was taken, to the history of the Broome area. The people of the Kimberley were subjected to successive waves of dispossession and terror from the late nineteenth century. Armed resistance was out of the question in open country, with only spears and boomerangs against guns. Protection came down to some kind of diplomacy: artful storytelling in Paddy Roe's case.

Artful diplomacy was Paddy Roe's version of Goolarabooloo 'foreign policy', literally a strategy for survival. In the face of colonial violence, people had to protect themselves and their communities by thinking in terms of shields, real and metaphoric. The metaphoric role of the shield is confirmed when it is doubled up by the little medal-as-shield, and their relationship of diplomacy is made explicit through the dialogue. A shield has power; the *garbina* has a design that reproduces the 'lightning' power of the *bugarrigarra*, and so does the figure of speech, the metaphor that animates the *garbina* and gives it words addressed to the colonisers – but only obliquely, for Paddy has thought to animate the objects and make them address each other like diplomats between the worlds of coloniser and colonised.

It's a clever composition, don't you think? It draws you into a sympathetic relationship with him, his people and their Dreaming. It's that sympathy that is the real protection. Even now, some decades later, it can draw you in again, to reflect upon history and what people need to do to survive.

WALKING
TOGETHER

LOVING

David Ritter

Tap. Tap. Tap.

It is a late afternoon in May in Townsville in 2019 and I'm standing in a small group of twenty or so, gathered together in a semicircle, watching four dancers who are performing in front of us in a rectangular grass courtyard at the rear of a hotel. The smallest is a little boy, who is aged, I guess, around three or four. He rhythmically strikes two sticks together in sync with the movements of those who are dancing, his face inwardly absorbed and not really engaging with the adults around him. The child is sensorily immersed in the present, focused in concentration, an occasional stomp the largest movement coming from the body that he's still learning how to use.

Tap. Tap. Tap.

I'm wearing the tropical sun. My back feels molten, a sensation fit for the times: sweat now richly running.

Tap. Tap. Tap.

The troupe are members of the Bindal and Wulgurukaba people, welcoming a group of visitors to Townsville. We visitors stand a little awkwardly, self-consciously accepting the greeting, our mood balanced ambiguously between the sombre and the festive. The atmosphere would be almost congregational, were it not for the informality of things, including the cheerful sounds of holiday-makers carrying over from the nearby swimming pool. I glance around and see that the eyes of many of us are directed towards the boy. Faces are radiating with love for this child, who we don't know, his small hands striking out the seconds.

How can we not smile? How can we not feel tenderness for such a boy, this tiny scion of humankind? How can we not hope with our whole selves that he will live long and grow strong, the little tyke – so evidently oblivious to our adoring gaze – who should still be alive in 2100?

And on this same day, the atmospheric research station at Mona Laua in Hawaii records 415 parts per million of carbon dioxide in the Earth's sky, for the first time in more than a million years.

Tap. Tap. Tap.

Later in the afternoon, the group gathers again; a collection of some of the leaders within the climate and environmental movement in Queensland and nationally. The tone of our gathering is ambivalent, caught between the joy and the shadow of the child's marking of the passage of time.

Tap. Tap. Tap.

I'VE KNOWN ABOUT GREENPEACE FOR ABOUT AS LONG AS I can remember. The first voyage of the inaugural Greenpeace ship, a doughty fifty-year-old wooden-hulled former herring and halibut seine fishing boat, the *Phyllis Cormack*, began in Vancouver around a fortnight after I was born, with the aim of halting planned US nuclear testing in the North Atlantic. The name 'Greenpeace' was coined in a moment of action as a statement of visionary intent when one of the founders, Bill Darnell, called out 'Make it a green peace!' Thereafter, the organisation never became known as anything other than the vision; not the 'foundation of this' or 'the society of that', but just straight out *green peace*. In truth, Greenpeace has always been both a movement and a thing; a machine that is nothing without its spirit; an essence that is given focused force by the strength of institutional capabilities. The objective isn't to stop bad stuff, per se, but to create the conditions to grow, build and nourish the good. 'Making it a green peace' is, after all, a mission of creation: of what we might do together if truly animated by our best instincts as a species. Greenpeace was founded on an idea of *agape*: love for the stranger and for the natural world. The imperative is to peacefully challenge the harm being done to the Earth in the name of love. In a note found posthumously in his papers, one of Greenpeace's most significant early figures, Bob Hunter, wrote that:

> Ecology has taught us that the entire Earth is part of our body and that we must learn to respect it as we respect ourselves.
> As we love ourselves, we must also love all forms of life in the planetary system.

It is a love of the world that sees people and the environment as miraculous and of intrinsic worth.

When I was a young teenager I had a picture of Greenpeace's most famous ship, the *Rainbow Warrior*, on my wall, up there with dozens of other posters and cards. There was no predestination in this: Alan Border and Blondie and who knows what else was displayed too, and I didn't grow up to play cricket for Australia or sing in a rock band or any of the other glamorous things that were puttied onto the garish candy-stripe wallpaper. I remember being in that very same room in the moment when I heard on the radio that the *Rainbow Warrior* had been bombed and sunk in Auckland Harbour. It was an instant of pure revulsion; my teenage self sickened at the notion that someone – as it turned out, the French state – had blown up a boat dedicated to seeking peace and disarmament, murdering one of the crew in the process. Memories slide, though. Maybe the picture went up on my wall in memorial, after the bombing.

Years later, when a street fundraiser approached me on Perth's Hay Street outside the now-demolished Cinema City (a movie complex finished with an exterior of harsh reflective glass that had opened in 1980 – the year after Western Australia's sesquicentenary – and exemplified a certain kind of stylistic self-consciousness in that particular *fin de la décennie* moment of provincial futurity), I signed on enthusiastically to become a monthly donor to Greenpeace. It was the mid-nineties by then and I had just started in the general litigation department of a large commercial law firm. Despite the joys of working for two intellectually dynamic, interpersonally humane and delightfully eccentric members of the partnership, neither of whom remotely conformed to the grey caricature of the corporate lawyer, the culture shock was real and often brought out the worst in me. Signing on to Greenpeace felt like something true, an expression of self communicated through a regular commitment of cash to be converted into power for change, as a private statement of where I really stood, within a lived reality of client deadlines, false front, and productive value determined through the number of billable six-minute units next to my initials at the end of the month. I remember opening the paper newsletters that came through the post and looking at pictures of investigators, campaigners and activists, all over the world, from the Arctic to the Amazon, and wondering who they were and how one became more involved.

AFTER A DECADE OR SO IN PRACTICE IN PERTH AND THROUGH a mixture of circumstances, I belatedly followed the familiar trail of many earlier Australians who were seeking, searching for something, in London. I needed work and was astonished by the depth of employment possibilities within civil society in the United Kingdom. After some anxious weeks, I saw a senior campaigner role advertised at Greenpeace. The truth is, I didn't really know what such a role entailed, but as my spouse Frances and I read through the list of skills and attributes required, they seemed analogous to at least some of the things I'd done as a lawyer and we agreed that I should give it a go. Happily, my application was rewarded with a hearing, and after a fairly miserable start to the interview (I was lost, late, overdressed and my pen didn't work), and with three vacancies to fill, the panel decided to take a risk on me. Apart from my logistical bungling, one of my abiding memories of the interview process was being asked about my will to win. I liked that question very much.

In Greenpeace terms, I would learn, 'winning' meant achieving the goals of a campaign in accordance with a carefully articulated strategy. Investigations, both field and desktop, would often be a pre-condition to deciding on an approach. Tactics, from boats and banner drops, to videos and lobbying, would only come into play once strategy had been determined. Campaigning of this kind is actively inter-ventionist and seeks to shift social, political, economic and cultural power in order to achieve objectives. The practice of campaigning is fundamentally different from 'awareness raising' or 'educating' or 'encouraging responsible consumer behaviour'. I was impressed, too, by not only the strategic considerations but the moral seriousness that accompanied all decisions around peaceful civil disobedience. Radi-calism and sophistication could be mutually self-supporting.

The basic structure of a campaign involved identifying an envi-ronmental problem and a solution, working out what decisions would have to be made by whom to get the latter implemented, and then shifting whatever ignorance, inertia and vested interests stood in the way. The job is done not when more people know about a problem, but when power has been shifted, causing an actual change to happen in the physical world. There was, I learned, always an emphasis on systems change; not simply preventing some particular outrage or atrocity or ameliorating symptoms, but reorienting entire structures of production and consumption to secure a just and sustainable world.

By the time I joined Greenpeace in 2007 the issue of global warming had already been our top campaign priority for some time. As early as 1990, Oxford University Press published *Global Warming: The Greenpeace Report*, which concludes with the words:

> The uniquely frustrating thing about global warming – to those many people who now see the dangers – is that the solutions are obvious. But there is no denying that enacting them will require paradigm-shifts in human behaviour. That is the challenge for the 1990s. There is no single issue in contemporary human affairs that is of greater importance.

Greenpeace's other great focus – though the two are of course intimately interwoven – is biodiversity, which includes both marine and terrestrial streams of work. My first principal area of work was the oceans. Here I had to confront the truth of my own ignorance because I actually knew very little about the challenges facing the ecology of the oceans, so there was a lot of reading to be done and a lot of listening. Apart from climate change, the principal threat to life in the oceans now came from industrial-scale overfishing. As I learned, my commitment deepened.

One of the first things I was given to read was English journalist Charles Clover's *The End of the Line*. I made my way through the book in a single intense sitting, tucked up on a cracked wooden bed in the one-room apartment that Frances and I were sharing in Marylebone. The book seriously got to me, but it was not the appalling chronicle of extinction, loss and destruction that finally brought the tears – though learning that history was staggering, and both psychologically and politically transformative – so much as the author's closing envisioning of what the oceans of the future *could yet be like*, if we just did the right thing. Clover imagined himself in the historic English fishing port of Lowestoft in September 2090 and evocatively described European seas returned to a state of ecological, cultural and economic flourishing:

> What children growing up today think of as entirely normal, we as educated adults know to be a great achievement.

The solutions for achieving this marine redemption were neither utopian nor unknown, but a solid mix of practical changes to the way that people interact with the ocean. It would simply be a matter of doing a whole bunch of things that we already knew how to do. Together, these could create the conditions for the magnificent resurgence of the oceans, with both more wildlife and the revitalisation of local fishing communities. All that stood in the way of this achievable future was a complex of vested interests blowing human society from the calm sailing of wise long-term stewardship, towards the murderous rocks of frenzied short-term value-extraction. Clover's analysis mapped on to Greenpeace's theory of change: if you could just shift vested interests, then solutions would be enabled to change the world for the better. This truth applies to virtually every major environmental and social problem.

The official mission of Greenpeace, hung on the wall in my workplace today, is 'to secure an earth capable of nurturing life in its magnificent diversity'. The essence of that mission has probably never had a greater or more urgent focus. Unhappily, the degree of difficulty is also unprecedented.

Tap. Tap. Tap.

TIME IS CHANGING AROUND US. IT IS IN THE ARRHYTHMIA of globalised social media and the convulsions of late capitalism, and, more deeply, in the multiple anthropogenic disruptions to chrono-biological cycles. Our conceptions of future times are changing too, as the numbers of parts per million and degrees Celsius, and their consequences, cast shadows over our collective destiny.

Every morning part of my ritual involves reviewing a digest of headlines from the previous twenty-four hours, curated by a dedicated Greenpeace volunteer. It is quaintly reassuring in form, in a way, because the very construct of 'headlines' evokes a more orderly and predictable information cycle in beat with the social certainties of industrial modernity that, in truth, no longer pertain. Each day there are usually around thirty articles and often the news is grim. One recent offering included the following:

Scientists Alarmed as Lightning Near North Pole Seen as Latest Sign of Climate Breakdown
Australia Seeks to Water Down Climate Declaration at Pacific Summit
It's Raining Plastic: Microscopic Fibres Fall from the Sky in Rocky Mountains
India's Holiest River Is Drying Up
Trump Administration Guts Endangered Species Act

It is not all like that, of course. Staggering breakthroughs in clean-energy tech and regenerative agriculture are reported like twinkling lamps, and all over the world human beings are politically active, demanding change. Nonetheless, the scale of the bad stuff is undeniable. There is a sense that night is closing in, a feeling that is manifest in each fresh study or news report detailing some incident presaging an ending in the world. There is a real risk of being overwhelmed, or of succumbing to a sense of creeping paralysis induced by dread, or of being devoured by anger and frustration at the political leaders and business executives who are ultimately responsible but failing to act.

Already, severe climate damage is here, but this is only a tiny foretaste of the suffering and chaos that lie ahead if we cannot change direction. According to the best available science, business as usual means the probable collapse of civilisation within current lifespans, making a mockery of every human's dream of the good life for future generations. I hide from none of this. Yet these descriptions are pallid when rendered in the abstract. It is in the deaths of wood and coral and people, the vanishing of our fellow creatures and the dying of whole places, from rivers to nations, where the trend lines land with unbearable pain. And for anyone with children in their lives, the possible foreclosure is unthinkably bitter; a crucifixion of the soul from which there is no rising. It is to imagine being on the trains of no returning.

Most recently the pixellated tidings have been full of burning. Scientists have been warning for years that global warming would mean more and worse conflagrations, occurring in places that are not meant to ever be on fire. In the course of 2019, as I read the news each day, it seemed that the blazes were everywhere: Brazil, Siberia, Indonesia, Greenland, Equatorial Africa, the Canary Islands, Alaska. And then, in New South Wales, Queensland, Victoria, South Australia, Tasmania and Western Australia, an unprecedented spring of fire. As nature at its grandest is put to the torch, what is happening feels like a pyre of human hope and expectation: the wilful sacrifice of our community of fate.

As spring becomes summer, the scale of the incendiary thing unleashed on Australia becomes monstrous and multiheaded. An area of more than 17 million hectares – an area bigger than Belgium, the Netherlands, Switzerland, Denmark and Slovenia combined –

has burned before summer is even half over. Thirty-four people killed already. Thousands of homes and other structures incinerated. More than a billion animals burned alive and the complete extinction of some species seeming likely. World Heritage areas destroyed. And the towns and cities of the eastern seaboard become enveloped in toxic smoke for days on end, with children kept indoors and scared citizens emptying Bunnings of face-masks. The Harbour Bridge disappears from view as David Williamson's Emerald City is turned brown. On 1 January 2020, Canberra begins the new decade as the most polluted capital in the world. And the images you cannot unsee are ubiquitous: skies turned black in the middle of the day; whole landscapes in flame. Ironically, though, it is in the most intimate images that the vast tragedy of the thing reaches deepest inside: a child in a mask, fleeing his burning town by boat; a young kangaroo immolated against barbed wire, paws crossed as if in prayer.

Yet everywhere too, are signs of all that is best: generosity, kindness, community spirit, bravery, the stoic performance of the firefighters and other emergency response workers, and the vocational commitment of our great public institutions, including the ABC and the Bureau of Meteorology. Love in the face of these multiple catastrophes becomes an act of purpose and will. The impact of the fire crisis is so profound that it is as if, over Christmas, we have travelled through time and space and woken up in another country. Contemplating this, the moral imperative is clear: not to assume the position of supplicating to the inevitability of despair, but to understand the truth as our operational terrain and to get to work. Raymond Williams once noted that 'to be truly radical is to make hope possible, rather than despair convincing'. The terrible noise outside should not be mistaken for the sounds of a planet dying; rather, should be understood as the just rage of life fighting for life. Love means an honesty of grief in what is lost and a fearless facing of the science, but also a resolution to win through, regardless of the odds. Inside Greenpeace and in deep co-operation and collaboration with our allies, the task is clear; to scaffold and amplify the voices of climate disaster survivors, and to ensure that the connection between the fires and rising emissions – and rising emissions and the coal and broader fossil fuel industries – is reinforced ad infinitum to drive the necessary transformation at speed and scale. We enable one survivor, Melinda Plesman, to bring the remains of her incinerated home from Nymboida, near Grafton, to the lawns of Parliament House in Canberra, in dignified demand for political witness and action to reduce emissions. 'It's happening now and this is what climate change looks like', she says simply.

AUSTRALIA HAS BECOME DISMALLY ACCUSTOMED TO THE shadow-face of national leadership. Our current prime minister will forever be the man who carried a lump of coal – our number one driver of global warming – into the parliament of Australia and told fellow MPs not to be scared, with all the cunning showmanship of a two-bit spruiker. Even the prop wasn't honest – as someone pointed out to me, the coal was varnished so that the one-time ad-man wouldn't be caught with soot on his hands. As fire conditions deepened to catastrophic and the prospect of death and destruction became inevitable, our PM quietly disappeared to Hawaii on a family holiday – an act that, once revealed, prompted outpourings of rage across Australia.

A decent prime minister would hear the moral drum-beat and turn to say, in the full face of the climate emergency, Australia will be there. Instead we have delinquency, denial and the dereliction of duty. And yet, to make it all about the abundance of the failure of the PM, who – given Australia's recent political history, may not even be in the role by the time this collection is published – is to miss the greater point. Institutional corruption has long been the first order of the day in Australia, as the vested interests of the coal, oil and gas industries are routinely preferred to the common good. The country writhes in fire under a system of political economy that has vigorously auspiced the conditions generative of our national immolation. There have been numerous warnings that rising emissions and global temperatures will lead to catastrophic fire conditions – my team counts eighteen expert warnings since 2013 alone. The fossil fuel industry, business peak bodies and their servants within the political system continue to thwart any serious emissions reduction efforts in Australia. Even as the bushfire crisis unfolds, Australia is rated zero for our efforts and is the subject of global opprobrium for obstructing progress in international negotiations. Yet the climate emergency is a truth that can only be avoided for so long. When the homes of your people are burning and tens of thousands of others face evacuation; when millions are waking with the acrid taste of inaction in their mouths or literally choking on the consequences of denial; when the malignancy of misused power has blackened the skies and rained ash on the hallowed beaches; then the conceit has become visceral. Acknowledgment of the truth, that Australia should transition to a clean energy economy and society – with all of the challenges and opportunities that come with that – with the speed of full national mobilisation, must entail the downfall of the fossil fuel order that has become so disastrously intrinsic to Australian politics, business and government. As the country blazed and bathed in smoke, there was a sense that this could be Australia's Chernobyl moment, an historic turning point, bringing on a crisis of legitimacy to render the status quo as untenable. At the time of writing, all is in the balance: the future of Australia and that of the world astride the hinge of fate.

FOUNDATIONAL TO LOVE IS WHAT YOU CHOOSE TO NOTICE. Apart from the headlines of disaster and tweets of outrage, there are other things in the mornings too, even on the days of heaviest smoke. Life flowing into your body with the first conscious breath and stretch. Even though we live in the inner city, the first noises I hear at daybreak are the squawks and chirrups of the remaining birds. Then there is the infinite nourishment of sleepy conversation, hugs with my partner and kids or, if they are asleep when I get up to leave for work, kisses delivered to slumbering cheeks. Loving those closest to you in these years of ecological crisis has added weight, but this is capable of expression with deeper tenderness and is an infinitely renewable resource of resolve. James Bradley said to me once that having children puts a floor on your despair, but I think the presence of kids in your life also creates a vaulted ceiling lit with the promise of what is yet possible, if we can get our act together.

In our tiny front garden, strange things are happening as the weather behaves unnaturally, but every day I witness the sublime of nature in dogged persistence as I head off to the bus. Last year a seed planted itself in a pot. We didn't know what the plant was, but we decided to let the plucky seedling be, and it has grown into a sapling, maybe four-foot high, with parakeet-green lanceolate leaves covered in fine thread-like trichomes. I noticed a few months ago that a bright emerald common garden katydid (*Caedicia simplex*) was resting in the upper leaves. The creature was present for a week or more and I assume was responsible for the grasshopper's-breakfast sized holes that began appearing in the foliage. I took to exchanging glances with the katydid each morning, the animal's bulging butter eyes with black pupils glancing back with insectine superciliousness over the top of long green antennae. The *memento mori* are now all about us, but so too are the *memento vivere*. In the midst of the summer of fire, a single Christmas beetle – the only one I have seen this year – flies through a slight gap in the window and lands directly in my lap. I can't help but imagine the creature as a tiny Pheidippides and I swear a silent oath that we are coming.

Enabling knowledge of what will happen to the world if nothing changes is the truth that sets us free, but should not to be confused with fatalism that our doom is inevitable. The most recent report of the United Nations Intergovernmental Panel on Climate Change (IPCC) found that keeping global warming to under 1.5°C 'can be done within laws of physics and chemistry'. Yet even if the best available science told us that hope was gone, to be animated by love is to continue to strive, not only because it is the right thing to do, but because even the greatest of our Nobel Laureates cannot be altogether certain of what comes next. Nor is the future binary; global warming is not a matter of being damned or saved, off or on like the switch of a light. Our biosphere is not lifeless, even with the carnage of this year, vast forests still stand, reefs hang on, and creaturedom, though severely reduced, will bounce back mightily if given the chance. The wounds are severe, but life on Earth remains beautiful beyond measure. The rise of the sun is inevitable, but events are contingent. Progress is non-linear. History is inherently unpredictable. The future is still open.

THERE IS AN IRONIC SYMMETRY IN THE CHEMICAL AND physical processes that created coal and the work that we must do now to bring the fossil fuel era to an end. The black rock that burns was brought into being by the application of unfathomable heat and pressure over time. Now it is our campaign strategy, too, that is being wrought in heat and fire. As researchers Neville Ellis and Ashlee Cunsolo have written, 'collective experiences of ecological grief may coalesce into a strengthened sense of love and commitment to the places, ecosystems and species that inspire, nurture and sustain us'. Amid the ashes of our homes and forests, through what we choose to notice and do, we are able to undertake an alchemy of remaking, turning grief and anger into strategy and action, forcing the wheel of history towards the light. In the face of the great ecological crisis, love mandates that hope must be neither passive nor wishful, but active and having a plan.

Inside Greenpeace Australia Pacific the immoral intransigence of the national political leadership is met with determined resilience. In 2019 we experienced an extraordinary and unprecedented surge of participation. The phenomenon is not confined to Greenpeace, of course. All over Australia, communities are organising anew, to demand the early closure of ageing, dirty, dangerous, polluting coal-fired power stations. At the time of writing, more than eighty local jurisdictions representing five million Australians have declared climate emergencies. The climate strike marches of Friday 20 September 2019 draw huge crowds – the largest ever in some cities. Inspired and organised by children, the school climate-strikers, the rallies are acts of *agape* en masse. Standing under the trees in the Sydney Domain where, at the request of the school-strikers, Greenpeace is supplying the back-of-house support for the main-stage, I witness the emotions of the adults: aunties, uncles, parents and grandparents, carers, teachers and friends. Frances and our two daughters are present too, carrying homemade placards. I lift my youngest daughter on to my shoulders so that she can see clearly the marchers, cascading across the parkland in every direction, united in will. Nobody here has acquiesced to disaster. We cry tears of love, not despair, and we march in our hundreds of thousands in resolute steps of hope through action. Tens of thousands are back on the streets in early January, demanding action in the face of the fire disasters.

Love commands that we do our utmost to achieve a world of future flourishing every day, whatever our situation. There are many years of bad news ahead: so much is locked in and clear. We must be braced and resilient: kind in our stoicism, creative in our determination. It will require monumental effort and take the labour of millions of human hands, but we can get there; through all the disasters that will come, we can still secure the conditions for recovery and regeneration. We human beings, when we work together, can achieve practically anything. Let's make it a green peace. In the name of love, we can yet do this.

So that children growing up in the distant future may take for granted our great achievement.

Tap. Tap. Tap.

Readings

Australian Associated Press, 'Woman Brings Remains of Home Lost in NSW Bushfires to Parliament in Climate Protest', *Guardian*, 2 December, 2019, <bit.ly/guardian-plesman>.

Charles Clover, *The End of the Line: How Overfishing Is Changing the World and What We Eat*, Ebury Press, London, 2005, p. 287.

Neville Ellis and Ashlee Cunsolo, 'Hope and Mourning in the Anthropocene: Understanding Ecological Grief', *The Conversation*, 5 April 2018, <bit.ly/conversation-ellis-cunsolo>.

Robert Hunter, *Warriors of the Rainbow: A Chronicle of the Greenpeace Movement from 1971 to 1979*, Greenpeace & Fremantle Press, Amsterdam, 2011 (40th anniversary edition), p. 12.

Jeremy Leggett (ed.), *Global Warming: The Greenpeace Report*, Oxford University Press, Oxford, 1990.

David Ritter, 'Australia's Politicians Face a Crisis of Legitimacy As Fire and Smoke Chokes the Country', *Guardian*, 13 December 2019, <bit.ly/guardian-ritter>.

Jeff Sparrow, 'The Humming of Christmas Beetles Was Once a Sign of the Season. Where Have They Gone?', *Guardian*, 23 December 2019, <bit.ly/guardian-sparrow>.